THE MOVIE BOOK
THE 1930's

THE MOVIE BOOK
THE 1930's

Alfred Brockman

Editor
Leonard Matthews

Consultant
Ann Lloyd

Crescent Books
New York

The editor is happy to acknowledge the generous help extended during the production of this book by John Hall of Edgbaston, Peter Peplow of Syndication International, London, Jerry Ohlinger and Steve Sally of New York and Eddie Brandt of Los Angeles; also for their provision of several hundred movie stills.

Produced and edited by Martspress Limited

For copyright reasons this edition is for sale only within the U.S.A.

First English edition published by
The Hamlyn Publishing Group Limited
Bridge House, Twickenham, Middlesex TW1 3SB, England

This 1987 edition is published by Crescent Books
Distributed by Crown Publishers, Inc.
225 Park Avenue South, New York, New York 10003

ISBN 0-517-62603-9

h g f e d c b a

Printed in Yugoslavia

CONTENTS

Picturegoer Weekly cover featuring John Boles — "REAL LOVE in Hollywood SEE PAGE 16"

Norma Shearer with Henry Kolker and Ralph Forbes in *Romeo and Juliet* (MGM)

Charles Laughton in *The Barretts of Wimpole Street* (MGM)

INTRODUCTION

There never was such a time. There can never be such a time again. The Second World War put paid to all that.

Only those people who lived and went to the cinema once, twice, thrice and even four times a week can know what it was like to live through the exciting (despite the Great Depression) days of the movies in the Twenties and Thirties, the Roaring Twenties and Glamorous Thirties.

This book is devoted to the movies of the Thirties when long queues, stretching to hundreds of yards waited patiently outside cinemas in rain, snow, biting cold and over-powering heat to see the latest release.

Not then was there a television set in nearly every home in the country, churning out modern and old-time movies by the scores.

To see a film one had to visit a cinema and to the cinema they went in their millions all over the world.

Film fans went to see their current idols, the latest smash hits. They went to be thrilled by mighty action films – the Robin Hoods, Captain Bloods and Cimarrons – to roar with laughter at the antics of Charlie Chaplin in *Modern Times*, Laurel and Hardy in *Way Out West* and the Marx Brothers in *A Night at the Opera* – to gasp at the gangland crimes of *Scarface* and *Little Caesar* – to ride to glory with Gary Cooper in *The Lives of a Bengal Lancer* and Errol Flynn in *The Charge of the Light Brigade* – to gallop with John Wayne, Tom Mix and Buck Jones as those practitioners of the six-gun put the Old West to rights – to stare incredulously at the ghoulish exploits of the vampire in *Dracula*, the man-made monster in *Frankenstein* and the towering King Kong as he falls for the undeniable but – compared with his immensity – minescule charms of beautiful Fay Wray. Then there were the 'women's' films as opposed to the roistering 'men's' films and in these Bette Davis, Norma Shearer, Luise Rainer, Ruth Chatterton, Barbara Stanwyck and above all, Greta Garbo, suffered, loved, lost and 'died.' Fred Astaire and Ginger Rogers, Dick Powell and Ruby Keeler danced their way to fame and fortune and Jeanette MacDonald and Nelson Eddy, Irene Dunne and Allan Jones sang their hearts out in many spectacular musicals.

Although Hollywood dominated the scene, European stars were also scintillating brilliantly – Francoise Rosay, Jean Gabin, Danielle Darrieux, Dorothea Wieck, Marlene Dietrich, Lilian Harvey, Anna Neagle, Charles Laughton and many others were in there, making names that even

Mae West and leonine co-star in *I'm No Angel* (Par)

Francoise Rosay

Lilian Harvey

Dorothea Wieck

today, half-a-century later, are still honoured adornments of that filmic period.

It was all a veritable wonderland that enchanted the picturegoers who little dreamed of the nightmare war years that awaited them during the Forties.

During the Twenties and Thirties, movie buffs were regaled with several periodicals, weeklies and monthlies, devoted to the activities of the film world. Such magazines proliferated in all countries where films were regularly shown. Amongst the foremost in Britain was *Picturegoer*, launched in 1921 as a monthly and then re-launched in 1931 as a weekly. It is from the archives of *Picturegoer* that many of the stills reproduced in this book have been culled.

Fantastic 'facts' and gossip were given in the cartload to omnivorous readers who lapped up such titbits as 'Mae West in her new Paramount picture *I'm No Angel* will be obliged to perform one of the most daring stunts ever essayed by a screen star. She will put her head smack in a lion's mouth!' Then again, as the weekly periodical *Picture Show* reported in the August 19th 1933 issue 'Nancy Carroll's hair is red. It was red when she was born, and it has been red ever since.' Unbelievable? But true.

On the following pages are highlights from hundreds of the decade's most popular films, the Academy Award Winners and films that perhaps have won no high critical praise across the years but that were applauded in their own time. These stills are accompanied by portraits of the stars who helped to create the only new art form of the Twentieth Century – the moving film.

WARNER BROS. SUPREME TRIUMPH

AL JOLSON

IN

The JAZZ SINGER

'Wait a minute, wait a minute,
you ain't heard nothin' yet!'

CHAPTER ONE
1930
EVERYBODY'S TALKING

Buck Jones

Tom Mix

George O'Brien

With the arrival of the Thirties silence was no longer golden for the film industry. Every studio had hitched its future to sound. No longer was it necessary for cinema audiences to read unlikely dialogue while imagining that the words were in fact being spoken by the characters in the film. Now cinemagoers could concentrate on the action, without having their attention diverted every few seconds to partake in the marathon reading exercise necessary to grasp all that was supposedly being said or related on the screen before the caption vanished.

Prior to 1930, the USA virtually had the world market for films to itself. Silent pictures had been acceptable in any language, for it had been a simple matter to change the dialogue captions. But talkies altered all that.

However, the American producers had something else to worry about when, in 1930, the world was hit by a gigantic depression. As the stock markets tumbled and businesses collapsed, so the world unemployment figures rose. Money was in such short supply that worried film moguls wondered how the masses would be able to afford the regular visits to the cinema they had made in the Twenties.

As it happened, it was a problem that never matured, for the depressive times made people want to get away from the drab realities of their everyday lives. The cinema offered the right escape. Their own and the world's troubles faded as audiences rode with their cowboy heroes across the prairie, experienced the luxury of great wealth as they mixed with the rich, shuddered happily at the shoot-outs of desperate gangsters, or hummed an afternoon or evening away, watching a fast-moving musical.

Contrary to all expectations and certainly unique in the industrial world at the time, 1930 was, in fact, the beginning of a boom period for the film industry. With few interruptions, it lasted well into the Forties.

Not only had talkies become established by the Thirties, but now colour was beginning to make an impact, following the success of Warner Brothers' 1929 film, *On With the Show*, which used an early version of a process that has

Al Jolson

Billie Dove

Charles Chaplin

lasted to this day – Technicolor. It was, of course, Warners, who had in 1927, introduced the all-talking and singing film, *The Jazz Singer*, starring the great Al Jolson.

By 1930 the star system had become well established, although with the arrival of the talkies many stars who had been big names during the silent era were unable to make the transition. Those with shrill or squeaky voices fell by the wayside. Among the silent greats who were unable to survive were Billie Dove, John Gilbert and Norma Talmadge. A number of foreign actors who had made names for themselves in American films found their accents unacceptable for English-speaking audiences and were dropped by the studios. Most notable were Vilma Banky, Emil Jannings and Pola Negri, international stars of the Twenties.

Yet some foreign players with pronounced accents survived in American talkies. Marlene Dietrich's German accent was an extra plus in her appeal to English-speaking audiences, while the Swedish tones of Greta Garbo were as acceptable as her face. Charles Boyer gave his love scenes an extra touch of romanticism with his French accent.

Incidentally, it was some three years after sound was first introduced to films in 1927 that Greta Garbo consented to make her first talking picture. In 1930, she made her speaking debut in MGM's *Anna Christie*, and her first lines spoken at a dockside bar: 'Gif me a visky, ginger ale on the side, and don't be stingy, baby', have become immortal. However, Charles Chaplin waited until 1940 before he uttered his first words on film in *The Great Dictator*.

A number of silent stars found that the talkies did not interrupt their careers at all. Indeed some, like Gary Cooper, Norma Shearer, William Boyd, Joan Crawford, Edward G. Robinson, Constance Bennett and the comedy duo Laurel and Hardy saw their reputations grow with their appearance in talkies.

And with the expansion of the industry, with more films than ever before being made, new stars were being sought by the studios. Some of the 'finds' among the newcomers to the screen were Clark Gable, James Cagney, Humphrey Bogart and Carole Lombard.

A certain starlet was ready for the big chance when Jeanne Eagles, a celebrated beauty who had made five films, died. She had been earmarked to star in *The Devil's Holiday*, but with her demise the role went to Nancy Carroll, a popular New York-born beauty who had scored as ingenue heroines in light musical comedies. Here was a chance for her to show her talent as a dramatic actress, playing a hard-boiled, man-hating fortune-hunter who deserts her husband after relieving his father of $50,000 dollars as a compensation for divorcing his son.

Alone, she finds she has a conscience, which she tries to ignore by attending a round of parties and drinking. When she learns that her husband is seriously ill, her love for him comes to the fore. She returns to him, hands back the money to his father and is all set to live happily ever after.

After her flighty roles of the past, Nancy Carroll gave a surprisingly convincing performance that led her to being nominated for an Oscar award. Her co-star in the film was Phillips Holmes, who was also acclaimed for his performance. Among the strong cast were ZaSu Pitts, Paul Lukas, Ned Sparks, Hobart Bosworth and the singing star, Morton Downey.

It was in 1930 that the Hays' Code was first introduced to Hollywood film-makers. Will H. Hays was brought into the industry by the Hollywood moguls to set standards on the screen that would be obeyed by all producers, and so avoid official censorship.

Many of the rules laid down would be considered laughable today but at the time, when moral standards were still important, it was felt necessary to have a watchdog, paid jointly by all the studios, to ensure that morality on the screen was not relaxed.

The code rules on such things as screen kissing, the *double-entendre* and the sleeping arrangements for married couples, when one of them had to have at least one foot on the ground, set the moral standards in film-making that lasted several years.

In 1930, there were five dominant Hollywood studios. The biggest was Metro-Goldwyn-Mayer (MGM); the others were RKO Radio Pictures, Paramount, Fox (which was to merge with Twentieth Century Pictures in 1935) and Warner Brothers.

The roar of Leo the lion was the familiar introduction to MGM films throughout the world. Their lot was the largest in Hollywood, occupying some 100 acres of land with no fewer than 22 sound stages.

Columbia and Universal were two smaller studios that produced a number of notable films, while even smaller companies like Republic and Monogram enjoyed a steady output, especially Westerns.

By the Thirties, the British film industry was also making an impact – but not in the world market. A number of quality films were produced but the 'quota' system, which by law made it necessary for all British cinemas to show a percentage of films that were made in the home country, had a detrimental effect. 'Quota-quickies' were being made cheaply and without too much attention to quality in order to satisfy the quota law. Cinemas had little alternative but to show them.

While American films were swamping the British market, British producers, with one or two exceptions, found it impossible to break the monopoly of the American cinema, as it was not viable for them to make films on the same lavish scale as their American counterparts. There were, of course, some good films made but until Alexander Korda and Herbert Wilcox managed to gain showings for their movies in the late Thirties, British films were held back through the lack of overseas markets.

In the early Thirties, the British film industry was domi-

Nancy Carroll and Phillips Holmes in *The Devil's Holiday* (Par)

Emil Jannings

The lion roars

Charles Boyer

Donald Calthrop

Fritz Kortner

nated by British International Pictures (BIP) and Gaumont British. BIP was a member of the British Associated Cinema group. Its studios, comprising nine sound stages in 40 acres of ground, were located at Elstree, Buckinghamshire, a few miles outside London. The first British talkie to be shown commercially was Alfred Hitchcock's *Blackmail* (made in 1929), which was shot as a silent film and then almost entirely remade as a talkie. Donald Calthrop as the shabby little blackmailer was superb.

The first British musical, *Elstree Calling,* was released in 1930. It comprised a collection of music-hall acts, loosely strung together, with top billing being given to Tommy Handley, the famous English comedian who became the BBC's top radio entertainer during the Second World War in a comedy series called 'Itma'.

The Japanese were active film-makers in the Thirties, and in the first year of the decade Yasujiro Ozu made three pictures. *I Flunked, But ...* starred Tatsuo Saito. It was a comedy and had much of the American style, with the star basing his performance on the work of Harold Lloyd. *Walk Cheerfully* included a revealing insight into Japanese society. The plot was based on a man's success in saving a woman from being swept into the underworld. *That Night's Wife* was a touching tale of a man who robbed a bank in order to save his sick child. The story's theme plays on the sympathy the detective has for the quarry he is pursuing.

Ozu made over 50 films before his death in 1963, and almost all of them dealt with the problems and lives of the Japanese lower-middle class.

The Thirties was, of course, the period of the Third Reich in Germany. It was an active time for film-making, with many of the films being produced specifically for propaganda purposes. However, one German film, called *Der Andere*, starring Fritz Kortner, was based on the book *Dr Jekyll and Mr Hyde*.

The most famous film made in Germany in 1930 was produced and directed by Josef von Sternberg. He had met a young and at that time an amply curvaceous film and stage actress. He saw great possibilities in her and cast her as Lola, the seductive temptress in *Der blaue Engel (The Blue Angel)* which he shot in both English and German. The actress was Marlene Dietrich, whose performance in the film led her to becoming an international star.

By clever means of the camera, Sternberg gave Dietrich, playing a cabaret singer, a sexual abundance that never strayed from her for the rest of her career. Her long legs, sheathed in silk stockings with black suspenders, her sensual looks and that now famous husky voice rendering 'Falling in Love Again' could not fail to attract attention. However, it was not until Dietrich had become an international star, that the English version of the film received worldwide showing.

Naturally Hollywood was not going to ignore a star of Dietrich's potential and she and Sternberg were invited

there by Paramount. By the time she arrived in the film capital she had, under Sternberg's guidance, slimmed down her figure considerably. At the same time, she developed an air of mystery that became her stock in trade.

Her first film in Hollywood was *Morocco*, in which she was cast opposite another rising star, Gary Cooper. Sternberg directed. Dietrich's performance in the film won her a nomination for an Academy Award.

Today, Australia has an impressive output of highly entertaining films made with a skill that equals any in the world but in 1930, things were different. Many producers were at work but they had to be content with satisfying the home market. They also had to face fierce competition from the highly professional films being produced overseas. These were allowed into the country because there was no quota system to restrict their showing.

Its favourable climate makes Australia an ideal location for film making but there was only one major film studio operating in 1930. This was Cinesound, which had its main film studio in Sydney, producing comedies and outdoor dramas that made the most of the country's impressive landscape. Its chief producer, who also directed, was Ken G. Hall who, from time to time, would make a popular melodrama. Bearing in mind the restricted capital resources available, Hall's movies were well produced and enjoyed a strong following in their own country.

Although Russia had been making films for several years, they had progressed little with sound until 1930, when Abram Room made *The Plan for Great Works*, a documentary about the Five Year Plan, with a musical score, sound effects and a voice that made political appeals throughout.

Most of the films that came out of Russia during the Thirties had a propaganda link, for the industry was rigidly controlled by its government with Boris Shumyatsky in charge. Until 1938, when he was fired by Stalin for failing to ensure that sufficient films of the 'right' kind were being produced, it was Shumyatsky who had the final word as to what could be made.

Nevertheless there were a number of worthwhile films produced in Russia during the Thirties, many of them now considered classics. These are mentioned in the section devoted to the year in which they were made.

As well as *The Blue Angel*, another outstanding film was produced in Germany in 1930. It was *Westfront 1918*, made by the veteran director G.W. Pabst, and it was a fine example of the German film at its best. It has as its principal characters four young German First World War soldiers, and their fortunes, in one of the most ghastly periods of world history, are followed with great tenderness and understanding. The film rivals Hollywood's *All Quiet on the Western Front* (1930), as the best anti-war film made between the two World Wars.

With the spread of the Nazi movement in Germany, numerous films were made from 1930 onward to further

Marlene Dietrich in *Der blaue Engel* (US *The Blue Angel*) (UFA) and *Morocco* (Par)

Erich von Stroheim

Conrad Veidt

Louis Wolheim and Lew Ayres in *All Quiet on the Western Front* (Univ)

Marie Dressler

its aims. There was a definite trend toward military subjects. Two such films were *Das Flötenkonzert von Sanssouci (The Flute Concert in Sanssouci)* directed by Gustav Ucicky and *Die Letzteh Kompanie (The Last Company)* directed by Kurt Bernhardt. Such pictures with their patriotic flavour provided excellent propaganda for the Nazi party that was to rule the country within three years.

Germany's neighbour, Austria, had been making films since 1908. However, the industry did not flourish, although a number of future international stars had appeared in films made there, including Marlene Dietrich, Nita Naldi and Conrad Veidt. Even so, Austrian audiences saw the early works of such legendary figures as Erich von Stroheim and Fritz Lang.

The first sound picture to be produced in Austria was *Geld auf der Strasse (Money in the Street)* directed by Georg Jacoby. Film-making there did not get into its stride until some time later, although during the Thirties the country picked up awards at the Venice Film Festival.

France maintained a thriving film industry all through the Thirties. One of its best-known and most prolific directors was René Clair, who will be dealt with at length in the next chapter.

Another French director to become internationally famous was Jean Grémillon. After his first sound film, *La Petite Lise*, in 1930, he made films in Germany and Spain. Returning home, he found that France had become the base for a number of producers and directors from Germany who had fled from the prospect of working under the Nazi regime.

The close proximity of Canada to America may account for the failure of its film industry to establish itself. Films from the United States filled the Canadian screens and it would appear that it was not worth the effort to compete. Those who had tried failed miserably. Rita Hayworth did appear in a Canadian film which, with its title, was soon forgotten. It was not until the Forties that Canada took a serious interest in making films.

In the Scandinavian countries, Sweden led the film-makers, but after the silent era had passed there was little progress and few films were produced in the Thirties that are worth recalling.

The film industries of both Norway and Finland have been even less progressive than Sweden. Although both countries have dallied with film producing, neither have achieved any real success.

In the English-speaking world it is natural that the best-remembered films are those made in the USA and England. With its vast home audiences providing huge revenues, America has always been in the position to produce top-grade pictures. But both countries have contributed a wealth of screen entertainment since the industry really started to take off in the early Twenties. The year 1930 saw a number of small-part players take their first steps to fame in films that are destined to live for ever.

Anna Christie, first shown in 1930, and already mentioned, was not only notable as Garbo's first talkie. Marie Dressler had a feature part in the film, and her outstanding performance in it made her a star at the age of 60. In the same year, Wallace Beery appeared in his first talkie, *The Big House*, and he, too, won stardom when he went on to team up with Marie Dressler in such films as *Min and Bill* (1930) and *Tugboat Annie* (1933).

All Quiet on the Western Front won the Academy Award for the 1929/1930 season. It made a tremendous impact when first shown; its grim, anti-war story of two young men facing death in the First World War gave a realistic insight into the horror of trench warfare. Produced by Carl Laemmle for Universal, and directed by Lewis Milestone, the film won instant stardom for Lew Ayres, playing a disillusioned young soldier who loses his life from a sniper's bullet as he tries to reach out for a settled butterfly – truly a memorable scene.

When Howard Hughes directed *Hell's Angels* for United Artists release, he had just completed four years as a film-maker. His first film produced in 1926, when he was only 21 years old, was called *Swell Hogan*. *Hell's Angels* was originally shot as a silent film, for it went into production in 1927, the year that heralded the first talkie. Hughes, with the backing of a huge personal fortune, decided it should have sound, and at an enormous expense all the dialogue scenes were reshot. Ben Lyon, James Hall and Greta Nissen were the original stars, but, because of her Norwegian accent, Greta Nissen had to be replaced. The girl that Hughes chose for the part was a young bit-player named Jean Harlow. It was her performance that gave life to the film, although the thrilling flying sequences had audiences on the edge of their seats wherever the film was shown.

When the vogue for musicals came about in 1930, Paramount jumped on the bandwagon by launching a 'super colossal' production that would have everything – stars, songs, comedy and lavish production numbers – to surpass anything that had gone before. When completed the film was titled *Paramount on Parade*, and was able to boast no fewer than 11 directors.

Jack Oakie, Skeets Gallagher and Leon Errol acted as compères, introducing musical numbers performed by such prestigious stars as Maurice Chevalier, Clara Bow, Charles 'Buddy' Rogers, Nancy Carroll, Ruth Chatterton, Nino Martini, Lillian Roth and Mitzi Green.

Other stars taking part in the sketches included Virginia Bruce, Fay Wray, Gary Cooper, Richard Arlen, Clive Brook, Warner Oland and Fredric March.

When Hollywood dug into history for film subjects, the results were generally satisfactory, if not always historically accurate. Such was the case with *Abraham Lincoln*, starring Walter Huston, who was later to add to an already illustrious career by appearing on Broadway in *Knicker-*

Wallace Beery

Jean Harlow

Maurice Chevalier

15

Kay Hammond and Walter Huston in Abraham Lincoln (UA)

Robert Montgomery and Norma Shearer in *The Divorcee* (GB *The Divorce*) (MGM)

George Arliss and Joan Bennett in *Disraeli* (WB)

Edward G Robinson in *Little Caesar* (FN)

bocker Holiday, in which he sang Kurt Weill's *September Song*, which he later recorded.

Abraham Lincoln was the first talkie for the director David Wark Griffith. The film had some good moments, and had much to offer in both its visual charm and fine acting from such sterling performers as Una Merkel, Henry B. Walthall and Kay Hammond.

During the Thirties, the undoubted Queen of Hollywood was Norma Shearer. Married to Irving Thalberg, MGM's production chief, she had influence, beauty, and a reasonable amount of acting talent. Her career was already progressing when she won the Academy Award for her role in *The Divorcee*. She played a woman who, after divorcing her husband, followed his example by playing the field before finally returning to him to live happily ever after. The film was a winner and kept the box offices round the world busy for many months. Her fellow stars in the film were Chester Morris, Robert Montgomery, Conrad Nagel and Florence Eldridge. Norma Shearer was now numbered among the front-rank actresses in Hollywood. Incidentally, the Englishman George Arliss won the Best Actor Oscar this same year for his part in *Disraeli*.

When the English producer Michael Balcon was unable to make his first talkie in the Gainsborough studios in England because they did not have any sound facilities, he looked to America for help. He found it at Tiffany, a lesser Hollywood studio that was wired for sound.

The film Balcon wanted to make was *Journey's End*, from R.C. Sherriff's play about life in the trenches during the First World War. Colin Clive, who had played in the West End production, repeated his role in the film. *Journey's End*, directed by James Whale, was a great success for Balcon, and is often shown today in presentations of classic films of this period.

Mention must now be made of a new movie genre which began with a roaring success in 1930. This was *Little Caesar* from the Warner Brothers stable.

Edward G. Robinson was a short, square-faced Broadway-trained actor, hoping to make his way in films. *Little Caesar* gave him the chance and as a result he reached the top ranks of movie stardom.

Based on a story by W.R. Burnett, it traces the rise and fall of a small-time crook who eventually becomes a gang leader. His short stature disguises the determined nature of a big-shot in the underworld. As the cocky Rico Brandello, eager to control the mob while destroying anyone who gets in his way, Edward G. Robinson is superb.

The film also won Mervyn LeRoy praise as a 'great director' (with a small 'g' according to studio boss Jack Warner) early in his career.

In singing the merits of Robinson's performance there is a tendency to forget other talented players who contributed to the success of the film. They include Douglas Fairbanks Jr, William Collier Jr, Ralph Ince and Glenda Farrell.

Silents may go and talkies may come but way back in 1930 Hollywood seemed to be going on forever. Here are some of the stars and films who helped to make that year the commencement of what is considered today to be the Golden Decade of Movies.

George Arliss in *Disraeli* (WB) for which role he won the Academy Award for Best Actor 1929/30

Buster Keaton

Gary Cooper and Marlene Dietrich in *Morocco* (Par)

Edward G Robinson and Douglas Fairbanks Jr in *Little Caesar* (FN)

Right: Wallace Beery (c) and Johnny Mack Brown in *Billy the Kid* (MGM)

Bernice Claire and Alexander Gray in *Song of the Flame* (FN) an early Technicolor musical

Amos (Freeman Gosden) and Andy (Charles Correll) in *Check and Double Check* (RKO) an unexpected box-office success

Ralph Morgan and Nancy Carroll in *Laughter* (Par)

William Powell in *For the Defense* (Par)

Above: Jeanette MacDonald and Dennis King in the very popular operetta *The Vagabond King* (Par)

Right: Phillips Holmes and Nancy Carroll in *The Devil's Holiday* (Par)

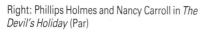

Jeanette MacDonald

Greta Garbo and George Marion in *Anna Christie* (MGM) which was Garbo's first talkie

Paul Whiteman in *King of Jazz* (Univ)

Jean Harlow who sprang to fame in *Hell's Angels* (HH)

Stan Laurel and Oliver Hardy

Right: John Wray greets the new recruits in *All Quiet on the Western Front* (Univ)

Picture Gallery for 1930

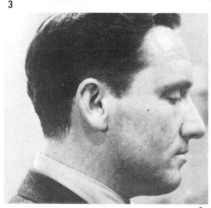

1. Chico and Groucho Marx in *Animal Crackers* (Par)
2. Frances Dee and Maurice Chevalier in *Playboy of Paris* (Par)
3. Lon Chaney
4. Ferdinand Gottschalk
5. Philippe De Lacey and Ruth Chatterton in *Sarah and Son* (Par)
6. Spencer Tracy
7. Gary Cooper
8. Tyrone Power Snr
9. William 'Stage' Boyd and Gary Cooper in *The Spoilers* (Par)

1

2

3

4

5

6

7 △ ▽ 10

8 △ ▽ 11

9

1. Cedric Hardwicke
2. Louis Armstrong
3. Lupe Velez
4. Leo Carillo
5. Lillian Gish
6. Dean Jagger
7. Ward Bond
8. Rex Harrison
9. Dorothy Gish
10. Mae Marsh
11. Godfrey Tearie

21

1

2

3

4

5

6 △ ▽ 9   7 △ ▽ 10   8 △ ▽ 11

12

13

14   15   16   17

18 △ ▽ 21   19   20 △ ▽ 23

22 △ ▽ 24

1. Walter Woolf, Vivenne Segal and Noah Beery Snr in *Golden Dawn* (WB)
2. Fay Wray, Emma Dunn, Oscar Apfel, Gary Cooper and Soledad Jiminez in *The Texan* (Par)
3. Cyril Maude and Halliwell Hobbes in *Grumpy* (Par)
4. Regis Toomey, William Powell and Jean Arthur in *Street of Chance* (Par)
5. Beryl Mercer and Gary Cooper in *Seven Days Leave* (GB *Medals*) (Par)
6. Evalyn Knapp
7. Harry Carey
8. Tom Moore and Lola Lane in *Costello Case* (WW)
9. Noah Beery Snr
10. Tom London and Rex Lease in *Troopers Three* (Tif)
11. Richard Arlen and Fay Wray in *The Sea God* (Par)
12. Nancy Carroll and Stanley Smith in *Honey* (Par)

24

1   2   3

4   5   6

7   8   9

10 △▽12   11 △▽13

1. William Haines and Billie Dove in *Sweethearts and Wives* (FN)
2. Hugh Williams and Charles Ruggles in *Charley's Aunt* (Col)
3. Stuart Erwin, Skeets Gallagher and Mitzi Green in *Love Among the Millionaires* (Par)
4. Mary Brian, Skeets Gallagher and Jack Oakie in *The Social Lion* (Par)
5. Bela Lugosi
6. Edmund Lowe in *Good Intentions* (Fox)
7. Alice White
8. Madeleine Carroll and Basil Gill in *School for Scandal* (B & D)
9. Dorothy Boyd
10. Leon Errol and Richard Arlen in *Only Saps Work* (Par)
11. Eugene Pallette
12. Harry Richman and James Gleason in *Puttin' on the Ritz* (JS)
13. Regis Toomey

1

2

3

5

4

6

7

8

1. Matthew Betz and Wynne Gibson in *Outside the Law* (Univ)
2. Nancy Carroll and Charles 'Buddy' Rogers in *Follow Thru* (Par)
3. Alice White and Neil Hamilton in *Widow from Chicago* (FN)
4. Henry Armetta, Robert Montgomery and Louis Mann in *Sins of the Children* (MGM)
5. Dennis King in *The Vagabond King* (Par)
6. Jeanette MacDonald and Dennis King in *The Vagabond King* (Par)
7. Marion Nixon and William Janney in *The Pay Off* (GB *The Losing Game*) (RKO)
8. Theodore Von Eltz, Raymond Hackett and Helen Twelvetrees in *The Cat Creeps* (Univ)
9. Billie Dove in *Painted Angel* (FN)

9

1. Lewis Stone and Greta Garbo in *Romance* (MGM)
2. Alan Curtis and Ilona Massey in *One Romantic Night* (UA)
3. Raymond Walburn and Dorothy Hale in *The Laughing Lady* (Par)
4. George Bancroft and Esther Ralston in *The Mighty* (Par)
5. William Austin, Loretta Young and John Barrymore in *The Man from Blankley's* (WB)
6. Warren Hymer, William Harrigan and Edmund Lowe in *Men On Call* (Fox)
7. Frank Albertson and Dixie Lee in *The Big Party* (Fox)
8. Mitchell Lewis, Reginald Sharland and Sally O'Neil in *Girl of the Port* (RKO)
9. William Powell and Hal Skelly in *Behind the Makeup* (Par)
10. Loretta Young and Ronald Colman in *The Devil to Pay* (SG)

1

2

3

5

4

6

7

8

9

10

27

Abraham Lincoln (UA) was another American Civil War epic directed by the famous director D W Griffith. In 1915 he had also directed that milestone in the world of films, *The Birth of a Nation*. Henry B Walthall, the hero of the latter movie, was cast again in *Abraham Lincoln*, but the title role went to Walter Huston.

1. E Alyn Warren and Walter Huston
2. Ian Keith (c)
3. Ian Keith
4. Hobart Bosworth and Henry B Walthall
5. Kay Hammond and Walter Huston
6. The Battle of Gettysburg
7. Walter Huston and Jimmie Eagles
8. Walter Huston
9. Walter Huston and young Gordon Thorp
10. Walter Huston
11. Walter Huston and Una Merkel
12. Ford's Theatre in Washington. Walter Huston is standing in the box
13. Walter Huston and Una Merkel
14. The Assassination
15. Kay Hammond and Walter Huston

10

11

12

13

14

15

1

2 3

4△▽6

5△▽7 8▽

9 10 11

1. Genevieve Tobin
2. Richard Arlen and Mary Brian in *Burning Up* (Par)
3. Claire Dodd
4. Eddie Cantor and Betty Grable (r) in *Whoopee* (SG/FZ)
5. Grace Moore in *A Lady's Morals* (MGM)
6. Jack Egan and Marie Saxon in *The Broadway Hoofer* (Col)
7. Betty Compson and Gary Cooper in *The Spoilers* (Par)
8. Charles King and Bessie Love in *Chasing Rainbows* (MGM)
9. Reginald Denny and Kay Johnson in *Madam Satan* (MGM)
10. Frank Morgan and Helen Kane in *Dangerous Nan McGrew* (Par)
11. Fifi D'Orsay
12. Leon Janney, Irene Rich and Lewis Stone in *Father's Son* (FN)
13. Kenneth MacKenna, Joan Bennett and Jason Robards in *Crazy that Way* (Fox)
14. Helen Johnson, Kenneth Thomson and Lawrence Gray in *Children of Pleasure* (MGM)
15. Marion Davies

▽13   12 △▽14   ▽15

1. Paul Whiteman
2. Jack Mulhall, El Brendel, Marjorie White and Sue Carol in *The Golden Calf* (Fox)
3. Jeanette Loff and Marie Prevost in *Party Girl* (Tif)
4. Helen Chandler, George O'Brien and Antonio Moreno in *Rough Romance* (Fox)
5. Guinn Williams and Lola Lane in *The Big Fight* (SAWW)
6. Charles Farrell and Janet Gaynor in *High Society Blues* (Fox)
7. Natalie Moorhead and William Powell in *The Benson Murder Case* (Par)
8. Kate Price, Charles Murray, George Sidney and Vera Gordon in *The Cohens and Kellys in Scotland* (Univ)
9. Grant Withers and Loretta Young in *The Second Floor Mystery* (WB)
10. Gibson Gowland, John Miljan and Boris Karloff in *The Sea Bat* (MGM)
11. Claude King, Aileen Pringle and Ian Keith in *Prince of Diamonds* (Col)
12. Beryl Mercer, Arthur Hoyt, Barbara Kent and Julia Swayne-Gordon in *Dumbbells in Ermine* (WB)

10 △ ▽ 11   12 ▽

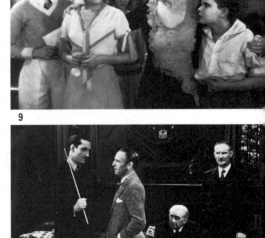

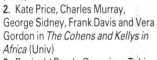

1. Charles Middleton, Mitchell Lewis and Rod La Rocque in *Beau Bandit* (RKO)

2. Kate Price, Charles Murray, George Sidney, Frank Davis and Vera Gordon in *The Cohens and Kellys in Africa* (Univ)

3. Reginald Pasch, Genevieve Tobin, Conrad Nagel and Bertha Mann in *Free Love* (Univ)

4. Fredric March and Claudette Colbert in *Manslaughter* (Par)

5. Monte Blue

6. Richard Arlen

7. Kenneth McKenna and Dorothy Mackaill in *Man Trouble* (Fox)

8. Ginger Rogers, Frank Morgan and Charles Ruggles in *Queen High* (Par)

9. Byron Sage, Marion Nixon, Belle Bennett and Don Marion in *Courage* (WB)

10. Charles Murray and George Sidney in *Around the Corner* (Col)

11. Basil Rathbone, Alec B Francis and Roland Young in *The Bishop Murder Case* (MGM)

12. Alan Roscoe, Mae Clarke, Jack Mulhall, Tom Kennedy, Pat O'Malley and Wynne Gibson in *The Fall Guy* (RKO)

13. Claudia Dell and John Harron in *Big Boy* (WB)

10 △ ▽ 12

11 △ ▽ 13

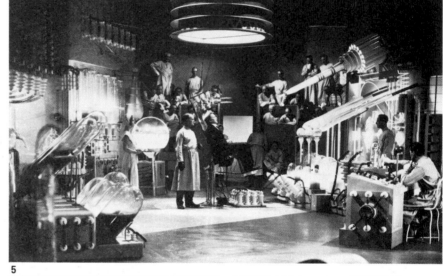

1. Ernest Torrence
2. Kay Francis
3. George O'Brien (l) in *Fair Warning* (Fox)
4. Helen Twelvetrees and Phillips Holmes in *Her Man* (Pat)
5. El Brendel in *Just Imagine* (Fox)
6. Charles Farrell and Janet Gaynor in *Happy Days* (Fox)
7. Ralph Lynn and Winifred Shotter in *Plunder* (B & D)
8. Sue Carol and George O'Brien in *The Lone Star Ranger* (Fox)
9. Harry Bannister and Ann Harding in *Girl of the Golden West* (FN)
10. Ramon Novarro and Dorothy Jordan in *Call of the Flesh* (MGM)

1. Tom Walls
2. Billie Dove
3. Madge Bellamy
4. Reginald Denny and Jeanette MacDonald in *Oh For a Man!* (Fox)
5. Charles Morton and Anita Page in *Caught Short* (Cos/MGM)
6. Maurice Chevalier and Claudette Colbert in *The Big Pond* (Par)
7. Bert Lytell and Claire MacDowell in *Brothers* (Col)
8. Barbara Stanwyck
9. Chester Morris and Norma Shearer in *The Divorcee* (MGM)
10. Thomas Meighan

1

3

4 5

The Blue Angel (Ufa) was intended to be a new starring vehicle for the great German actor Emil Jannings. In the event it proved to be Marlene Dietrich's greatest movie. Even today, mention of *The Blue Angel* evokes the memory of Marlene in her top hat and stockings, singing throatily the film's theme song 'Falling in love again.'

1. Marlene Dietrich
2. Marlene Dietrich and Rosa Valetti
3. & 4. Marlene Dietrich
5. Marlene Dietrich and Emil Jannings
6. Kurt Gerron and Marlene Dietrich
7. Emil Jannings
8. Marlene Dietrich and Emil Jannings
9. Reinhold Bernt, Emil Jannings, Marlene Dietrich and Rosa Valetti

▽8

6 △ ▽9 7

1. John Wray (c) in *Czar of Broadway* (Univ)
2. Joseph Schildkraut and Myrna Loy in *Cock o' the Walk* (SAWW)
3. Jack Oakie (r) in *Hit the Deck* (RKO)
4. J Harold Murray and Norma Terris in *Cameo Kirby* (Fox)
5. Elissa Landi
6. Rex Lease, star of *The Utah Kid* (Tif)
7. George Arliss and Alice Joyce in *The Green Goddess* (WB)
8. George Moran and Charles Mack in *Anybody's War* (Par)
9. Joseph Schildkraut and Edward G Robinson in *Night-Ride* (Univ)

6 △ ▽ 8   7 △ ▽ 9

1

2

3

4 △ ▽ 6

5 △ ▽ 7

King of Jazz (Univ) was one of the earliest musicals. On release it proved a great success, featuring as it did many famous stars of the time. Today it is probably best remembered as Bing Crosby's first movie. He was a member of a group called The Rhythm Boys

1. Paul Whiteman (f) and his band with the chorus girls
2. Jeanette Loff with John Boles who sings 'It Happened in Monterey'
3, 5 & 12. Chorus Line
4. Charles Murray and George Sidney
6. Otis Harlan and Slim Summerville
7. Slim Summerville
8. The spectacular 'Bridal Veil' number
9. Jeanette Loff
10. Paul Whiteman
11. The Sisters G

8 △ ▽ 9

10 △ ▽ 12   11

The Big Trail (Fox) was John Wayne's first big movie. After minor roles in seven films, he was still carrying props around the movie lot when he was spotted by director Raoul Walsh. Gary Cooper, offered the role of leading man, had evinced little interest and Walsh was seeking a suitable substitute. Wayne jumped at the chance but the film did not come up to Fox's expectations and Wayne had to wait until *Stagecoach* in 1938 before reaching true star status.

1. David Rollins, Ian Keith and Marguerite Churchill
2. John Wayne and Marguerite Churchill
3. El Brendel (r)
4. John Wayne and Marguerite Churchill
5. John Wayne and Tyrone Power Snr.
6. Ward Bond (leaning against wagon.)
7. El Brendel
8. John Wayne (l), Tyrone Power Snr (c) and Charles Stevens (r)
9. David Rollins and Marguerite Churchill

1

2

3

4

5

6

7

8

9

10

Morocco (Par) was the film that launched Marlene Dietrich on her Hollywood career. Paramount hoped for a big success and Dietrich did not disappoint the studio. For her performance, she was nominated for an Academy award.

1. and 9. Adolphe Menjou and Marlene Dietrich
2. Adolphe Menjou, Ulrich Haupt, Gary Cooper and Francis McDonald.
3. Gary Cooper, Marlene Dietrich and Adolphe Menjou
4. Gary Cooper and Marlene Dietrich
5. Marlene Dietrich and Gary Cooper
6. Gary Cooper and Francis McDonald
7. Marlene Dietrich
8. Gary Cooper (c) and fellow legionaires make their farewells.
10. Marlene Dietrich

41

1. Leila Hyams
2. Reginald Denny and Virginia Sale in *Embarrassing Moments* (Univ)
3. Mary Duncan and Charles Farrell in *City Girl* (Fox)
4. Mae Clarke
5. Fred Scott and Helen Twelvetrees in *Swing High* (Pat)
6. Billie Dove in *Notorious Affair* (FN)
7. Ralf Harolde and Robert Emmett O'Connor in *Framed* (RKO)
8. Betty Pierce and Bebe Daniels in *Alias French Gertie* (GB *Love Finds a Way*) (RKO)
9. Greta Garbo and Charles Bickford in *Anna Christie* (MGM)
10. Greta Garbo and Marié Dressler in *Anna Christie* (MGM)

1

2

4

5

6

7

8

9

10

1. Wallace Beery and Marie Dressler in *Min and Bill* (MGM)
2. Paul Lukas and Clive Brook in *Anybody's Woman* (Par)
3. Raquel Torres
4. Dolores Del Rio and Edmund Lowe in *The Bad One* (UA)
5. George Bancroft and Jessie Royce Landis in *Derelict* (Par)
6. Basil Rathbone and Ruth Chatterton in *The Lady of Scandal* (MGM)
7. Noah Beery Jr
8. William Bakewell
9. Walter Huston
10. Owen Moore and Gloria Swanson in *What a Widow!* (UA)

1

2

3

4

5

6

7 △ ▽ 9

8

Billy the Kid (MGM) was Metro's attempt to promote Johnny Mack Brown, hitherto leading man in several 'B' features, as one of their major stars. Their aim was unsuccessful and Johnny continued his movie career as lead in more 'B' films, mostly Westerns. He was listed among the leading money-making Western stars for each year from 1942 to 1950

1. Johnny Mack Brown, Warner Richmond and Kay Johnson
2. Blanche Frederici, Johnny Mack Brown and Russell Simpson
3. Roscoe Ates and Johnny Mack Brown
4. Kay Johnson and Johnny Mack Brown
5. Wyndham Standing and Kay Johnson
6. Johnny Mack Brown and Wallace Beery
7. Roscoe Ates, Chris-Pin Martin, Soledad Jiminez, Blanche Frederici, Russell Simpson, Johnny Mack Brown, Kay Johnson and Wyndham Standing
8. Johnny Mack Brown, Chris-Pin Martin, Roscoe Ates and Wyndham Standing
9. Johnny Mack Brown, Chris-Pin Martin, Kay Johnson, Roscoe Ates, Russell Simpson and Blanche Frederici

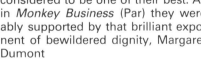

Animal Crackers (Par) The Marx Brothers' second movie is generally considered to be one of their best. As in *Monkey Business* (Par) they were ably supported by that brilliant exponent of bewildered dignity, Margaret Dumont

1. Margaret Irving and Harpo
2. Harpo and Robert Greig
3. Margaret Dumont, Margaret Irving, Harpo and Chico
4. Groucho and Margaret Dumont
5. Louis Sorin, Groucho and Margaret Dumont
6. Zeppo, Louis Sorin, Groucho and Margaret Dumont
7. Robert Greig, Louis Sorin, Groucho, Hal Thompson, Harpo, Zeppo and Chico.
8. Louis Sorin, Harpo and Chico
9. Chico, Groucho, Harpo and Margaret Dumont
10. Chico and Harpo
11. Harpo and Robert Greig
12. Chico, Groucho, Harpo and Zeppo
13. Hal Thompson, Lillian Roth and Chico
14. Chico, Louis Sorin, Hal Thompson and Lillian Roth

10 △ ▽ 13

12 △ ▽ 14

1. Kenneth Thomson and Billie Dove in *The Other Tomorrow* (FN)

2. Richard Arlen and Nancy Carroll in *Dangerous Paradise* (Par)

3. Dorothy Revier and Douglas Fairbanks Jr in *The Way Of All Men* (GB *Sin Flood)* (FN)

4. Basil Rathbone and Kay Johnson in *This Mad World* (MGM)

5. Dorothy Jordan and Robert Montgomery in *Love in the Rough* (MGM)

6. Lois Moran and Walter Byron in *Not Damaged* (Fox)

7. Myrtle Stedman and Winifred Westover in *Lummox* (UA)

8. Bert Lytell and Patsy Ruth Miller in *The Last of the Lone Wolf* (Col)

9. Vivienne Segal and Walter Pidgeon in *The Bride of the Regiment* (GB *Lady of the Rose)* (FN)

1. William Austin, Tully Marshall and Jeanette MacDonald in
Let's Go Native (Par)
2. Richard Arlen, Eugene Pallette and Jack Holt in *The Border Legion* (Par)
3. William Haines and Karl Dane in *Navy Blues* (MGM)
4. Joe E Brown
5. Randolph Scott
6. John Gilbert and Wallace Beery in *Way for a Sailor* (MGM)
7. H B Warner, Frank Albertson, Sharon Lynn and Joyce Compton in *Wild
Company* (Fox)
8. Richard Barthelmess
9. Bela Lugosi in *Wild Company* (Fox)
10. Rod La Rocque
11. Emil Jannings

1

2

3

4

5

6

7

8

9 △ ▽ 12

10

11 △ ▽ 13

14

15 16

17 18

19 △ ▽21 20△ ▽22

All Quiet on the Western Front (Univ) was completely different from Hollywood's previous attempts at portraying war. Hitherto audiences were persuaded to believe that war was a glorious adventure. This film showed war as it really is, grisly, ruthless, filthy, gory and above all glamourless. It won the Academy Award for the best picture of 1930 and its director, Lewis Milestone, was given the award for best direction.

1. Lew Ayres and Owen Davis Jr
2. Lew Ayres and Ben Alexander
3. Lew Ayres and Raymond Griffith
4. Lew Ayres and John Wray
5. Lew Ayres
6. Lew Ayres, Scott Kolk, Russell Gleason, William Bakewell, Louis Wolheim, Owen Davis Jr, Harold Goodwin and Slim Summerville.
7. The casualty ward
8. Ben Alexander, Lew Ayres, Owen Davis Jr, Russell Gleason and William Bakewell.
9. Bertha Mann, Beryl Mercer and Owen Davis Jr
10. Lew Ayres
11. Russell Gleason, Lew Ayres and Louis Wolheim
12. Over the top
13. Yola D'Avril and Lew Ayres
14. Training for the war
15. Yola D'Avril and Lew Ayres
16. Off-set coffee break during filming
17. Louis Wolheim and Lew Ayres
18. Lew Ayres
19. Lew Ayres, Scott Kolk, William Bakewell, Yola D'Avril, Poupée Andriot and Renée Damonde
20. Louis Wolheim and Slim Summerville
21. On the way to the front
22. Lew Ayres and Beryl Mercer

12

13

11

14   15

Hell's Angels (HH) was directed by Howard Hughes who was always fascinated with flying. In this film he indulged himself to such an extent that he produced a movie that is still talked about today as one of the greatest aerial war films ever made. During the filming two fliers and a mechanic were killed. *Hell's Angels* launched Jean Harlow as the Vamp of the Thirties, par excellence.

1. Jean Harlow and Ben Lyon
2. The destruction of the German Zeppelin
3. Douglas Gilmore, Jean Harlow, James Hall and Ben Lyon
4. A dog-fight
5. Ben Lyon and Jean Harlow
6. Lucien Prival and Ben Lyon
7. James Hall
8. Ben Lyon and Jean Harlow
9. Examining a crashed German bomber
10. Carl Von Haartman
11. Jean Harlow and Ben Lyon
12. James Hall and Ben Lyon
13. Douglas Gilmore, Jean Harlow and James Hall
14. Interior of German Zeppelin
15. Ben Lyon (seated centre) and James Hall (r)
16. Jean Harlow and Ben Lyon

16

51

1

2

3

4

5

6   7

1. Sally Starr, Elliott Nugent and
Jack Mulhall in *For the Love O' Lil*
(Col)
2. Everett Marshall, Ralf Harolde and
Bebe Daniels in *Dixiana* (RKO)
3. William Powell
4. Lupe Velez, Gibson Gowland and
Jean Hersholt in *Hell Harbor* (UA)
5. Walter Byron and Lois Moran in
The Dancers (Fox)
6. Ian Keith and Mary Duncan in
Boudoir Diplomat (Univ)
7. Robert Montgomery and June
Walker in *War Nurse* (MGM)
8. Grant Withers, Kate Price and Sue
Carol in *Dancing Sweeties* (WB)
9. Jack Oakie and Ginger Rogers in
The Sap From Syracuse (Par)
10. Robert Armstrong, DeWitt
Jennings and Jean Arthur in *Danger
Lights* (RKO)
11. Zelma O'Neal and Glenn Tryon
in *Dames Ahoy* (Univ)

8   9

10   11

1. Dorothy Lee, Robert Woolsey and Bert Wheeler in *Half Shot at Sunrise* (RKO)
2. William Farnum and Norma Talmadge in *Dubarry, Woman of Passion* (UA)
3. Dorothy Mackaill in *The Office Wife* (WB)
4. Jeanette MacDonald in *Monte Carlo* (Par)
5. Gary Cooper and June Collyer in *A Man From Wyoming* (Par)
6. Charles Ruggles, Clara Bow and Ralph Forbes in *Her Wedding Night* (Par)
7. Marguerite Churchill, William Collier Snr and Rex Bell in *Harmony at Home* (Fox)
8. Raymond Hackett, Jed Prouty, Nancy Price and Bessie Love in *Girl in the Show* (MGM)
9. William Boyd and Dorothy Sebastian in *His First Command* (Pat)

1. Helen Kane, Charles 'Buddy' Rogers and Margaret Breen in *Heads Up!* (Par)

2. Bernice Claire and Alexander Gray in *Spring is Here* (FN)

3. Buck Jones and Miriam Seegar in *The Dawn Trail* (BeP)

4. Edward G Robinson, Lupe Velez, Lew Ayres and Henry Kolker in *East is West* (Univ)

5. Lupe Velez and Edward G Robinson in *East is West* (Univ)

6. Dixie Lee and Arthur Lake in *Cheer Up And Smile* (Fox)

7. Sidney Blackmer and Otis Skinner in *Kismet* (FN)

8. Wallace Beery and Chester Morris in *The Big House* (MGM)

9. Mary Brian and Gary Cooper in *Only the Brave* (Par)

10. Buck Jones and Vera Reynolds in *Lone Rider* (BeP)

11. Nancy Carroll and Hobart Bosworth in *Devil's Holiday* (Par)

12. Fifi D'Orsay and Harold Murray in *Women Everywhere* (Fox)

13. Jack Holt

10 △ ▽ 12

54

1
2
3

5

6

7

8

10

11 △ ▽ 14

1. Robert Armstrong and Louis Wolheim in *Danger Lights* (RKO)
2. Warner Baxter and Myrna Loy in *Renegades* (Fox)
3. Alec B Francis and Leslie Howard in *Outward Bound* (WB)
4. Ralph Graves, Dorothy Sebastian and Jack Holt in *Hell's Island* (Col)
5. Lois Wilson
6. Henry B Walthall, Joan Peers and Richard Cromwell in *Tol'able David* (Col)
7. Mary Nolan
8. James Gleason, Eddie Quillan and Robert Armstrong in *Big Money* (Pat)
9. Fay Wray, Richard Arlen, James Hall, Jean Arthur, Gary Cooper, Mary Brian, Phillips Holmes, Joan Peers, David Newell and Virginia Bruce in *Paramount on Parade* (Par)
10. Bessie Love
11. Spencer Tracy, Claire Luce and Warren Hymer in *Up the River* (Fox)
12. Theodore Von Eltz
13. Barbara Kent
14. Vivienne Segal and John Boles in *Song of the West* (WB)

12 △ ▽ 13

1

2

3

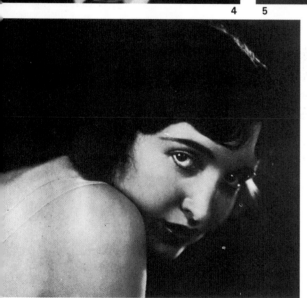

4

5

6

7

8 △ ▽ 10

9 △ ▽ 11

1. Eleanor Boardman
2. Marjorie Rambeau
3. Agnes Ayres
4. William Farnum
5. James Cagney
6. Anna Q Nilsson
7. Alice Joyce
8. Don Alvarado
9. George K Arthur
10. William Haines
11. Marilyn Miller

1. Ruth Chatterton
2. June Collyer
3. Margaret Bannerman
4. Elliott Nugent
5. Helen Twelvetrees
6. Donald Cook
7. Jessie Ralph
8. Warwick Ward
9. Pat O'Malley
10. Corinne Griffith
11. Jackie Coogan
12. Irvin S Cobb

57

1

2

4

3

1. Edward G Robinson
2. Lon Chaney and Lila Lee in *The Unholy Three* (MGM)
3. Annie Ondra in *Blackmail* (WW)
4. Slim Summerville and Harry Langdon in *See America Thirst* (Univ)

CHAPTER TWO
1931
NEW STARS SPARKLE

Joan Crawford and Harry Langdon in *Tramp, Tramp, Tramp* (HaL) a 1926 Frank Capra comedy

By 1931 the two biggest film-producing companies were Metro-Goldwyn-Mayer and Fox who between them were responsible for 40 per cent of the films being made in the USA. Warner Brothers and its associates produced about 25 per cent, while Paramount made about a quarter of the remaining 35 per cent.

One natural development was that the film-makers also became cinema owners, so that they not only gained more profit from the films being produced, they were also in a position to decide when and where their pictures would be shown.

The majority of both British and American audiences were going to the cinema in 1931 to be entertained by talkies. They were by now considered the norm.

It was a year when new names were being flashed on the screens; many of them rapidly became familiar. Not only were there new stars – some 26 of them – but now producers and directors were becoming equally well-known and could command followers among cinema audiences.

Frank Capra, for instance, had spent his time during the silent years making Harry Langdon comedies. They were among the best of their day but talkies offered Capra new opportunities, of which he made the most, to become recognized as one of the world's top directors.

Having directed 23-year-old Barbara Stanwyck to stardom in the 1930 Columbia film *Ladies of Leisure*, he did the same in 1931 for Jean Harlow in *Platinum Blonde*. She plays the daughter of a wealthy family who loses her man (Robert Williams), a newspaper man, to a fellow reporter (Loretta Young) when he realizes he would lose his own personality married to a socialite. After the film, Jean Harlow was always known as 'the platinum blonde'.

Capra made two other films for Columbia the same year. One was *The Miracle Woman*, in which he again starred Barbara Stanwyck, playing an evangelist. The other was *Dirigible*, an exciting drama of an airship on a scientific mission to the Arctic, starring Jack Holt.

In 1930 and 1931 Warner Brothers set out to prove that

Barbara Stanwyck

Loretta Young

James Cagney in *The Public Enemy* (GB *Enemies of the Public*) (WB)

Eddie Woods and Joan Blondell in *The Public Enemy* (WB)

James Cagney and Jean Harlow in *The Public Enemy* (WB)

James Cagney and Joan Blondell in *Blonde Crazy* (GB *Larceny Lane*) (WB)

Ray Milland

crime did not pay by producing two films which are today recognized as cinema classics.

The films were *Little Caesar* (1930) and in the following year *The Public Enemy* (GB: *Enemies of the Public*.) They made an impact that has never been lost, for they can still stir audiences to this day. In fact, for the whole of the decade Warners always had a gangster movie in the pipeline.

James Cagney, an actor and song-and-dance man trained on Broadway, was in his second year of films when he was cast as the leading man's friend in *The Public Enemy*. It was a role that he did not retain for long. Soon after the film began shooting, his dynamic performance showed him to be a natural for the leading role. The original star of the film, Eddie Woods, became the friend and Cagney was given the part of Tom Powers, a deprived kid from the slums of Chicago who lived by petty crime during the Prohibition era.

Probably the scene that has left the most lasting impression is when Cagney, during an argument, smashes a grapefruit into leading lady Mae Clarke's face.

Cagney's performance was compulsive watching and marked him as a superstar, a position he enjoyed throughout his long screen career. Director William Wellman's work on the film brought highly deserved praise, while Mae Clarke also earned star status from her role. Others in the impressive cast are Jean Harlow, Joan Blondell, Beryl Mercer, Donald Cook and Leslie Fenton.

Before the year passed director Mervyn LeRoy and Edward G. Robinson were to follow their previous year's success, *Little Caesar*, with another film that gave Robinson's personality as a screen tough guy full scope. *Five Star Final* is a drama that features a New York newspaper engaged in muckraking and exploiting people in order to increase its circulation.

Others in the cast are Marian Marsh, H. B. Warner, Boris Karloff, Aline MacMahon, making her debut for the studio, Anthony Bushell and Ona Munson.

Another James Cagney film released in 1931 was *Blonde Crazy* (GB *Larceny Lane*). Cagney displays his rare versatility as a sharp hotel porter who spends his time conning the clientele. In his nefarious activities he has the perfect partner in Joan Blondell who, as a chambermaid, assists him in his petty swindles.

The film was directed by Roy Del Ruth who kept the action moving at a fast pace. The supporting cast was headed by Ray Milland and Louis Calhern.

Norma Shearer, Leslie Howard, Lionel Barrymore and Clark Gable – any one of these names would have been enough to entice members of the public to pay a visit to the cinema. *A Free Soul* boasts all four stars in a cast that has an impressive list of supporting players.

The film not only won Barrymore an Oscar for Best Actor playing Norma Shearer's alcoholic lawyer-father, but it so impressed the bosses at MGM that he was given a contract for life. There is little doubt that Barrymore out-shone his fellow members of the cast. Even so, Miss Shearer was nominated for an Academy Award for her performance, as was Clarence Brown for his sparkling direction. The film was also important to Clark Gable's career as it led to him becoming classed as one of MGM's superstars.

Gable was able to display his talent enacting a sexually attractive gangster who plays an aggressive game of love with the lawyer's beautiful daughter.

Dishonored was the third Marlene Dietrich film to be directed by Josef von Sternberg. It has weathered the years well and even today endorses Dietrich's right to be classed among the legends of the silver screen. She appears, somewhat surprisingly, as a Russian spy opposite Victor McLaglen.

Incidentally, the film was based on a story *X-27* which was written by Sternberg himself. The cast list also included Barry Norton, Lew Cody and Wilfred Lucas.

When Lon Chaney died in 1930, he left a vacancy for the title role in *Dracula* which was to be made the following year. Chaney at the time was recognized as the master of horror movies. His successor would have to be equally menacing with a voice that could chill, as well as thrill, an audience. The choice was a Hungarian actor with a talent that matched Lon Chaney's in its originality. He was Bela Lugosi. He played the part with such effect and conviction that his name has been linked forever with that of Count Dracula. Lugosi became the Vampire Count and no actor playing the part since has been able to get close to Lugosi in his interpretation.

Lugosi's Count Dracula, swathed in a black cloak beneath which he wears full evening dress, shows little of the sophistication expected of the modern player of such a part; today Lugosi's acting would probably be described as 'wooden'. But that he is always a threat, a terrifying monster, with fangs ever ready to bury in the throat of a victim, does not fail to stir some sense of fear in those watching him on the screen. Helen Chandler has the feminine lead and others in the cast are David Manners, Dwight Frye, Edward Van Sloan and Herbert Bunston.

Six months after *Dracula* came to the screen another strange creature was introduced. This time it was in the film *Frankenstein*. There was, thought the Universal bosses, only one man for the title role – Bela Lugosi again, but they were in for a shock. Lugosi's most menacing feature was his voice and this was not required for *Frankenstein*. At most he emits only a few grunts and groans. There is no dialogue at all. His screen test for the part did not reveal the right image for the new monster. It was agreed that another actor must be found for the role.

The choice was a gentle, softly-spoken, cricket-loving Englishman born William Pratt, a name he had changed to the more formidable-sounding Boris Karloff. The film gave Karloff the break he needed and was the start of a

Clark Gable

Lew Cody

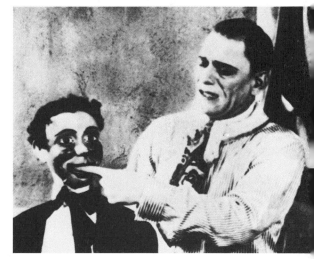
Lon Chaney

William Pratt – later to become Boris Karloff

Boris Karloff in *Frankenstein* (Univ)

Phillips Holmes and Sylvia Sidney in *An American Tragedy* (Par)

Phillips Holmes

Ronald Colman in *Arrowsmith* (SG)

career that lasted some 40 years. Just as Lugosi has always been 'Dracula' so Karloff will always be remembered as the gruesome man-made ghoul created by Dr. Frankenstein.'

The film, based on the Gothic classic written by Mary Shelley, wife of the famous poet, tells the story of a mad scientist who creates a human monster from corpses and accidentally uses the criminal brain of one of them. The monster with his square face, stiffened neck and unreal movements terrorizes the community, although, as the film unfolds, audiences get a combined feeling of revulsion and sympathy for the creature.

It took make-up man Jack Pierce four hours each morning to create the monster before the day's shooting. During the filming, Karloff's own height of 1.8 m (6 ft) was increased by 45 cm (18 in), while his heavy attire made him 27 kg (60 lb) heavier. The actor himself lost 13.5 kg (30 lb) in weight during the time the film was in production.

The year 1931 saw the first showing of two major Hollywood films, *An American Tragedy* and *Arrowsmith*.

Paramount's *An American Tragedy* was taken from Theodore Dreiser's famous novel. The film deals with a young man who is due to marry his pregnant girlfriend (Sylvia Sidney), when he meets a rich girl (Frances Dee). Dazzled by all the trappings of wealth he sees around her, he decides to rid himself of his dowdy girlfriend by murdering her, which he does by taking her out in a boat on a lake and drowning her – a crime for which he pays the ultimate price by a one-way trip to the electric chair.

This sombre story was directed by Josef von Sternberg in a more subdued manner than usual, and the film starred Phillips Holmes, a sensitive actor, whose career ended when he was killed in an air collision in 1942, during his Second World War service.

Arrowsmith, produced by Sam Goldwyn, was taken from a novel by the Nobel Prize-winning author, Sinclair Lewis. It starred Ronald Colman as an idealistic doctor who gives up a lucrative career only to have his scientific ideals shattered. The film, directed by John Ford, had a strong supporting cast which included Helen Hayes, Myrna Loy and Beulah Bondi.

When German director Ernst Lubitsch was casting for the leads in *The Smiling Lieutenant*, based on the Oscar Straus operetta 'A Waltz Dream', and previously filmed in Germany in 1925, he chose Maurice Chevalier and Claudette Colbert.

The Smiling Lieutenant proved to be a happy picture, a light-hearted piece of nonsense that was tailor-made for its stars. Lubitsch's clever direction was good enough to win a nomination for the year's best picture. Miriam Hopkins and Charles Ruggles provided the stars with worthy support.

Walter Forde was a prominent British director in the early Thirties. He was noted for his comedies but he enjoyed some success with films of a more serious nature. He had acted for Gainsborough Pictures, a leading British studio, and no doubt his previous experience as a music-hall performer stood him in good stead when he devoted his talents to directing.

During 1931 he made three movies: *Third Time Lucky*, starring Bobby Howes, Gordon Harker and Dorothy Boyd; the Edgar Wallace story, *The Ringer*, starring Franklyn Dyall, Gordon Harker, Carol Goodner and John Longden; and *The Ghost Train* with Jack Hulbert and his wife, Cicely Courtneidge. All the films were well made for their time and proved popular with British audiences.

At this period Herbert Marshall and his wife, Edna Best, were appearing in films for Gainsborough Pictures. In 1931, they co-starred in *Michael and Mary*, and then in Edgar Wallace's *The Calendar*.

René Clair made two sound films (as distinct from talkies) in France during 1931. *Le Million* and *A Nous la Liberté* both had songs instead of dialogue. The films displayed the light humour that has become the hallmark of Clair's work for the cinema. *Le Million* told the story of a hunt for a missing lottery ticket. *A Nous la Liberté* is described by Clair himself as being about 'two convicts who break jail and meet years later when one is owner of a gramophone factory and the other works for him. The owner eventually gives his factory to the workers and takes to the road with his friend.'

Jean Renoir, son of the celebrated French artist, began his climb to international fame with *On Purge Bébé*, a farce that took only three weeks to complete, including scripting, writing and editing. The film starred the wonderful French actor Michel Simon who also appeared in Renoir's *La Chienne* the same year. In this film he plays a solid, faithful bank employee who seeks his soul's escape first through his painting and then with a lovely mistress, when his boring, orderly life turns to much more rewarding chaos.

Two films from the German veteran G.W. Pabst caused a stir in the same year. *Die Dreigroschenoper* (*The Threepenny Opera*) based on the Brecht stage play, is mainly remembered for the author's disapproval of the screen version of his work.

Pabst's other film was *Kameradschaft (Comradeship)*, which had political overtones in the telling of a group of German miners working on the French-German border who defy the orders of their bosses and rescue French miners trapped underground.

Berlin Alexanderplatz made by Piel Jutzi followed the vogue of German movies at the time by containing a message. It wove fiction with documentary fact. Based on the story by Döblin, it deals with one Franz Biberkopf who, after taking a series of hard knocks that would cripple weaker men, emerges as a man refusing to be browbeaten by the ill-luck that comes his way.

As a sop to the Nazi movement which was already on its way to ultimate power, some 'soft' films were made full of

Miriam Hopkins and Maurice Chevalier in *The Smiling Lieutenant* (Par)

Cicely Courtneidge and Jack Hulbert

Herbert Marshall

Kameradschaft (Nero)

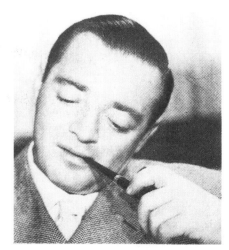

Peter Lorre

Peter Lorre in *M* (Nero)

Hedy Lamarr

sentimentality with the principal characters displaying a definite leaning towards fascism. A special genre of these films grew up called 'mountain films'. They used the drama of the mountain scenery and the struggles of men to conquer them as heroic elements in their plots. The director Luis Trenker made several of these films including, in 1931, *Berge in Flammen (The Doomed Battalion.)*

Before he answered the call to Hollywood, Fritz Lang made one of the most remarkable films to come out of Germany. It was called simply *M* and has been making its impact felt throughout the world whenever it has been shown since it made its Berlin premiere in 1931. The story is based on an actual happening in Dusseldorf and follows the activities of a group of beggars engaged in tracking down a child murderer who, when apprehended, is given a kangaroo trial before the police intervene. The film was loaded with suspense and has earned the status of being a classic. It is also notable for starting its star, Peter Lorre, on the road to international fame.

In 1931 the Russian film industry was still in the experimental stage with sound. Leonid Trauberg and Grigori Kozintsev co-directed *Alone* which, originally planned as a silent movie, was switched to sound. It told the story of a young lady teacher who is sent to a poverty-stricken village in a remote region – and had a wonderful score by the young Shostakovitch.

The first Russian film that was produced especially to take sound was *Road to Life*, directed by Nikolai Ekk. It follows the factual story of a group of youngsters left orphans after a civil war who are running wild in the streets. When an understanding teacher takes them in hand and forms a settlement where they live and learn to cope with normal lives, they become worthwhile citizens. Technically, the film was a big advance on any film made in Russia previously.

Czechoslovakia has always been a nation of film-makers. They were among the pioneers of the art. One of the best-known is Gustav Machatý who in 1931 completed the 'social-realism' story *From Saturday to Sunday*. Machatý gained the world's attention in 1933 for his film *Ecstase* which featured nude scenes of a young lady later known as Hedy Lamarr.

Hungary had a flourishing industry in the early days of cinema, but by the late Twenties filming was in the doldrums. This lasted until 1931 when, with the backing of the government, a revival came about. The country's first two talkies were made that year. One of these was *Hyppolit the Butler* and it clearly showed its maker, István Székely, to be one of the best Hungarian directors of the Thirties. It told of the fortunes of an engaging member of the *nouveau-riche* in the grip of his tyrannical butler and socially ambitious wife.

India also showed its first talkie in 1931. This was Ardeshir Irani's *Alam Ara.*

Warner Oland in *Daughter of the Dragon* (Par)　　Boris Karloff in *Frankenstein* (Univ)

Horror, crime, sex and Westerns were becoming the dominant themes for movies of the Thirties. In 1931, Boris Karloff, Bela Lugosi, James Cagney, Joan Crawford and Richard Dix all responded dutifully to the summons.

Marlene Dietrich and Victor McLaglen in *Dishonored* (Par)

Charles Chaplin, Virginia Cherrill in *City Lights* (UA)

Hedda Hopper in *Good Sport* (Fox)

David Manners and Richard Barthelmess in *The Last Flight* (FN)

65

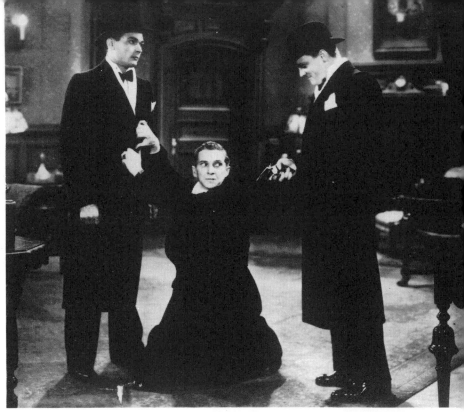

Edward G Robinson, Nel Francis and James
Cagney in *Smart Money* (WB)
Right: Edward Woods, Murray Kinnell and James
Cagney in *The Public Enemy* (GB *Enemies of the
Public*) (WB)

James Cagney in *Blonde Crazy* (WB) (GB *Larceny Lane*)

Mae Clarke and James Cagney in *The Public Enemy*
(GB *Enemies of the Public*)

Richard Dix in *Cimarron* (RKO)

Right: Lester Vail and Joan Crawford in *Dance
Fools, Dance* (MGM)

The spectacular Oklahoma landrush in *Cimarron* (RKO)

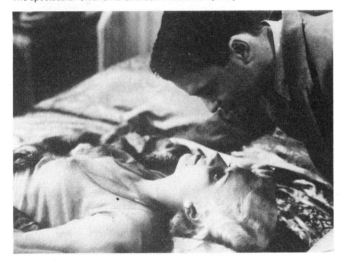

Lew Ayres and Jean Harlow in *The Iron Man* (Univ)

Barbara Stanwyck and Ben Lyon in *Night Nurse* (WB)

Norma Shearer

Left: Phillips Holmes and John Huston in *The Criminal Code* (Col)

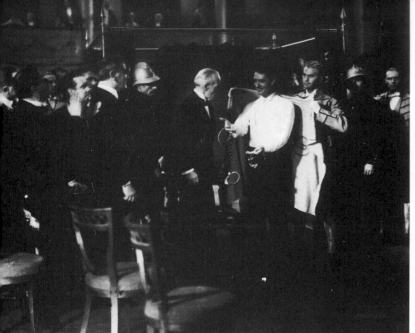

Picture Gallery for 1931

5 △ ▽ 8   6   7 △ ▽ 9

10   11

1. Lewis Stone and John Gilbert in *The Phantom of Paris* (MGM)
2. Maureen O'Sullivan, William Farnum and Will Rogers in *A Connecticut Yankee* (Fox)
3. Buster Keaton and Anita Page in *The Sidewalks of New York* (MGM)
4. John Wayne, Buck Jones and Susan Fleming in *The Range Feud* (Col)
5. Gary Cooper and Claudette Colbert in *His Woman* (Par)
6. Jeanette MacDonald in *Annabelle's Affairs* (Fox)
7. Clark Gable and Skeets Gallagher in *Possessed* (MGM)
8. Ralph Forbes, C Aubrey Smith, Halliwell Hobbes, Edgar Norton, Marian Davies, Ray Milland and Nena Quartaro in *The Bachelor Father* (MGM)
9. Fay Wray and Ronald Colman in *The Unholy Garden* (SG)
10. Laurel and Hardy in *Pardon Us* (HR)
11. Johnny Mack Brown, Elliott Nugent, Richard Barthlemess, Helen Chandler and David Manners in *The Last Flight* (FN)
12. Lupe Velez and John Boles in *Resurrection* (Univ)
13. Laurence Olivier and Elissa Landi in *The Yellow Ticket* (GB *The Yellow Passport*) (Fox)
14. Marian Marsh and John Barrymore in *Svengali* (WB)
15. Joan Crawford in *Paid* (GB *Within the Law*) (MGM)
16. Edmund Gwenn, C V France and Jill Esmond in *The Skin Game* (BIP)
17. Buck Jones in *Desert Vengeance* (BeP Col)

12

13

14 △ ▽ 16

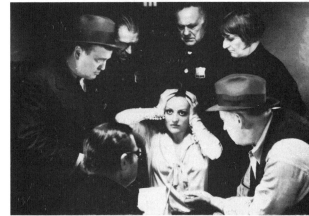

15 △ ▽ 17

8 △ ▽9

1. Dorothy Revier and Buck Jones in *The Avenger* (BeP/Col)
2. Harold Goodwin
3. Mae Simon and Seymour Rechzeit in *My-Yiddishe-Mama* (XX)
4. Hedda Hopper
5. Buster Keaton and Anita Page in *The Sidewalks of New York* (MGM)
6. Mickey Rooney
7. Sylvia Sidney in *City Streets* (Par)
8. Irene Delroy in *Men of the Sky* (FN)
9. Helen Jerome Eddy and Robert Coogan in *Sooky* (Par)

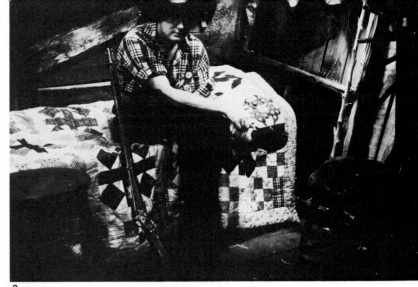

5 △ ▽ 8

6 △ ▽ 9

7 △ ▽ 10

1. Cliff Lyons, Ruth Mix, Al Ferguson and Jim Corey in *Red Fork Range* (Big)
2. Lew Ayres in *Heaven on Earth* (Univ)
3. Estelle Taylor and Ronald Colman in *Unholy Garden* (SG)
4. Stan Laurel
5. Douglas Fairbanks (I) in *Around the World in 80 Minutes* (UA)
6. Charles Ray
7. Stanley Holloway
8. Frank Fay and Dorothy Mackaill in *Bright Lights* (FN)
9. Clive Brook
10. Hardie Albright and Dorothy Jordan in *Young Sinners* (Fox)

71

1   2

3   4   ▽ 7

1. Louise Closser Hale, Jean Harlow and Robert Williams in *Platinum Blonde* (Col)
2. Peter Lorre in *M* (Nero)
3. Ralph Graves and Fay Wray in *Dirigible* (Col)
4. Mae Clarke, Ricardo Cortez and Matt McHugh in *Reckless Living* (Univ)
5. Edward Woods and Joan Blondell in *The Public Enemy* (GB *Enemies of the Public*) (WB)
6. Leslie Howard and Norma Shearer in *A Free Soul* (MGM)
7. Warner Baxter in *The Cisco Kid* (Fox)
8. Vladimir Sokoloff
9. Charlotte Greenwood
10. Joseph Cawthorn
11. Kathleen Harrison
12. Richard Dix
13. Lawrence Gray
14. Russell Gleason
15. Kathlyn Williams
16. Dorothy Gulliver
17. Charles Starrett
18. Lillian Bond
19. Mitzi Green
20. Virginia Grey
21. Sonnie Hale

5 △ ▽ 6

72

8

9 10

11

12

13 14

15

16 △ ▽ 19

17 △ ▽ 20

18 △ ▽ 21

1. Billie Dove and Edward Everett Horton in *The Age for Love* (HH)
2. James Hall and Dorothy Sebastian in *The Lightning Flyer* (Col)
3. Lewis Stone and Joan Crawford in *Dance Fools Dance* (MGM)
4. Genevieve Tobin, Ivan Lebedeff and Betty Compson in *The Gay Diplomat* (RKO)
5. Lowell Sherman, Irene Dunne and Charles Coleman in *Bachelor Apartment* (RKO)
6. Frank Albertson, Sally O'Neil and Alan Dinehart in *Brat* (Fox)
7. Mary Astor and Ricardo Cortez in *Behind Office Doors* (RKO)
8. H B Warner, Anthony Bushell and Dolores Costello in *Expensive Woman* (FN)
9. John St Polis and Kay Francis in *Transgression* (RKO)
10. Dorothy Sebastian and Warner Oland in *The Big Gamble* (Pat)
11. Ricardo Cortez, Helen Twelvetrees and John Garrick in *Bad Company* (Pat)
12. Ricardo Cortez and Loretta Young in *Big Business Girl* (FN)

1
2
3

4
5
6

7
8
9 △ ▽ 11

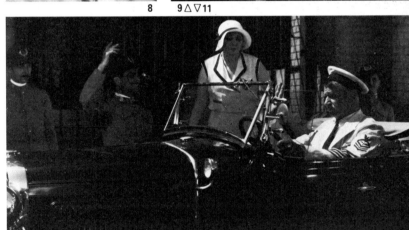

10 △ ▽ 12

1. Charles Delaney and Kenneth Harlan in *Air Police* (WW)
2. Bert Wheeler and Robert Woolsey in *Cracked Nuts* (RKO)
3. Sally Eilers, Minna Gombell and James Dunn in *Bad Girl* (Fox)
4. Vivienne Osborne, Paul Lukas, Dorothy Jordan and Charles Ruggles in *The Beloved Bachelor* (Par)
5. Ralph Morgan
6. Anthony Bushell, Rose Hobart and Douglas Fairbanks Jr in *Chances* (FN)
7. Edward Martindel, Mae Murray, Maude Turner Gordon, Ethel Levey and Lowell Sherman (r) in *High Stakes* (RKO)
8. Olive Borden
9. Monroe Owsley (c) in *Honor Among Lovers* (Par)
10. Clara Bow and Norman Foster in *No Limit* (Par)
11. Marjorie Rambeau and Wallace Beery in *Hell Divers* (MGM)
12. Ona Munson, Joe E Brown, Frank McHugh, Laura Lee and Lawrence Gray in *Going Wild* (WB)

75

Cimarron (RKO) was based on Edna Ferber's best-selling novel of the same title. There can be little doubt that the movie's winning of an Academy Award was largely due to its spectacular scenes and to Richard Dix's unsurpassable performance as Yancey Cravat, the footloose crusading pioneer of Old Oklahoma.

1. Richard Dix, Douglas Scott and Irene Dunne
2. Estelle Taylor and Richard Dix
3. Richard Dix, Douglas Scott and Irene Dunne
4. Richard Dix
5. Estelle Taylor (s)
6. Irene Dunne and Richard Dix
7. William Collier Jr and Richard Dix
8. Richard Dix, Irene Dunne and Stanley Fields
9. Richard Dix and Estelle Taylor
10. Douglas Scott, Irene Dunne, Nance O'Neil, Richard Dix and Frank Beal

9 ▽

8 △

1   **2**

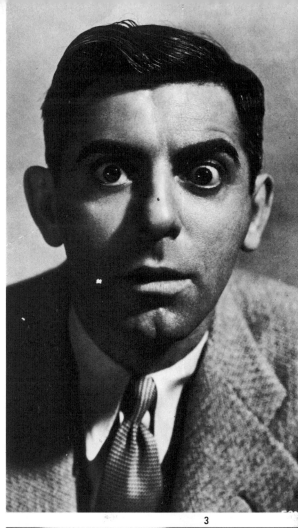
3

4   **5**

6 △ ▽ 9   **7 △ ▽ 10**

8

1. Gordon Harker
2. Willy Fritsch
3. Eddie Cantor
4. Willard Robertson
5. Jameson Thomas
6. Seymour Hicks
7. Bert Lytell
8. Joan Bennett
9. Al Jolson
10. Dennis King

1. John Loder
2. Regis Toomey
3. Jeanne de Casalis
4. Sig Rumann
5. Monty Banks
6. J M Kerrigan
7. Arthur Lake
8. Tom Keene
9. Edward Everett Horton
10. Dolores Costello
11. Jetta Goudal
12. Robert Warwick
13. Jane Darwell

9 △ ▽ 11

12 △ ▽ 13

78

1

2

3

4

5 6

7 △ ▽13

8 9 △ ▽ 12

10 △ ▽ 11

1. Norman Foster
2. Ian Keith
3. Ina Claire
4. Sydney Howard
5. Betty Compson
6. Arthur Treacher
7. Fay Compton
8. Sophie Tucker
9. Guy Kibbee
10. Belle Bennett
11. Edna Best
12. Dorothy Sebastian
13. Bobby Howes

14

15

16

17

18

19

20

21

22

23

1. John Gilbert
2. Leslie Howard and Mary Duncan in *Five and Ten* (GB *Daughter of Luxury*) (MGM)
3. Irene Rich
4. Ricardo Cortez and Bebe Daniels in *The Maltese Falcon* (WB)
5. Sylvia Sidney, Norman Foster and Phillips Holmes in *Confessions of a Co-ed* (GB *Her Dilemma*) (Par)
6. George O'Brien and Marguerite Churchill in *Riders of the Purple Sage* (Fox)
7. Paul Lukas and Sidney Fox in *Strictly Dishonorable* (Univ)
8. Carole Lombard, Skeets Gallagher, Lucien Littlefield and Norman Foster in *It Pays to Advertise* (Par)
9. George Bancroft and Frances Dee in *Rich Man's Folly* (Par)
10. Kay Francis and William Powell in *Ladies' Man* (Par)
11. Alison Skipworth, Melvyn Douglas and Gloria Swanson in *Tonight or Never* (SG/UA)
12. Dorothy Sebastian and Lloyd Hughes in *The Deceiver* (Col)
13. Bob Steele in *Near the Trail's End* (Tif)
14. Jack Oakie and Stuart Erwin in *Dude Ranch* (Par)
15. Robert Young and Constance Cummings in *Guilty Generation* (Col)
16. John Darrow, Edna May Oliver and Rochelle Hudson in *Fanny Foley Herself* (GB *Top of the Bill*) (RKO)
17. Helen Twelvetrees and John Halliday in *Millie* (RKO)
18. Leon Errol, Mitzi Green, Jackie Searle and ZaSu Pitts in *Finn and Hattie* (Par)
19. Paul Lukas and Eleanor Boardman in *Women Love Once* (Par)
20. Pat O'Brien and Irene Dunne in *Consolation Marriage* (GB *Married in Haste*) (RKO)
21. Leila Hyams, Norman Foster and Adolphe Menjou in *Men Call it Love* (MGM)
22. Conchita Montenegro and Leslie Howard in *Never the Twain Shall Meet* (MGM)
23. William Powell and Carole Lombard in *Man of the World* (Par)

1

3

4

5

6

7 △ ▽ 10

8 △ ▽ 11

9 △

12
13
14

15
16

17
18

1. Frances Dade and Bela Lugosi in *Dracula* (Univ)
2. Bela Lugosi and Helen Chandler in *Dracula* (Univ)
3. Jack Holt and Ralph Graves in *A Dangerous Affair* (Col)
4. Irving Pichel and Peggy Shannon in *The Road to Reno* (Par)
5. Edmund Lowe and Myrna Loy in *Transatlantic* (Fox)
6. Neil Hamilton, Henry Kolker and Kay Johnson in *The Spy* (Fox)
7. Boris Karloff and Mae Clarke in *Frankenstein* (Univ)
8. Charles Bickford playing a dual role in *River's End* (WB)
9. Franklin Pangborn, ZaSu Pitts, William Bakewell and Helen Twelvetrees in *A Woman of Experience* (Pat)
10. Tim McCoy and Doris Hill in *The One Way Trail* (Col)
11. Constance Cummings, Stanley Fields, Gwen Lee, Hugh Herbert, Dorothy Peterson and Frank McHugh in *Traveling Husbands* (RKO)
12. Adolphe Menjou and Leila Hyams in *Men Call it Love* (MGM)
13. Warner Baxter and Joan Bennett in *Doctors' Wives* (Fox)
14. Bela Lugosi, Marjorie White and Joe E Brown in *Broadminded* (FN)
15. Charles Chaplin and Virginia Cherrill in *City Lights* (ChC)
16. Mary Astor and Edward Everett Horton in *Smart Woman* (RKO)
17. Lili Damita and Gary Cooper in *Fighting Caravans* (Par)
18. Gary Cooper (r) in *Fighting Caravans* (Par)
19. Gary Cooper, Charles Trowbridge and Carole Lombard in *I Take This Woman* (Par)
20. Dorothy Mackaill and Walter Byron in *The Reckless Hour* (FN)
21. Robert Montgomery and Constance Bennett in *The Easiest Way* (MGM)
22. Joan Blondell and James Cagney in *Blonde Crazy* (GB *Larceny Lane*) (WB)
23. Lionel Atwill

19 △ ▽ 21
20 △ ▽ 22
23

12 13

14

15 16

1. Peggy Shannon and Richard Arlen in *The Secret Call* (Par)
2. Janet Gaynor in *Delicious* (Fox)
3. Grant Withers and Mary Astor in *Other Men's Women* (WB)
4. Richard Dix, Paul Hurst and Boris Karloff in *Public Defender* (RKO)
5. Rene Clama and Garry Marsh in *The Man They Couldn't Arrest* (G'boro)
6. Eric Linden and Arline Judge in *Are These Our Children?* (RKO)
7. Ernest Torrence and Adolphe Menjou in *The Great Lover* (MGM)
8. Warner Baxter in *Surrender* (Fox)
9. Joel McCrea and Dorothy Mackaill in *Once A Sinner* (Fox)
10. Gene Raymond and Nancy Carroll in *Personal Maid* (Par)
11. Karen Morley
12. Lilyan Tashman and Kay Francis in *Girls About Town* (Par)
13. Lucille Powers and Phillips Holmes in *Man to Man* (WB)
14. Thelma Todd
15. Madge Evans and Ramon Novarro in *Son of India* (MGM)
16. Laura La Plante
17. Bette Davis and Emma Dunn in *Bad Sister* (Univ)
18. Janet Gaynor and Warner Baxter in *Daddy Long Legs* (Fox)
19. Fay Wray and Richard Arlen in *The Conquering Horde* (Par)
20. Sylvia Sidney
21. Thomas E Jackson

17 18

19 20 21

1. Jack Holt, Constance Cummings and Gaylord Pendleton in *The Last Parade* (Col)

2. Peggy Shannon

3. Leila Hyams and Charlotte Greenwood in *Stepping Out* (MGM)

4. Pat O'Brien in *Flying High* (GB *Happy Landing*) (MGM)

5. Greta Garbo and Clark Gable in *Susan Lennox, Her Rise and Fall* (GB *The Rise of Helga*) (MGM)

6. Madge Evans, Charles Farrell and John Arledge in *Heartbreak* (Fox)

7. Claude King, Owen Moore and Joan Bennett in *Hush Money* (Fox)

8. Ben Lyon and Marilyn Miller in *Her Majesty, Love* (FN)

9. Charles Murray and George Sidney in *Caught Cheating* (Tif)

10. Lewis Stone, Elissa Landi and Paul Cavanagh in *Always Goodbye* (Fox)

11. Chrissie White

12. Clive Brook and Tallulah Bankhead in *Tarnished Lady* (Par)

86

1

2

3

4

5

6

7

8

1. Ruth Chatterton in *Once a Lady* (Par)
2. Buck Jones (I) in *Fighting Sheriff* (BeP)
3. Buck Jones and Harry Woods in *Range Feud* (Col)
4. Eddie Dowling, June Collyer and Noah Beery Snr in *Honeymoon Lane* (Par)
5. Mady Christians
6. Paul Gregory and Tom Patricola in *Children of Dreams* (WB)
7. Noah Beery Snr in *Homicide Squad* (Univ)
8. Fredric March and Nancy Carroll in *The Night Angel* (Par)
9. Frances Dee and Charles 'Buddy' Rogers in *Along Came Youth* (Par)
10. Marjorie Rambeau and Clive Brook in *Silence* (Par)
11. Louise Huntington and George O'Brien in *Fair Warning* (Fox)
12. Bob Steele and Dorothy Dix in *Nevada Buckaroo* (Tif)

9 △ ▽ 11

10 △ ▽ 12

1

2   3

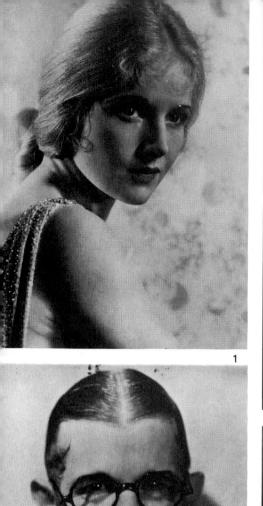

4   5

6 △ ▽ 9

7   8

10 △ ▽ 12   11 △ ▽ 13

14

15

16

17

18

19

20

21 △ ▽ 23

22

1. Ann Harding
2. Richard Arlen, Tom Kennedy and Louise Dresser in *Caught* (Par)
3. Rosita Moreno and Garry Marsh in *Stamboul* (Par)
4. Lew Cody, Harry Myers, Laura La Plante and Claud Allister in *Meet the Wife* (Col)
5. Warren Hymer and Spencer Tracy in *Goldie* (Fox)
6. Robert Woolsey

7. Olsen and Johnson in *Fifty Million Frenchmen* (WB)
8. Bebe Daniels and Warren William in *Honor of the Family* (FN)
9. Merna Kennedy
10. John Darrow, Robert Woolsey and Anita Louise in *Everything's Rosie* (RKO)
11. Robert Armstrong, Jean Arthur and George Brent in *Ex Bad Boy* (UA)
12. Tallulah Bankhead and Irving Pichel in *The Cheat* (Par)
13. Pat O'Brien and Adolphe Menjou in *The Front Page* (HH)
14. Owen Nares, Renate Muller and Jack Hulbert in *Sunshine Susie* (G'boro)
15. Lil Dagover
16. Mary Nolan
17. George Bancroft and Kay Francis in *Scandal Sheet* (Par)
18. Richard Arlen, William 'Stage' Boyd and Mary Brian in *Gun Smoke* (Par)
19. Lilian Roth
20. Dorothy Gulliver, Rex Lease and Harry Woods in *In Old Cheyenne* (SAWW)
21. John Garrick, Marguerite Churchill and Warner Oland in *Charlie Chan Carries On* (Fox)
22. Joan Barry
23. Anthony Bushell, Mary Astor and Lowell Sherman in *The Royal Bed* (GB *The Queen's Husband*) (RKO)

89

1. Elizabeth Allan
2. Helen Hayes and Ronald Colman in *Arrowsmith* (SG)
3. Robert Montgomery and Constance Bennett in *The Easiest Way* (MGM)
4. Lili Damita and Adolphe Menjou in *Friends and Lovers* (RKO)
5. Jack Oakie and June MacCloy in *June Moon* (Par)
6. Neil Hamilton and Joan Crawford in *This Modern Age* (MGM)
7. Charles Farrell and Elissa Landi in *Body and Soul* (Fox)
8. Elinor Fair
9. Leila Hyams and John Gilbert in *Gentleman's Fate* (MGM)
10. Elissa Landi and Theodore von Eltz in *Wicked* (Fox)
11. Charles Farrell and Janet Gaynor in *Merely Mary Ann* (Fox)
12. Monte Blue and Eleanor Boardman in *The Flood* (Col)

8

9 △ ▽ 11

10 △ ▽ 12

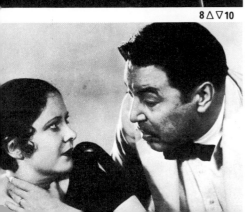

1. Joan Barry and Jack Buchanan in *Man of Mayfair* (Par/Brit)
2. Alan Mowbray and Kay Francis in *Guilty Hands* (MGM)
3. Irene Dunne.
4. Regis Toomey and Clara Bow in *Kick In* (Par)
5. Jeanette MacDonald and Edmund Lowe in *Don't Bet on Women* (Fox)
6. Joel McCrea and Dorothy Mackaill in *Kept Husbands* (RKO)
7. Lawrence Tibbett and Lupe Velez in *Cuban Love Song* (MGM)
8. Robert Montgomery and Greta Garbo in *Inspiration* (MGM)
9. David Manners and Evalyn Knapp in *The Millionaire* (WB)
10. Warner Oland in *The Black Camel* (Fox)
11. John Barrymore and Carmel Myers in *Mad Genius* (WB)
12. Bebe Daniels

1. Olga Baclanova
2. Fay Wray
3. Constance Bennett in *Bought*
(WB)
4. Brandon Hurst, Gustav von
Seyffertitz and Chester Morris in
The Bat Whispers (UA/RW)
5. Rose Hobart and George
Renavent in *East of Borneo* (Univ)
6. Billie Dove in *The Lady Who
Dared* (FN)
7. Charles Boyer, Ruth Chatterton
and Sam Hardy in *The Magnificent
Lie* (Par)
8. Sidney Fox
9. Edward G Robinson and Boris
Karloff in *Five Star Final* (WB)
10. Neil Hamilton, Billie Haggerty
and Judith Barrie in *Ex-Flame* (Tif)
11. Minor Watson, Adrienne Ames,
Kay Francis and Clive Brook in *24
Hours* (GB *The Hours Between* (Par)
12. Joe E Brown in *Sit Tight* (WB)
13. Charles Ruggles and Sue Conroy
in *The Girl Habit* (Par)
14. Isobel Elsom
15. Kay Strozzi, John Halliday,
Arthur Edmund Carewe and William
B Davidson in *Captain Applejack*
(WB)
16. Victor Varconi in *Captain
Thunder* (WB)
17. William 'Stage' Boyd and Jack
Oakie in *The Gang Buster* (Par)
18. Irene Rich and Evelyn Brent in
The Mad Parade (Lib/Par)
19. Joan Bennett and Lew Ayres in
Many a Slip (Univ)
20. Henry Kendall and Benita Hume
in *The Flying Fool* (BIP)

1   2

3

4

5

6

7

8

9

10

11   12

13   14   15

16   17

18   19   20

Greta Garbo

John Barrymore in *Grand Hotel* (MGM)

Maureen O'Sullivan and Johnny Weissmuller in
Tarzan the Ape Man (MGM)

The year 1932 saw the use of star names to promote films. Sets, stories, dialogue, script and camera-work were important to any production, but the biggest attraction at the box office was star names.

Greta Garbo had a huge following of fans. So did John Barrymore, his brother Lionel, Joan Crawford and Wallace Beery. Put all these super stars in one film and add for good measure players of the stature of Jean Hersholt, Lewis Stone and Tully Marshall, and one could rely on a hit at the box office. And so it was with *Grand Hotel*, adapted from the successful Broadway play which had been culled from a novel by the German best-selling writer Vicki Baum.

The story of life, love and death at a Berlin hotel between the two World Wars gives every opportunity to present various characters in differing roles: Greta Garbo as a ballet star on her way out, John Barrymore as a debonair jewel thief whose love brings new hope to the fading ballerina, and Joan Crawford as a secretary whose morals could only be described as questionable.

The film was directed by an Englishman, Edmund Goulding, who had already made several films for MGM. It was a film of some distinction, with each star's performance raising their status in the profession and it was *Grand Hotel* that gave Garbo the line that was to haunt her for the rest of her career: 'I vant to be alone!'

One of the great 'fun' films of the year was MGM's *Tarzan the Ape Man*. The Tarzan character has been one of the most endurable characters in films since he was first introduced in 1918. Since then, many actors playing Tarzan have come and gone but none captured the public's imagination more than Johnny Weissmuller, the US and Olympic swimming champion. Co-starring in the film with him is Maureen O'Sullivan, who is playing Jane.

The film was a smash hit that won the stars long-term contracts with the studio. They are supported by an excellent cast that includes Neil Hamilton, C. Aubrey Smith and Doris Lloyd. It was directed by W.S. Van Dyke, who used some left-over jungle footage from his *Trader Horn*.

Tarzan the Ape Man was the first talking Tarzan film

and it led to Weissmuller and Maureen O'Sullivan starring in a number of other Tarzan films, none of which matched the quality or had the appeal of this one.

One of the most constant stars of the Thirties was Herbert Marshall, an Englishman, who did not allow the loss of a leg during the First World War to impede his work as an actor. He had settled in Hollywood in 1932 and was continuously in demand by the studios, starting off with one of his best movies, *Trouble in Paradise*. His co-stars were Miriam Hopkins, Kay Francis, C. Aubrey Smith and Charles Ruggles. The film became a comedy classic, thanks to the deft touches of Ernst Lubitsch, the producer and director. In the same year, Lubitsch made *One Hour With You*, the story of a philandering Parisian doctor, starring Maurice Chevalier and Jeanette MacDonald, with Roland Young and Charles Ruggles giving them excellent support.

I Am a Fugitive From a Chain Gang was a film with a message. And the message was wrapped up in a drama that made it one of the best films of 1932. It won for Paul Muni, its star, an Oscar nomination for his performance as a war veteran who gives up his job as a clerk to become a construction worker. He becomes implicated in a robbery, and as a result is wrongly convicted of the crime and sentenced to ten years hard labour to be served on a chain gang, where he experiences savage brutality at the hands of the guards.

The film brought to the notice of the public the unsavoury truth about the American penal system and caused an outcry. Muni gives a performance that equals the best of his career. He made a nation sit up and take notice and probably did as much for penal reform as did any politician. The love interest was provided by Glenda Farrell. The strong cast includes Preston Foster, Helen Vinson and Allen Jenkins.

Paul Muni gave another powerful performance in *Scarface*, a gangster melodrama modelled on the life of Al Capone. Produced by Howard Hughes, it remains one of the best gangster films of the period and it afforded George Raft the best role of his career as Muni's henchman, who is eventually shot down by Muni. The supporting cast also includes Ann Dvorak and Boris Karloff.

One of the most talked about films of 1932 was *If I Had a Million*. Not only was it packed with the highest-ranking stars, it contained a novel story that was split into eight episodes, each showing the reactions of one of the ordinary people whose names are picked at random from a telephone directory by an eccentric millionaire, who then leaves each of them a million dollars.

What happens when the lucky eight receive their money, gives the film drama, humour and above all permits some superb acting from George Raft, Charles Laughton, Gary Cooper, W.C. Fields, Jack Oakie and Mary Boland.

The directors employed on the film were Norman Taurog, Stephen Roberts, James Cruze, Ernst Lubitsch, Norman Z. McLeod, H. Bruce Humberstone and William Seiter. No fewer than 18 scriptwriters contributed to the production.

RKO's *A Bill of Divorcement* saw the screen debut of a

Kay Francis

Paul Muni in *Scarface* (HH)

W C Fields

Jack Oakie

Katharine Hepburn

Frank McHugh

Dolores Del Rio in *Bird of Paradise* (RKO)
Below: Joel McCrea and Dolores Del Rio in *Bird of Paradise* (RKO)

young actress named Katharine Hepburn. It was a triumphant start to a career that was to make her one of the cinema's greatest actresses. In the film she matched her talents against another screen legend, John Barrymore, who gave a restrained performance. And making her talkie debut was a star of the silent days, Billie Burke.

Based on a Clemence Dane play, the film has Barrymore playing an inmate of a mental home where he has spent 25 years of his life. He decides to escape on the same day that his wife (Billie Burke) divorces him. Katharine Hepburn is their daughter who meets the father she has never really known. Because there is mental instability in the family, the girl decides she will not risk having children of her own and that she must part from her boy friend, played by David Manners.

Like so many films of the period, it now seems dated. But Katharine Hepburn's performance in particular survives and gives more than a hint of the great actress she was to become. The strong supporting cast includes Paul Cavanagh, the English actor, Elizabeth Patterson and Henry Stephenson.

Although *Public Enemy* propelled James Cagney to stardom as a tough gangster, it was *The Crowd Roars* that gave him the opportunity to display his versatility as an actor. In the film, he forsook thuggery for the role of a cocky, devil-may-care racing driver who, because of the dangers, does everything he can to discourage his younger brother (Eric Linden) from following in his footsteps as a racing driver. His concern is not welcomed by his brother, and there is further discord between them when the latter takes up with and eventually marries a girl (Joan Blondell) of whom the older brother disapproves.

The younger brother eventually becomes a successful racing driver, while his brother loses his pre-eminence in the sport. Reconciliation between them comes after the death on the track of a friend.

The film's story line is not strongly developed but the fast-moving action and the excitement on the race track keep the picture very much alive. Needless to say, Cagney retains a firm hold throughout the whole film. The romantic interest is provided by Ann Dvorak and other members of the cast include Guy Kibbee and Frank McHugh.

One of the more interesting films of the year was *Bird of Paradise* – not because of the high quality of its acting but for its glamour. First, there was the female star, the lovely Dolores Del Rio, whose glamour is matched by the outstanding scenery of its locale in Hawaii, which was stunningly photographed by Clyde De Vinna, with a number of breathtaking panoramic views of still lagoons, tall, forbidding mountains and sweeping beaches. All provide the backcloth to a story which has Dolores Del Rio playing a Polynesian girl who falls in love with a white adventurer, (Joel McCrea), but who realizes too late that in doing so she has offended the gods. She refuses to believe her lover's assurance that her fears are groundless and dramatically solves her problem by throwing herself into a fiery volcano.

Well directed by King Vidor, the film has a rich musical score written by Max Steiner. The native dance sequences were choreographed by Busby Berkeley and the supporting cast includes John Halliday, Richard 'Skeets' Gallagher and Lon Chaney Jr.

After working for six years with MGM, where he had never felt at home and had achieved very little, Cecil B. DeMille returned to the Paramount studios in 1932. There was an air of expectancy when he arrived, for DeMille was a great showman as well as a highly professional director. His films were lavish, often outrageous, but always full of spectacle.

His first film under his new contract was *The Sign of the Cross*, a Roman saga that was to be made on a low budget. Normally low-budget pictures and DeMille were not compatible but it was a film he had set his heart on making.

He cast Claudette Colbert in the role of Empress Poppaea. ('The wickedest woman in history' is how he described the character to Miss Colbert). Charles Laughton had the role of Emperor Nero who fiddled while Rome burned, while Fredric March played the Captain of the Guard, Marcus Superbus, loved by a Christian girl (Elissa Landi) and wooed by Nero's wicked wife.

What greater spectacle could one find than an arena filled with lions ready to devour the Christians, or Nero's wife bathing in a sunken bath filled with asses' milk? DeMille did not miss out on a trick on either count. It all added up to a glorious production to mark DeMille's homecoming. Admittedly, it was kitsch of the first order, but it was all so well done that it won the admiration of most critics. Its supporting players included Ian Keith and Nat Pendleton.

Another of the year's successes was *Love Me Tonight*, starring Maurice Chevalier and Jeanette MacDonald. Directed by Rouben Mamoulian, this frothy concoction follows the adventures of a Parisian tailor who suddenly finds himself moving in aristocratic circles, with highly amusing and often witty results. With superb songs by Richard Rodgers and Lorenz Hart, it remains one of the very best musicals of its period. Myrna Loy and Charles Ruggles were in the supporting cast.

Shanghai Express, starring Marlene Dietrich, Clive Brook and Warner Oland, was another of the year's critical successes. Directed by Josef von Sternberg, basically the story deals with a British officer who has just met up with an old flame on the Shanghai Express, when the train is suddenly boarded by Chinese bandits. This leads to a whole series of dramatic confrontations. The film was brilliantly photographed by Lee Garmes, who won an Academy Award. The supporting cast includes Anna May Wong and Eugene Pallette.

In the same year Harold Lloyd made his first sound film with *Movie Crazy*. Lloyd, was not at his best in this film which deals with a film-struck callow young man who suddenly finds himself facing the camera for a film test.

Jeanette MacDonald and Maurice Chevalier in *Love Me Tonight* (Par)

Anna May Wong

Eugene Pallette

A 1932 caricature of Harold Lloyd.

Constance Cummings and Harold Lloyd in *Movie Crazy* (HL)

Leslie Howard

Gracie Fields

Nevertheless, with able support from Constance Cummings, Lloyd has his moments in what is in fact a nostalgic look at the early days of the cinema.

In 1931, Herbert Wilcox – one of Britain's top film producers – had given contracts to Jack Buchanan and Anna Neagle. Buchanan was a musical-comedy star, popular in both England and America. He had appeared in a few silent films, and a talkie which was made in Hollywood by Paramount. Anna Neagle was a young dancer who had appeared in Buchanan's stage show, *Stand up and Sing*.

Wilcox cast them in *Goodnight Vienna*, a musical with Buchanan playing an Austrian officer who had fallen on hard times. Anna Neagle plays a humble flower seller who eventually becomes a star. The film was a big success and was the first of a series of Wilcox films co-starring Buchanan and Anna Neagle. Miss Neagle eventually became Wilcox's wife – and he directed all but two of her films himself.

The previous year had also been notable in British film history for the arrival of Alexander Korda with a contract to make two pictures for Paramount.

His first British film was called *Service for Ladies*. The film stars George Grossmith playing a king, and a British stage actor named Leslie Howard had the role of a head waiter masquerading as a prince. Howard became an international star. The film was an immediate success, and in typical Korda style, he decided that he would prefer to produce his own films in future. He gave up his contract with Paramount and formed his own company London Film Productions, which was to produce some of the best British films of the Thirties.

After starring in *Sally in Our Alley*, the previous year, Gracie Fields, who had been on the boards since her early teens and who was to become the most popular performer in Britain during the Thirties, went on to make *Looking on the Bright Side* a musical with plenty of slapstick comedy in it.

A low-budget picture, *Jack's the Boy*, proved to be one of the most profitable British films of 1932. It starred Jack Hulbert with his wife Cicely Courtneidge, a lively comedienne from the British music halls and the legitimate stage. A comedy with songs, it featured Hulbert as a uniformed policeman (Hulbert actually became Head of London's Special Constabulary after World War II) whose ambition is to be a detective. The film was a well-paced farce, with a particularly hilarious sequence involving a very long ladder holding up the traffic. Directed by Walter Forde, it was one of the best British comedies of the year.

Rome Express, also directed by Forde, was a thriller that gave the German star Conrad Veidt his first part in an English film. Except for an introductory scene, all the action takes place aboard a train. Forde made good use of back projection shots to persuade audiences that the film was actually filmed on a train moving at fast speed. It was the first train thriller.

In France, the Danish director Carl Theodor Dreyer was

making *Vampyre: Der Traum des Allan Grey* (*Vampyr: The Strange Case of David Gray*). With this picture he tried to show that horror is not a part of the things around us but our own subconscious mind at work. Although this film is now regarded as a classic, at the time it was a miserable failure and ten years passed before Dreyer made another movie. It was a tragic situation for a director who had made the world-famous silent masterpiece, *La Passion de Jeanne D'Arc*. (*The Passion of Joan of Arc*).

It took Julien Duvivier 13 years of hard work before he found fame as one of France's leading directors with *Poil de Carotte*. He had already made a silent film of the Jules Renard novel some time earlier, but it was the new film that did so much for his career. The plot focusses on the Lepic family. The youngest is known as Poil de Carotte. It is a disturbed family in which the father does not speak to his wife; she releases her frustrations by making life miserable for her youngest son, who eventually tries to commit suicide. Harry Baur and Catherine Fontenoy play the parents, while Robert Lynen gives a superb performance as the son. Lynen, incidentally, was executed by the Germans in World War II for being a member of the Resistance.

Jean Renoir, probably the most famous of all French directors brought the first of Georges Simenon's books to the screen with *La Nuit du Carrefour*, a thriller that had the infallible policeman Maigret (played by the director's brother, Pierre Renoir) as the chief character.

In 1932 there appeared another little masterpiece from Jean Renoir with his *Boudu Sauve des Eaux* (*Boudu Saved From Drowning*) which starred Michel Simon. It concerns itself with a man who rewards the person who saved him from drowning by seducing both his wife and mistress. It humorously dwells on the clash between the two men, one a tramp, the other a member of conventional society.

The Russian leaders of the early Thirties were not slow to appreciate the important role that movies could play in inspiring the Russian people to meet the goals of their Five Year Plan for industrialization and reconstruction. With this in mind, every facility was given to the country's filmmakers. The directors Sergei Yutkevitch and Fredrich Ermler must have delighted their country's leader when they made *Counterplan*, which emphasized the advantages of 'collective labour'. It concerns a group of workers employed in a desperate effort to construct a gas turbine to meet a deadline. It traces the problems and conflicts of the workers which are little different from those experienced the world over. Although graced by some fine acting, the film must be remembered mainly for Shostakovitch's musical score.

In 1932 no fewer than 400 films were produced in Japan. The industry was experiencing vast expansion which left the producers short of good scripts, so quite often they had to rely on remakes. One film of quality that did emerge was *Yataro's Sedge Hat*, directed by Hiroshi Inagaki, who later won the Golden Lion, the top award at the Venice Film Festival, for his *The Rickshaw Man* (1958.)

A scene from *Vampyr: Der Traum des Allan Grey* (TK/CD)

Harry Baur and Robert Lynen in *Poil de Carotte* (GB *Carrot Head* (FrF)

Pierre Renoir

Film Favourites 1932

This was a big year for all the studios. Talkies were now on their grand and glorious way – MGM releasing *Red Dust*, *Rasputin and the Empress*, *As You Desire Me* and *Grand Hotel*; Paramount and RKO were hot on their heels with *Horse Feathers* and *Symphony of Six Million* respectively.

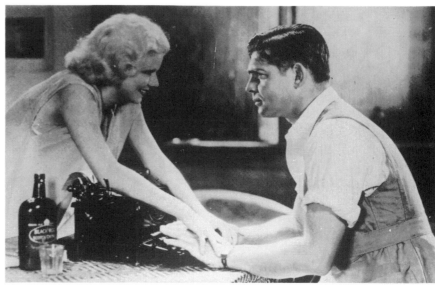

Above: Jean Harlow and Clark Gable in *Red Dust* (MGM)
Below: Charles Laughton and Dorothy Peterson in *Payment Deferred* (MGM)

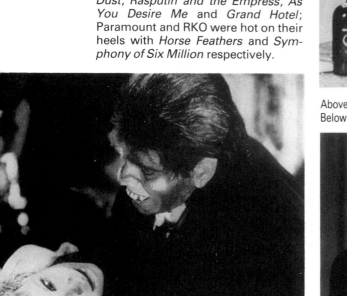

Miriam Hopkins and Fredric March in *Dr Jekyll and Mr Hyde* (Par)

James Cagney and Loretta Young in *Taxi!* (WB)

Lupe Velez and Lee Tracy in *Half-Naked Truth* (RKO)

Above: Paul Muni and C Henry Gordon in *Scarface* (HH)
Below: Edwin Maxwell, Paul Muni and George Raft in *Scarface* (HH)

Ethel Barrymore and John Barrymore in *Rasputin and the Empress* (GB *Rasputin the Mad Monk*) (MGM)

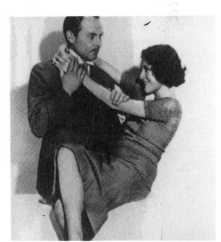

Charles Ruggles and Frances Dee in *This Reckless Age* (Par)

Left: Greta Garbo and Erik Von Stroheim in *As You Desire Me* (MGM)

Mary Carlisle, Lionel Barrymore, Joan Crawford and Lewis Stone in *Grand Hotel* (MGM)
Left: Joan Crawford and Wallace Beery in *Grand Hotel* (MGM)

Ricardo Cortez in *Symphony of Six Million* (GB *Melody of Life*) (RKO)
Left: Greta Garbo and John Barrymore in *Grand Hotel* (MGM)

Right: Constance Bennett in *Lady with a Past* (GB *Reputation*) (RKO)

Henry Stephenson, John Barrymore and Katharine Hepburn in *A Bill of Divorcement* (RKO DS)

James Cagney, Ann Dvorak and Joan Blondell in *The Crowd Roars* (WB)

Left: Groucho Marx in *Horse Feathers* (Par)
Right: Claudia Dell and Tom Mix in *Destry Rides Again* (Univ)

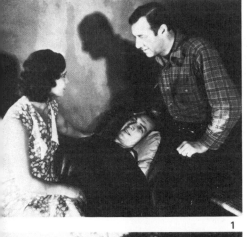

1

Picture Gallery for 1932

2

3

4

5

6

7

8

9

1. Betty Mack, Tom Tyler and John Elliott in *Galloping Thru* (MoP)
2. Matty Kemp, Dorothy Jordan and Will Rogers in *Down to Earth* (Fox)
3. Bill Cody (l) in *Ghost City* (MoP)
4. Dwight Frye and Barbara Weekes in *By Whose Hand* (Col)
5. John Miljan (sl) Una Merkel, Ernest Truex and Edward Arnold in *Whistling in the Dark* (MGM)
6. Dorothy Peterson and Frankie Darro in *Way Back Home* (RKO)
7. W C Fields
8. Marcelline Day and Walter Byron in *The Crusader* (Maj)
9. Victoria Hopper
10. Junior Durkin (s), Pat O'Brien and James Marcus in *Hell's House* (Cap)

10

1

2

3

4

5

6

7

8

9 △ ▽ 12

10 △ ▽ 13

11 △ ▽ 14

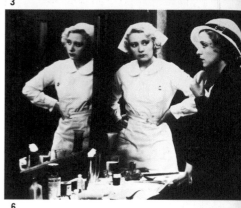

15

16

17

18 19

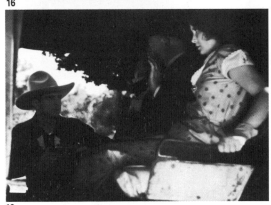

20

21

22

23 △ ▽ 25

24 △ ▽ 26

1. Lili Damita and Roland Young in *This is the Night* (Par)
2. Sylvia Sidney and Gene Raymond in *Ladies of the Big House* (Par)
3. Corinne Griffith and Colin Clive in *Lily Christine* (Par)
4. Barbara Stanwyck in *Shopworn* (Col)
5. Lloyd Hughes
6. Joan Blondell and Mary Doran in *Miss Pinkerton* (FN)
7. Jean Parker
8. George Bancroft and Wynne Gibson in *Lady and Gent* (Par)
9. Tom Mix and Lucille Powers in *The Texas Bad Man* (Univ)
10. Tom Mix in *Destry Rides Again* (Univ)
11. John Barrymore in *State's Attorney* (GB *Cardigan's Last Case*) (RKO)
12. John Wayne, Wallace MacDonald and Tim McCoy in *Two Fisted Law* (Col)
13. Tim McCoy and Shirley Grey in *Texas Cyclone* (Col)
14. Lew Ayres and Maureen O'Sullivan in *Okay America* (Univ)
15. Warren William and Marian Marsh in *Beauty and the Boss* (WB)
16. Richard Cromwell and Dorothy Jordan in *That's My Boy* (Col)
17. Gary Cooper and Toby Wing in *If I Had a Million* (Par)
18. Bradley Page (c) and Mae Clarke in *The Final Edition* (Col)
19. Bob Steele and Nancy Drexel in *Man from Hell's Edges* (SAWW)
20. Carmen LaRoux and Bob Steele in *Son of Oklahoma* (SAWW)
21. Tallulah Bankhead in *Faithless* (MGM)
22. Karen Morley and John Barrymore in *Arsene Lupin* (MGM)
23. Walter Miller, Joan Blondell and Adrienne Dore in *The Famous Ferguson Case* (FN)
24. Reginald Denny in *Strange Justice* (RKO)
25. Conway Tearle, Kay Francis and William 'Stage' Boyd in *The False Madonna* (GB *The False Idol*) (Par)
26. Gene Raymond

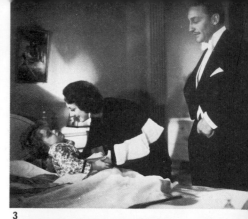

1. Claudette Colbert in *The Sign of the Cross* (Par)
2. Greta Garbo in *Mata Hari* (MGM)
3. Ann Dvorak and Warren William in *Three on a Match* (FN)
4. Charles Laughton, Claudette Colbert and Fredric March in *The Sign of the Cross* (Par)
5. Cary Grant and Marlene Dietrich in *Blonde Venus* (Par)
6. Boris Karloff, Myrna Loy, Jean Hersholt and Karen Morley in *The Mask of Fu Manchu* (MGM)
7. Greta Garbo and Lionel Barrymore in *Mata Hari* (MGM)
8. Boris Karloff in *The Mummy* (Univ)
9. Francis MacDonald in *Trailing the Killer* (WW)
10. Greta Garbo and John Barrymore in *Grand Hotel* (MGM)
11. Edmund Lowe and Bela Lugosi in *Chandu the Magician* (Fox)
12. Una Merkel and Jean Harlow in *Red-Headed Woman* (MGM)
13. George M Cohan and Claudette Colbert in *The Phantom President* (Par)

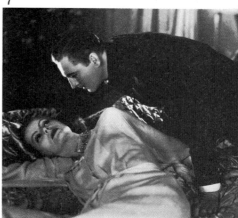

9 △ ▽ 12

10 △ ▽ 13

8 △ ▽ 11

1 & 2 Eddie Cantor in *The Kid from Spain* (SG)

3. Mary Brian, Lee Tracy and Emma Dunn in *The Blessed Event* (WB)

4. Ruth Hall, Robert Young and Eddie Cantor in *The Kid from Spain* (SG)

5. Edward G Robinson, Vivienne Osborne and J Carrol Naish in *Two Seconds* (FN)

6. Ruth Hall and Ken Maynard in *Between Fighting Men* (KBS/WW)

7. Henry B Walthall, Ralph Morgan and Norma Shearer in *Strange Interlude* (MGM)

8. George Brent, John Miljan and Ruth Chatterton in *The Rich Are Always With Us* (FN)

9. Lois Wilson and Theodore Von Eltz in *Drifting Souls* (Tow)

10. Jean Harlow, Clark Gable and Donald Crisp in *Red Dust* (MGM)

11. Melvyn Douglas and Greta Garbo in *As You Desire Me* (MGM)

12. Bela Lugosi and Boris Karloff in *Night World* (Univ)

13. Walter Huston and Helen Chandler in *A House Divided* (Univ)

8 △ ▽ 11

9 △ ▽ 12

10 △ ▽ 13

1. Ann Dvorak in *Scarface* (HH)
2. Paul Muni in *Scarface* (HH)
3. Karen Morley in *Scarface* (HH)
4. Vince Barnett and Paul Muni in *Scarface* (HH)
5. Paul Muni, George Raft and Vince Barnett in *Scarface* (HH)
6. Maurice Chevalier, Jeanette MacDonald, Genevieve Tobin and Roland Young in *One Hour with You* (Par)
7. Gary Cooper, Tallulah Bankhead and Charles Laughton in *Devil and the Deep* (Par)
8. Bette Davis and George Arliss in *The Man Who Played God* (GB *The Silent Voice*) (WB)
9. James Cagney and Clarence Muse in *Winner Takes All* (WB)
10. Helen Hayes and Gary Cooper in *A Farewell to Arms* (Par)
11. Walter Huston in *The Woman from Monte Carlo* (FN)

6 △ ▽ 9   7 △ ▽ 10   8 △ ▽ 11

1

2 3

1. Douglas Fairbanks and Maria Alba in *Mr Robinson Crusoe* (UA)
2. Jeanette MacDonald and Maurice Chevalier in *Love Me Tonight* (Par)
3. Anny Ondra
4. Boris Karloff and Lillian Bond in *The Old Dark House* (Univ)
5. Clark Gable, Donald Crisp and Tully Marshall in *Red Dust* (MGM)
6. Gloria Stuart and Pat O'Brien in *Laughter in Hell* (Univ)
7. Stan Laurel and Oliver Hardy in *Pack Up Your Troubles* (HR)
8. William Gargan, Guy Kibbee, Joan Crawford and Walter Catlett in *Rain* (UA)
9. Lee Tracy, Tommy Dugan, Frank McHugh and Ned Sparks in *The Blessed Event* (WB)
10. Guy Kibbee, George Chandler, Lee Tracy and Frank McHugh in *The Strange Love of Molly Louvain* (FN)

4 5

6 7 △ ▽ 9 8 △ ▽ 10

1. Lew Ayres and Mae Clarke in *The Impatient Maiden* (Univ)
2. Irene Dunne and Ricardo Cortez in *Symphony of Six Million* (GB *Melody of Life*) (RKO)
3. William Gargan and Maureen O'Sullivan in *The Silver Lining* (UA)
4. Charles Farrell and Janet Gaynor in *The First Year* (Fox)
5. David Manners and Kay Francis in *Man Wanted* (WB)
6. Gwili Andre and John Warburton in *Secrets of the French Police* (RKO)
7. Constance Cummings and Harold Lloyd in *Movie Crazy* (HL)
8. Joan Blondell and Stuart Erwin in *Make Me a Star* (Par)
9. Vince Barnett, Allen Jenkins and Victor McLaglen in *Rackety Rax* (Fox)
10. Ramon Novarro and Helen Hayes in *The Son-Daughter* (MGM)
11. Edward G Robinson and J Carrol Naish in *The Hatchet Man* (GB *The Honourable Mr Wong*) (FN)
12. Bill Robinson
13. Cora Sue Collins
14. Lupe Velez and Melvyn Douglas in *The Broken Wing* (Par)
15. Mae West and George Raft in *Night after Night* (Par)
16. Mae Clarke and Donald Cook in *Penguin Pool Murder* (RKO)
17. Tim McCoy

10 **11**

13

12 **14**

15 **16** **17**

1

2

3

4

5

6

7 △ ▽10   8 △ ▽11   9 △ ▽12

13 **14** **15**

16 **17**

18 **19**

1. Dickie Moore, Charles 'Chic' Sale and Lois Wilson in *The Expert* (WB)
2. Charles 'Chic' Sale
3. Kay Francis and Ronald Colman in *Cynara* (SG)
4. Leslie Howard and Ann Harding in *Animal Kingdom* (GB *The Woman in His House*) (RKO)
5. William 'Stage' Boyd, Ann Dvorak and Spencer Tracy in *Sky Devils* (Cad/HH)
6. Richard Tucker and Sally Blane in *The Reckoning* (Pee)
7. William Collier Jr (I) and Barbara Kent in *Exposed* (EaP)
8. Mickey Rooney and Tom Brown in *Fast Companions* (Univ)
9. Theodore Von Eltz and Mary Brian in *The Unwritten Law* (Maj)
10. Jack Hulbert and Winifred Shotter in *Jack's the Boy* (G'boro)
11. Lois Moran and John Gilbert in *West of Broadway* (MGM)
12. Walter Catlett and Irene Dunne in *Back Street* (Univ)
13. Reginald Owen (I) in *The Man Called Back* (Tif)
14. Betty Grable in *Probation* (Che)
15. June Clyde and Henry Armetta in *Steady Company* (Univ)
16. George Brent and Lyle Talbot in *Purchase Price* (WB)
17. Harry Welchman
18. James Gleason and Marion Davies in *Blondie of the Follies* (MGM)
19. James Durkin and Sidney Fox in *Nice Women* (Univ)
20. Joan Marsh and Arthur Pierson in *Bachelor's Affairs* (Fox)
21. Richard Barthelmess and Marian Marsh in *Alias the Doctor* (FN)
22. De Witt Jennings and Rex Lease in *Midnight Morals* (May)
23. Gibb McLaughlin and Jack Buchanan in *Magic Night* (UA)
24. Mary Jane Irving, Harry Carey and Gibson Gowland in *Without Honors* (Art)

20 △ ▽ 22 **21 △ ▽ 23** **▽ 24**

1 2

3 4 5

6 △ ▽9 7 △ ▽10 8 △

11 12

13 14

1. Warner Richmond, Jean Hersholt, Tully Marshall, Jean Harlow and Walter Huston in *The Beast of the City* (MGM)
2. Joe E Brown in *Fireman, Save My Child* (FN)
3. Tom Tyler in *Honor of the Mounted* (MoP)
4. Eric Linden and Joan Blondell in *Big City Blues* (WB)
5. Marion Davis and Clark Gable in *Polly of the Circus* (MGM)
6. James Dunn and Boots Mallory in *Handle with Care* (Fox)
7. Tim McCoy in *The Fighting Fool* (Col)
8. Victor McLaglen and Beryl Mercer in *The Devil's Lottery* (Fox)
9. David Manners, Merna Kennedy and Constance Bennett in *Lady with a Past* (GB *Reputation*) (RKO)
10. Kay Francis and William Powell in *Jewel Robbery* (WB)
11. William Collier Snr, Warren Hymer, Jack Oakie and William 'Stage' Boyd in *Madison Square Garden* (Par)
12. Marion Nixon, Frankie Darro and Warner Baxter in *Amateur Daddy* (Fox)
13. Ginger Rogers and Joe E Brown in *You Said a Mouthful* (FN)
14. Roscoe Karns
15. George Arliss and David Torrence in *A Successful Calamity* (WB)
16. Jean Hersholt
17. Sidney Fox, Lew Ayres, Boris Karloff and Genevieve Tobin in *The Cohens and Kellys in Hollywood* (Univ)
18. William Powell, Evalyn Knapp, Ben Alexander and Evelyn Brent in *High Pressure* (WB)

15 △ ▽ 17 16 △ ▽ 18

1. Sheila Mannors, Andy Shuford, Bill Cody and Gibson Gowland in *Land of Wanted Men* (MoP)
2. Richard Arlen and Robert Coogan in *Sky Bride* (Par)
3. Robert McWade and Alison Skipworth in *Madame Racketeer* (GB *The Sporting Widow*) (Par)
4. Conway Tearle and Karen Morley in *Man About Town* (Fox)
5. Chester Morris and Boris Karloff in *The Miracle Man* (Par)
6. Claud Allister and Adolphe Menjou in *Blame the Woman* (Pri)
7. Charlotte Henry
8. Will Rogers and Jetta Goudal in *Business and Pleasure* (Fox)
9. Tom Dugan, Glenn Tryon, Jason Robards Snr and Sally Eilers in *Pride of the Legion* (MaP)
10. Ann Dvorak, Joan Blondell and Bette Davis in *Three on a Match* (WB)
11. Jack Oakie and Miriam Hopkins in *Dancers in the Dark* (Par)
12. Joel McCrea and Constance Bennett in *Rockabye* (RKO)
13. Richard Dix, Ann Harding and Jason Robards Snr in *The Conquerors* (RKO)
14. Paul Lukas and Ruth Chatterton in *Tomorrow and Tomorrow* (Par)
15. Lee Tracy and Lupe Velez in *The Half Naked Truth* (RKO)
16. Claudette Colbert and Clive Brook in *The Man from Yesterday* (Par)
17. June Clyde and Frank Albertson in *Racing Youth* (Univ)
18. Joan Bennett and John Boles in *Careless Lady* (Fox)
19. Clara Bow and John St Polis in *Call Her Savage* (Fox)
20. Constance Cummings and Jack Holt in *Behind the Mask* (Col)
21. Phillips Holmes and Nancy Carroll in *Broken Lullaby* (Par)

1

2

3

4 △ ▽7   5 △ ▽8

6

9 10

11 12 13

14 15

16 △ ▽ 21

17 △ ▽ 19 18 △ ▽ 20

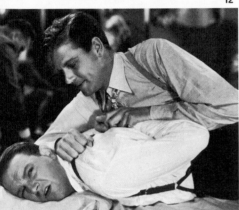

12　**13**

14

15

1. Robert Young, Clara Blandick and Walter Huston in *The Wet Parade* (MGM)
2. Edward G Robinson and Aline MacMahon in *Silver Dollar* (FN)
3. Joan Blondell and William Powell in *Lawyer Man* (WB)
4. Richard Tucker, Loretta Young and George Brent in *Weekend Marriage* (GB *Weekend Lives*) (FN)
5. Alexander Kirkland and Violet Heming in *Almost Married* (Fox)
6. Ralph Bellamy and Slim Summerville (r) in *Airmail* (Univ)
7. George 'Gabby' Hayes, Julian Rivero and Harry Carey in *The Night Rider* (Art)
8. Roland Young and Pola Negri in *A Woman Commands* (Col)
9. Frances Dee and Charles Ruggles in *This Reckless Age* (Par)
10. David Manners
11. Marie Dressler and Myrna Loy in *Emma* (MGM)
12. Sally Eilers, Monroe Owsley and Ginger Rogers in *Hat Check Girl* (Fox)
13. Marian Marsh and Warren William in *Under Eighteen* (WB)
14. William Gargan and Joel McCrea in *The Sport Parade* (RKO)
15. William Haines and Madge Evans in *Are You Listening?* (MGM)
16. Virginia Bruce, Paul Lukas and John Gilbert in *Downstairs* (MGM)
17. Jack Holt and Lillian Miles in *Man Against Woman* (Col)
18. David Manners, Ken Murray and Ann Dvorak in *Crooner* (FN)
19. George O'Brien and Bert Hanlon in *The Golden West* (Fox)
20. Irving Pichel and Sari Maritza in *Forgotten Commandments* (Par)
21. Paul Muni (l) and Preston Foster in *I Am a Fugitive from a Chain Gang* (WB)

16　**17**

18

19　**20**

21

1   2   3

4   5   6

8

7 △ ▽ 10

9 △ ▽ 13

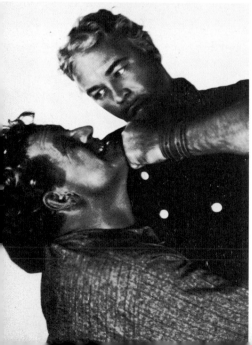

11 △ ▽ 12

14   15

16   17

1. Robert Young, Robert Warwick and Helen Twelvetrees in *Unashamed* (MGM)
2. Sally Eilers and James Dunn in *Dance Team* (Fox)
3. Belle Christall in *The Frightened Lady* (G'boro)
4. Johnny Weissmuller and Maureen O'Sullivan in *Tarzan the Ape Man* (MGM)
5. Clive Brook and Miriam Jordan in *Sherlock Holmes* (Fox)
6. Elizabeth Allan, Frank Lawton, Edna Best and Herbert Marshall in *Michael and Mary* (Gau)
7. Irene Purcell, Ben Lyon and C Henry Gordon in *The Crooked Circle* (WW)
8. Ken Maynard, Nat Pendleton and Lafe McKee in *Hell Fire Austin* (Tif)
9. Fay Wray and Lionel Atwill in *Dr X* (WB)
10. Fred Kohler and Bill Boyd in *Carnival Boat* (RKO)
11. Tarquini D'Or, Henri Garat, and Lilian Harvey in *Congress Dances* (Ufa)
12. Kay Francis, Herbert Marshall and Miriam Hopkins in *Trouble in Paradise* (Par)
13. Marlene Dietrich and Clive Brook in *Shanghai Express* (Par)
14. Buck Jones and Mitchell Lewis in *McKenna of the Mounted* (Col)
15. Mary Astor and Ricardo Cortez in *Men of Chance* (RKO)
16. Adolphe Menjou and Barbara Stanwyck in *Forbidden* (Col)
17. Sari Maritza and Herbert Marshall in *Evenings for Sale* (Par)
18. Bing Crosby, Stuart Erwin and Leila Hyams in *The Big Broadcast* (Par)
19. Loretta Young
20. Cary Grant, Nancy Carroll and Edward Woods in *Hot Saturday* (Par)
21. Wallace Ford, Joan Blondell and Guy Kibbee in *Central Park* (FN)
22. Edmund Lowe and Claudette Colbert in *Misleading Lady* (Par)
23. Charles Bickford and Helen Twelvetrees in *Panama Flo* (RKO)
24. Joan Bennett and Spencer Tracy in *Me and My Gal* (GB *Pier 13*) (Fox)

18   19

20 △ ▽ 22   21 △ ▽ 23   24

1

2

5

4

6

7

8

9

10

11

3

122

1. H B Warner, Richard Tucker and Sally Blane in *Cross Examination* (Art)
2. Cary Grant and Sylvia Sidney in *Madame Butterfly* (Par)
3. Sandy Roth and Richard Dix in *Hell's Highway* (RKO)
4. Lyle Talbot (l) in *Klondike* (MoP)
5. Spencer Tracy and Doris Kenyon in *Young America* (Fox)
6. Guy Kibbee and Warren William in *The Dark Horse* (WB)
7. Bob Steele (l) in *The Fighting Champ* (MoP)
8. Leo Carrillo and Dolores Del Rio in *Girl of the Rio* (GB *The Dove*) (RKO)
9. Dorothy Mackaill and Humphrey Bogart in *Love Affair* (Col)
10. Walter Connolly
11. Lili Damita and Warren William in *The Match King* (FN)
12. Sidney Toler, Buster Keaton and Jimmie Durante in *Speak Easily* (MGM)
13. Barbara Stanwyck
14. Barbara Leonard and Ruth Chatterton in *The Crash* (FN)
15. Cliff Edwards and William Haines in *Fast Life* (MGM)
16. Esther Ralston in *Rome Express* (Gau)
17. Peggy Shannon, Spencer Tracy and James Dunn in *Society Girl* (Fox)
18. Joel McCrea, Leslie Banks and Fay Wray in *The Most Dangerous Game* (GB *The Hounds of Zaroff*) (RKO)
19. Walter Huston, Kay Johnson and Gavin Gordon in *American Madness* (Col)
20. Diane Sinclair, Lionel Barrymore and Henry Kolker in *Washington Masquerade* (GB *Mad Masquerade*) (MGM)
21. Mary Carlisle and William Davidson in *Her Mad Night* (May)

12   13

14   15

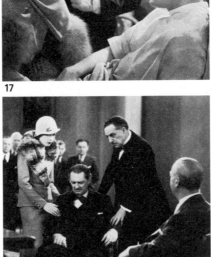

16   17

18

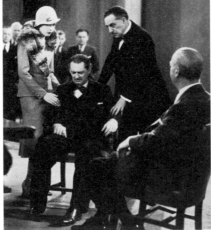

19   20

21

123

1

2

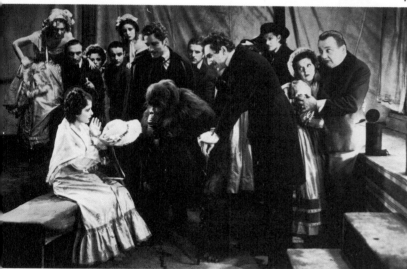

3

4

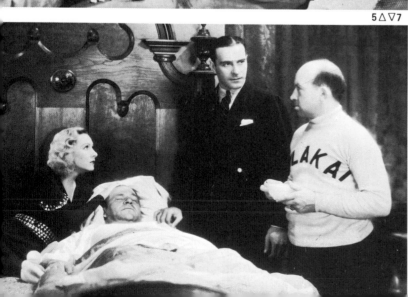

5 △ ▽ 7

6 △ ▽ 8

9 10

11

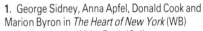

1. George Sidney, Anna Apfel, Donald Cook and Marion Byron in *The Heart of New York* (WB)
2. Buck Jones in *White Eagle* (Col)
3. Sidney Fox, Leon Waycoff, Bela Lugosi, Arlene Francis and Bert Roach (r) in *Murders in the Rue Morgue* (Univ)
4. Raymond Hatton, J Farrell MacDonald, Johnny Mack Brown and Evalyn Knapp in *The Vanishing Frontier* (Par)
5. Raymond Hatton, Walter Huston, Harry Carey and Harry Woods (r) in *Law and Order* (Univ)
6. Russell Hopton and Mae Clarke (r) in *Night World* (Univ)
7. Karen Morley, Wallace Beery, Ricardo Cortez and Vince Barnett in *Flesh* (MGM)
8. Ann Harding, Adolphe Menjou and Melvyn Douglas in *Prestige* (RKO)
9. Harry Gribbon, Otis Harlan, John Wayne, Ruth Hall and Henry B Walthall in *Ride Him Cowboy* (Vit/WB)
10. June Clyde, Andy Devine, Lila Lee, Robert Armstrong and Russell Hopton in *Radio Patrol* (Univ)
11. Ray Cooke, James Cagney, Loretta Young and George E Stone in *Taxi!* (WB)
12. Conrad Nagel, Jackie Cooper and Lois Wilson in *Divorce in the Family* (MGM)
13. Pat O'Brien, Walter Brennan, Glenda Farrell and Charles Bickford in *Scandal for Sale* (Univ)
14. Tully Marshall, Sidney Bracey, Pat O'Malley, Walter Byron and Mary Doran in *Exposure* (Cap)

12 △ ▽13   14 ▽

13

15

17

14

16

18

1. Marie Dressler and Polly Moran in *Prosperity* (MGM)
2. Juliette Compton and Fredric March in *Strangers in Love* (Par)
3. Robert Woolsey, Betty Grable , Edna May Oliver and Edgar Kennedy in *Hold 'Em Jail* (RKO)
4. Diana Napier, Ida Lupino and Arnold Riches in *Her First Affaire* (SGPS)
5. Tala Birell and Luis Trenker in *The Doomed Battalion* (Univ)
6. Conchita Montenegro and George O'Brien in *The Gay Caballero* (Fox)
7. Ken Maynard and Philo McCullough in *The Sunset Trail* (Tif)
8. Dorothy Stickney, Richard Arlen and Nancy Carroll in *Wayward* (Par)
9. Matt Moore, Chester Morris and Billie Dove in *Cock of the Air* (UA)
10. Grant Mitchell, Dorothy Mackaill and Clark Gable in *No Man of her Own* (Par)
11. Esther Ralston and Marie Burke in *After the Ball* (Gau)
12. Wallace MacDonald, Loretta Sayers and Buck Jones in *High Speed* (Col)
13. Theodore Von Eltz and Claudia Dell in *Midnight Lady* (Che)
14. Robert Montgomery and Madge Evans in *Lovers Courageous* (MGM)
15. Shirley Grey and Jack Oakie in *Uptown New York* (WW)
16. John Wayne in *The Big Stampede* (FN)
17. Bill Cody, Sheila Manners and LeRoy Mason in *Texas Pioneers* (MoP)
18. Phillips Holmes and Miriam Hopkins in *Two Kinds of Women* (Par)
19. Buster Phelps and Mitzi Green in *Little Orphan Annie* (RKO)
20. Douglas Fairbanks Jr and Mary Brian in *It's Tough to be Famous* (FN)
21. Richard Cromwell, Tom Brown, and Tyrone Power in *Tom Brown of Culver* (Univ)

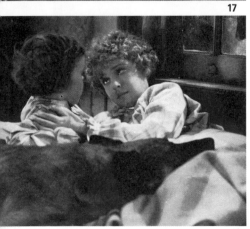

19

20

21

127

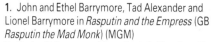

1. John and Ethel Barrymore, Tad Alexander and Lionel Barrymore in *Rasputin and the Empress* (GB *Rasputin the Mad Monk*) (MGM)

2. Spring Byington and Joan Davis in *Too Busy To Work* (Fox)

3. Berton Churchill, Richard Barthlemess and Bette Davis in *Cabin in the Cotton* (WB)

4. Henry Armetta and Ramon Novarro in *Huddle* (GB *The Impossible Lover*) (MGM)

5. Walter Huston and Virginia Bruce in *Kongo* (MGM)

6. C Aubrey Smith, Heather Thatcher and Robert Montgomery in *But the Flesh is Weak* (MGM)

7. Bela Lugosi and Brandon Hurst in *White Zombie* (ASC)

8. Charlotte Henry in *Lena Rivers* (Tif)

9. Clive Brook, Vivienne Osborn, Dickie Moore and Juliette Compton in *Husband's Holiday* (Par)

10. Tim McCoy in *The Riding Tornado* (Col)

11. Pat O'Brien, Lorena Layson, Thomas Jackson and Claire Dodd in *Hollywood Speaks* (Col)

12. Irene Rich and Nydia Westman in *Manhattan Tower* (Rem)

13. Jack Oakie and Andy Clyde in *Million Dollar Legs* (Par)

14. Walter Miller, Winnie Lightner, Joe Smith and Charles Dale in *Manhattan Parade* (WB)

15. Hermione Baddeley

16. Ramon Novarro and Madge Evans in *Huddle* (GB *The Impossible Lover* MGM)

17. Jason Robards Snr in *Docks of San Francisco* (May)

18. Helen Hayes

19. Tamara Desni

20. Buck Jones in *One Man Law* (Col)

21. Otto Kruger

22. Gibb McLaughlin

23. Paul Lukas

6 △ ▽ 8

5 △ ▽ 9

▽ 7

10   11

12   13   14   ▽23

15   16

17 △ ▽20

18 △ ▽21   19 △ ▽22

1

2 3

4 △ ▽7

5 △ ▽8 6

9 △ ▽10

1. Ann Dvorak
2. Benita Hume
3. Tom Mix
4. Ethel Barrymore
5. Raymond Hatton
6. Adolphe Menjou
7. Edward G Robinson
8. Paul Muni
9. Herbert Marshall
10. Charles Ruggles

130

1   2   3

4   5 △ ▽ 9   6 △ ▽ 10

7 △ ▽ 8

1. Maurice Chevalier
2. Richard Barthelmess
3. Buck Jones
4. Preston Foster
5. Joan Crawford
6. Mary Brian
7. Jean Harlow
8. Charles Boyer
9. Mary Carlisle
10. Wallace Beery

131

A page from a 1933 *Picturegoer Weekly*

Ginger Rogers in *Professional Sweetheart*
(GB *Imaginary Sweetheart*)

CHAPTER FOUR
1933
ENTER ASTAIRE AND ROGERS

A new chapter in film history began in 1933 when RKO Radio teamed Fred Astaire with Ginger Rogers to support Dolores Del Rio and Gene Raymond in *Flying Down to Rio*. Fred had appeared earlier that same year with Joan Crawford in *Dancing Lady* which was a big hit and gave him world exposure. Ginger Rogers was a veteran of 19 feature films, plus some shorts. Pert and bubbly, she was already popular in her own right. Brought together they added a new dimension to film entertainment. Their partnership lasted throughout the Thirties during which they made nine films.

Their big moment came in *Flying Down to Rio* when they danced 'The Carioca' which had little to do with the plot but gave what otherwise would have been a run-of-the-mill picture a place in cinema history. It was the only film in which they appeared together without having top billing.

The film was all good fun, ending with a beautifully choreographed aerial ballet of gorgeous dancing girls going through their routine strapped to the wings of airplanes.

Among the cast are Blanche Frederici, Walter Walker and Eric Blore. Directed by Thornton Freeland, the film has a number of memorable tunes, including 'Music Makes Me,' 'Orchids in the Moonlight' and 'Flying Down to Rio.'

One of the most exciting and imaginative films to come from Hollywood was *King Kong* also made by RKO. There had never been anything like it before and there has never been anything like it since, although it has inspired countless imitations (including a remake), none of which is worth remembering. *King Kong* is a classic adventure fantasy that will live forever.

The film is a masterpiece of film-making with the behind-the-scenes people deserving as much credit as the stars. The man of the picture was undoubtedly Willis O'Brien who masterminded the trick photography to create an ape who looked 15m (50 ft) tall, although in reality Kong was only a 45 cm (18 in) scale model. All the models of the prehistoric monsters were filmed using stop-action photography so that their limbs and eyes could be moved a fraction at a time before the camera took the next frame. This gives the impression of movement when the film is projected. It was a wonder of make-believe.

The action comes when Carl Denham (Robert Armstrong) a producer of travelogue films, takes an actress (Fay Wray) to a remote island for filming. The natives seize the girl and offer her to their god, an enormous and savage gorilla, who they hope will be placated by this unusual gift. Kong, in fact, is so delighted with the gift that he carries the girl away, pursued by the explorer and the film crew, most of whom are killed when Kong sweeps them off a bridge.

Armstrong and his assistant, Driscoll (Bruce Cabot), survive the tragedy, and have a chance later to rescue the girl while Kong is fighting a pterodactyl. Kong is eventually captured and taken to New York where he escapes, carrying the girl with him to the top of the Empire State Building. Here, after an aerial attack, Kong is riddled with bullets and dies and the girl is rescued.

The scenes of Fay Wray swaying in Kong's hand while the planes buzz round them like angry hornets, remain one of the great classic sequences of the early talkies. Merian C. Cooper, who conceived the whole idea, co-directed with Ernest B. Schoedsack. The music, which played an important role in the film, was written by Max Steiner.

In 1932 Greta Garbo went back to her native Sweden for a long holiday. She had been away for a year when MGM agreed to her request that she should star in *Queen Christina*, playing the title role. Written especially for her, the story dealt with an episode in the life of the seventeenth century Swedish monarch.

The film, as far as audiences are concerned, remains one of the most fondly remembered of Garbo's films, rivalled only in 1936 by *Camille* and in 1937 by *Conquest (GB Marie Walewska)*. The latter film's success owed a great deal to Charles Boyer's intense performance as Napoleon.

Playing opposite Garbo in *Queen Christina* was John Gilbert but Garbo might have done better for a partner had Laurence Olivier not been dropped from the film to make way for Gilbert. He would have made a more convincing lover, for Gilbert was by then past his best.

The film was directed by Rouben Mamoulian, with excellent support from a cast that included Lewis Stone, Ian Keith, C. Aubrey Smith and Reginald Owen.

In 1933 Warners presented two musicals, *42nd Street* and *Gold Diggers of 1933*, both enjoying the enormous advantage of Busby Berkeley devising and staging dance routines. They left little doubt that he was the best in the business. As a result both movies have survived the years and the changing tastes of filmgoers, and appear to be favourites with television-film programmers.

First off the mark was *42nd Street* which takes audiences to a theatre where a producer is having trouble with his temperamental leading lady. The problem is made worse for the unfortunate man because she is having an affair

Fay Wray in *King Kong*

Ruby Keeler and Dick Powell in *42nd Street*

Warner Baxter

Bebe Daniels

Billie Burke, Wallace Beery and Jean Harlow in
Dinner at Eight

Charles Laughton in *The Private Life of Henry VIII*

with the show's principal backer. The plot has all the ingredients one can expect in a musical based on life backstage, including the young understudy replacing the star and going on to stardom herself.

In the role of the producer is Warner Baxter, while Ruby Keeler plays the girl who gets her big chance. Ginger Rogers, Bebe Daniels, Dick Powell, George Brent, Una Merkel, Guy Kibbee and Ned Sparks all contribute to the success of the picture which was directed by Lloyd Bacon.

Gold Diggers of 1933 was another piece of cheerful escapism but this time Mervyn LeRoy was back in harness and directing. Interwoven with some catchy songs and production numbers are three love stories. Warren William, Joan Blondell and Aline MacMahon had top billing and singer Dick Powell and dancer Ruby Keeler were re-united to lead the musical numbers.

None of the films starring Mae West has lived up to the fame she gave them with her famous wisecracks like: 'It's not the men in my life that count, it's the life in my men.'

Starting her professional career back in 1916 as a male impersonator, she achieved a dubious fame in 1926 with a play she had written, produced and directed called 'Sex'. It was considered so obscene that she was sent to prison for ten days on a charge of obscenity. She first appeared on the screen in 1932 in *Night After Night* with George Raft. The following year she appeared in her now famous *She Done Him Wrong*, a watered down version of one of her stage hits, 'Diamond Lil', in which she played a Gay Nineties saloon keeper who falls in love with an undercover cop. It was a role which gave her ample opportunity to display to the full her own particular brand of humour.

The film offered a big break for Cary Grant. She had spotted him at the Paramount studio and demanded him as her leading man. Others in the cast were Gilbert Roland, Noah Beery, Rochelle Hudson and Owen Moore.

Mae West made a second film in 1933. It was *I'm No Angel* and once again Cary Grant went West to be her leading man. She obviously liked his style. *I'm No Angel* is thought by many to be her best film.

Dinner at Eight offered an impressive all-star cast the opportunity for some fine acting. Heading the list are Marie Dressler, John Barrymore, Lionel Barrymore, Wallace Beery, Jean Harlow, Lee Tracy, Billie Burke and Madge Evans. The film was a natural follow-up to *Grand Hotel*, the enormously successful MGM film of the previous year.

All the stars are ideally cast, give impressive performances and receive ample backing from the featured players including Louise Closser Hale, Phillips Holmes, May Robson, Grant Mitchell and Elizabeth Patterson. The excellent direction was carried out by George Cukor.

In 1933 Alexander Korda finished his most ambitious film to date. It was *The Private Life of Henry VIII* and starred Charles Laughton in the title role. The finished film not only confirmed Korda as one of the world's great film directors, it also boosted the British film industry internationally. Giving Laughton the title role was an inspired piece of casting. What other actor of the time could have played the part so convincingly? And what better story could be told than that of a man, a king to boot, who had so many wives? The film has everything, pathos, drama and comedy, and all in large doses.

Aiding Laughton in the picture is a bevy of royal wives played by Merle Oberon (as Ann Boleyn), Elsa Lanchester (as Anne of Cleves), Binnie Barnes (as Catherine Howard), Wendy Barrie (as Jane Seymour) and Everley Gregg (as Catherine Parr). Only five ladies were needed – Catherine of Aragon had already been dispensed with. Playing the part of Thomas Culpeper, Catherine Howard's lover, is Robert Donat. It was their performances in this film that made stars of both Laughton and Merle Oberon. For his performance Charles Laughton won the Oscar for the Best Actor of 1932-33, a rare honour for an Englishman at that time.

One of the big British productions of 1933 was the film version of J.B. Priestley's novel *The Good Companions*. Directed by Victor Saville, it had a large cast headed by Jessie Matthews, John Gielgud and Edmund Gwenn no lightweights in the British film world. In fact, it was owing to the persuasive powers of producers Michael Balcon that Jessie resisted the lure of Hollywood.

Another film directed by Victor Saville the same year was *I Was a Spy*, starring Madeleine Carroll, Herbert Marshall and Conrad Veidt. Based on the true experiences of a Belgian woman's work in espionage during the First World War, the action takes place in a Belgian town. This was created in a huge set built at the Welwyn Garden Studios near London. Although made as a drama, the picture gives a balanced insight into enemies at war and joined the succession of anti-war films made between the two World Wars.

In 1933 Jack Buchanan starred in and also made his directing debut with *Yes, Mr. Brown*. Buchanan was a light comedian, an excellent song-and-dance man, and a leading star of British musical films of the Thirties. (He was to impress Hollywood later with his role in *The Band Wagon*, 1953). Not only was the film successful but the title song was also a hit. His co-star is Elsie Randolph, a talented singer and dancer who partnered Buchanan in a number of his stage shows. Also in the cast are Margot Grahame and Hartley Power.

One of the most charming films made in France during 1933 was *La Maternelle* (Infant's School). It was directed by Jean Benoît-Levy, noted for his very realistic near-documentary style. The leading role of Rose was played by Madeleine Renaud. The story concerns Rose, a servant in a nursery school. When Marie, one of the pupils is left alone because her mother has run off with a lover, Rose takes pity on the child and adopts her. But complications set in

Edmund Gwenn in *The Good Companions*

Madeleine Carroll in *I was a Spy*

Hartley Power

135

Harry Baur

Scenes from *SA Mann-Brand* and *Hitlerjunge Quex*

when Rose receives a proposal from the school's doctor and it appears that Marie could be left alone again. The film well deserves the high praise it received when first shown and gives an authentic impression of what life was like at a French school of the period.

Raymond Bernard made his second version of *Les Miserables* in 1933, starring Harry Baur and Charles Vanel. *Les Miserables* proved to be a marathon of a picture with a running time of five hours and when first presented, was screened in three separate parts.

Zero de Conduite (Zero for Conduct) which also appeared in 1933, has become a famous French classic. Directed by Jean Vigo, the film is set in a boys' boarding school where the tyrannical behaviour of the under-sized headmaster and his staff make life so impossible for the boys that they revolt. It has a famous sequence in which the boys have a pillow fight until the air becomes filled with feathers – a sequence that was shot in slow motion. *The New Yorker* commented with some truth, that it was one of the most important films ever made.

When the Nazis took over Germany in 1933, Joseph Goebbels was appointed Minister of Public Enlightenment and Propoganda. He then turned his attention to the country's film industry. By 1934 he had introduced the Reich Film Law which meant that every script had to be submitted for scrutiny and any changes thought necessary had to be carried out.

Goebbels also banned all existing films that he considered undesirable, and set about ridding the film industry of its Jewish element.

Primarily, Goebbels wanted people to go to cinemas to watch pro-Nazi newsreels. He was quite happy to entice them in with harmless escapist nonsense. Propaganda films, he believed, should be kept down in number and when they did appear they were first-rate and had a strong effect.

The year 1933 started off with three such Nazi Propaganda 'specials'. There was *Hans Westmar*, directed by Franz Wenzler, a fictionalized film about the Nazi 'hero' Horst Wessel. It had to be a highly fictionalized biography because Wessel was, in fact, a very seedy, unheroic character – but he had written the words to one of the most popular Nazi anthems.

Then there were two 'Hitler Youth' films. The first, *SA Mann-Brand* directed by Franz Seitz, is the story of the conflicts between a Nazi youth and his Communist father. However, it was not very impressive, featured no star actors – and was not very popular. *Hitlerjunge Quex* fared much better. It was based on the real-life story of an upright Hitler Youth who was barbarously slaughtered by the unruly Communist kids who ruled the 'Red' district in which he lived. This film was well directed and was a public success.

Another film which would have appealed to the public as it had lots of drama and a good plot was Robert Siodmak's

Brennendes Geheimnis. It was, however, far from appreciated by Goebbels.

It was based on a story by Stefan Zweig, and the action takes place in a hotel in Switzerland, where a married woman (Hilda Wagener) on holiday is seduced by a rich philanderer (Willi Forst) to the great distress of her young son.

Goebbels attacked the film. He complained that it did not fulfil the high moral standards set by the regime and had it withdrawn from cinemas. This, coupled with the fact that Siodmak was Jewish, made the director realize it was time to leave Germany. He went first to France and then to Hollywood where he made some of the best thrillers of the Forties, including *The Spiral Staircase* (1945) and *The Killers* (1946).

Two days after he became German leader in 1933 Hitler attended the premiere of *Morgenrot (Dawn)*. This film clearly had a strong propaganda slant for the Nazis; heroism is the theme, as two crew-members of a U-boat are prepared to sacrifice their own lives for their comrades and the glory of the fatherland. The film did have one doubtful scene, when a distraught mother is shown crying for her son lost at sea – something a good German mother of the period was not supposed to do. However, overall the film seems to have been deemed highly 'suitable', and Gustav Ucicky, the Austrian-born director, went on to make many other such films for the Nazis.

There was much to disturb the Nazi leaders in Fritz Lang's masterpiece *M* (1931); comparisons between police methods and those of the criminal underworld were there for all to see. Whether or not Lang was consciously aiming these observations at the Nazis, he takes them further in *Das Testament des Dr. Mabuse (The Testament/Last Will of Dr. Mabuse* in which the insane Dr. Mabuse is locked up in a lunatic asylum surrounded by his plans for world domination – ideas which then pass to his psychiatrist after his death. Goebbels did not like the film and banned it but nevertheless offered Lang the job of the Third Reich's official film-maker. However, Lang was very suspicious of this offer – two films of his had met with disapproval and he had Jewish ancestry – so like Siodmak and many others he fled, first to Paris and then on to Hollywood.

That great master of the silent cinema, Vsevolod I Pudovkin, whose silent films *The End of St. Petersburg* (1927) and *Storm Over Asia* (1928), remain two of the milestones in the history of the cinema, made another major contribution with the sound film *Deserter*. The story deals with a young revolutionary who becomes involved in a dockyard strike in Hamburg.

A little piece of film history was made in Australia in 1933. Errol Flynn made his debut as an actor. A semi-documentary, *In the Wake of the Bounty* was a film in which neither he nor the film made any great impact, but it was the beginning of something big for Flynn.

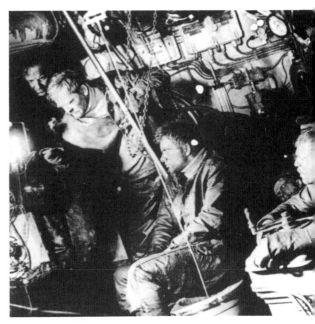

Members of the U-Boat crew in *Morgenrot*

Errol Flynn

Errol Flynn in *In the Wake of the Bounty*

In Germany Hitler was imposing a strict censorship on the films made there. Meanwhile Hollywood was dedicated to sheer escapism with Fred Astaire and Ginger Rogers and a giant ape called King Kong leading the way.

Stuart Erwin and Dorothy Wilson in *Before Dawn* (RKO)

Maureen O'Sullivan, Charles Murray and George Sydney in *The Cohens and Kellys in Trouble* (Univ)

The Last Stand of *King Kong* (RKO)

Grant Mitchell, Louise Closser Hale, Jean Harlow, Wallace Beery, Edmund Lowe, Karen Morley and Billie Burke in *Dinner at Eight* (MGM)

Clark Gable and Jean Harlow in *Hold Your Man* (MGM)

Conrad Veidt in *I Was a Spy* (Gau)

Ruby Keeler

Alec B Francis and Charlotte Henry in *Alice in Wonderland* (Par)

Fred Astaire and Ginger Rogers in *Flying Down to Rio* (RKO)

Clark Gable and Helen Hayes in *The White Sister* (MGM)

Robert Montgomery and Ann Harding in *When Ladies Meet* (MGM)

George Arliss in *Voltaire* (WB)

Barbara Stanwyck in *Baby Face* (WB)

Noel Francis and Joe E Brown in *Son of a Sailor* (FN)

Adolphe Menjou and Katharine Hepburn in *Morning Glory* (RKO)

Above: Bette Davis, Theodore Newton and George Arliss in *The Working Man* (WB)

Left: Lionel Atwill and Fay Wray in *The Mystery of the Wax Museum* (WB)

Grant Mitchell, Robert Barrat, Ruth Chatterton and Frank McHugh in *Lilly Turner* (FN)

Jean Parker, Katharine Hepburn, Joan Bennett and Frances Dee in *Little Women* (RKO)

Myrna Loy in *The Barbarian* (GB *A Night in Cairo* (MGM)

George Raft and Jackie Cooper in *The Bowery* (UA)

Greta Garbo

Carole Lombard

Above: Frances Fuller and Gary Cooper in *One Sunday Afternoon* (Par)

Right: Winnie Lightner and Joan Crawford in *Dancing Lady* (MGM)

Greta Garbo and John Gilbert in *Queen Christina* (MGM)　　　John Barrymore and Bebe Daniels in *Counsellor at Law* (Univ)

Kay Francis and John Halliday in *The House on 56th Street* (WB)　　　Hedda Hopper and Phillips Holmes in *Beauty for Sale* (MGM)

Kent Taylor and Irving Pichel in *The Mysterious Rider* (Par)
Buck Jones, John Boles and Nancy Carroll in *Child of Manhattan* (Col)

Paul Robeson in *The Emperor Jones* (UA)
Bette Davis and Monroe Owsley in *Ex-Lady* (WB)

Edward G Robinson and Kay Francis in *I Loved a Woman* (FN)
Warner Baxter and Martha Sleeper in *Penthouse* (GB *Crooks in Clover*) (HS/MGM)

Picture Gallery for 1933

1   2

3

4

5 △ ▽ 8

6 △ ▽ 9   7 △ ▽ 10

11 12

13

14 15

16 17

18 △ ▽ 20   19 △ ▽ 21

1. Front: Charles Bickford, Richard Arlen and George Meeker   Back: Louise Dresser and Jean Hersholt in *Song of the Eagle* (Par)
2. Stanley Lupino and Thelma Todd in *You Made Me Love You* (BiP)
3. Maureen O'Sullivan, Charles Murray and George Sidney in *The Cohens and the Kellys in Trouble* (Univ)
4. Mary Brian, Guy Kibbee and Glenda Farrell in *Girl Missing* (WB)
5. John Halliday, Verree Teasdale and Neil Hamilton in *Terror Aboard* (Par)
6. Phillips Holmes and Diana Wynyard in *Men Must Fight* (MGM)
7. Sally O'Neill and Lew Cody in *By Appointment Only* (Inv)
8. Zeppo, Groucho and Chico Marx in *Duck Soup* (Par)
9. George O'Brien and Greta Nissen in *Life in the Raw* (Fox)
10. ZaSu Pitts and Slim Summerville in *Her First Mate* (Univ)
11. Mary Pickford and Leslie Howard in *Secrets* (UA)
12. Jill Esmond, Gibb McLaughlin and Finlay Currie in *No Funny Business* (Jo St)
13. Kay Francis and George Brent in *The Keyhole* (WB)
14. Francis Rich, Rex Bell (c) and Lloyd Whitlock (r) in *The Diamond Trail* (MoP)
15. Wynne Gibson, Jean Hersholt and Stuart Erwin in *The Crime of the Century* (Par)
16. Gregory Ratoff, Texas Guinan and Paul Kelly in *Broadway Thru a Keyhole* (UA)
17. William Bakewell and Marian Marsh in *A Man of Sentiment* (Che)
18. Kay Francis in *Mary Stevens MD* (WB)
19. Richard Arlen, Jack Oakie and and Joseph Sawyer in *College Humor* (Par)
20. Claude King, Holmes Herbert and Lionel Atwill in *The Mystery of the Wax Museum* (WB)
21. Allen Jenkins, Glenda Farrell, Frank McHugh and Joan Blondell in *Havana Widows* (FN)

143

1. Barton MacLane
2. Robert Montgomery, Sterling Holloway and Ann Harding in *When Ladies Meet* (MGM)
3. Bradley Page and Judith Allen in *This Day and Age* (CdeM)
4. Cary Grant and Mae West in *I'm No Angel* (Par)
5. Kay Francis, Walter Huston and Nils Asther in *Storm at Daybreak* (MGM)
6. Carmen Miranda
7. Myrna Loy and John Barrymore in *Topaze* (DS)
8. Halliwell Hobbes
9. Tom Mix in *Terror Trail* (Univ)
10. Paul Muni and Mary Astor in *The World Changes* (WB)

6 △ ▽ 8

7

9

10

1. Katharine Hepburn in *Morning Glory* (RKO)
2. Wallace Beery and Jean Harlow in *Dinner at Eight* (MGM)
3. C Henry Gordon
4. Irene Dunne and Walter Huston in *Ann Vickers* (RKO)
5. Elsa Lanchester
6. Stuart Erwin, Spencer Tracy, Frank McGlynn and Marian Nixon in *Face in the Sky* (Fox)
7. J Farrell MacDonald, George Arliss, Bette Davis and Theodore Newton in *The Working Man* (WB)
8. Mary Astor, Anna Q Nilsson and Paul Muni in *The World Changes* (FN)
9. John Boles and Nancy Carroll in *Child of Manhattan* (Col)
10. Henry Victor

1

2

3

4

5

6

7

8

The Private Life of Henry the Eighth (LF) directed by Alexander Korda was one of the few British movies to prove a winner in the US. Charles Laughton was supreme in the role of the much-married King Henry.

1. Charles Laughton and Elsa Lanchester
2. Charles Laughton and Binnie Barnes
3. Charles Laughton and Elsa Lanchester
4. Elsa Lanchester and John Loder
5. Lady Tree and Claude Allister
6. Charles Laughton
7. Elsa Lanchester
8. Charles Laughton and Binnie Barnes
9. 10. Charles Laughton
11. John Loder, Charles Laughton and Robert Donat
12. Robert Donat
13. Charles Laughton and Binnie Barnes
14. Charles Laughton
15. Judy Kelly
16. Elsa Lanchester, Charles Laughton and Lady Tree

9   10

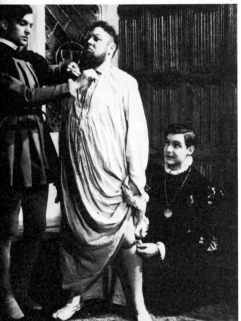

11   12

13

14   15   16

1

3

4

2

5

6

8

7 △ ▽ 11

10 △ ▽ 12

1. Matt McHugh, Spencer Tracy, Claire Trevor and Willard Robertson in *The Mad Game* (Fox)

2. Fay Wray and Jack Holt in *The Woman I Stole* (Col)

3. Mary Carlisle and Buster Crabbe (r) in *The Sweetheart of Sigma Chi* (MoP)

4. Ralph Morgan and Sally Eilers in *Walls of Gold* (Fox)

5. Charles Grapewin and Nancy Carroll in *The Kiss before the Mirror* (Univ)

6. Constance Bennett, and Leonid Snegoff in *After Tonight* (GB *Sealed Lips*) (RKO)

7. Evelyn Venable

8. Frank Morgan, Alice Brady and Russell Hardie in *Broadway to Hollywood* (GB *Ring up the Curtain*) (MGM)

9. Charles Grapewin, Randolph Scott, Kate Smith and Sally Blane in *Hello, Everybody!* (Par)

10. Ralph Forbes, Genevieve Tobin and Roland Young in *Pleasure Cruise* (Fox)

11. Dorothy Sebastian and Leon Waycoff (I) in *Ship of Wanted Men* (ShP)

12. May Robson, John Barrymore and Eduardo Ciannelli in *Reunion in Vienna* (MGM)

1

2

3

4

5

6

7

8

9 △ ▽ 11

10 △ ▽ 12

1. James Dunn, Kenneth Thomson and Sally Eilers in *Hold Me Tight* (Fox)

2. Victor Jory and Vivienne Osborne in *The Devil's in Love* (Fox)

3. Bette Davis, Douglas Fairbanks Jr and Frank McHugh in *The Parachute Jumper* (WB)

4. ZaSu Pitts, Charles Starrett and Will Rogers in *Mr. Skitch* (Fox)

5. William Gargan and Frances Dee in *The Headline Shooter* (GB *Evidence in Camera)* (RKO)

6. Gary Cooper, Fay Wray, Frances Fuller and Neil Hamilton in *One Sunday Afternoon* (Par)

7. Lee Tracy, Madge Evans and John Miljan in *The Nuisance* (GB *Accidents Wanted*) (MGM)

8. Walter Huston, Franchot Tone and Karen Morley in *Gabriel Over the White House* (MGM/WaW)

9. George Brent, Margaret Lindsay and Eugene Pallette in *From Headquarters* (WB)

10. Larry 'Buster' Crabbe

11. Loretta Young and Regis Toomey in *She Had To Say Yes* (FN)

12. John Wayne and J P McGowan in *Somewhere in Sonora* (WB)

1

2

3

4

5

6

7

8

9

10

11

1

2

3

1. Hugh Williams and H B Warner in *Sorrell and Son* (B&D)
2. Tully Marshall and Bela Lugosi in *Night of Terror* (Col)
3. Dorothy Mackaill and Tom Moore in *Neighbors Wives* (FR)
4. Noah Beery Snr and Dorothy Burgess in *Easy Millions* (FFA)
5. Earle Foxe, Vivienne Osborne and Leo Carrillo in *Men Are Such Fools* (RKO)
6. Victoria Hopper in *The Constant Nymph* (Gau)
7. Hugh Herbert, Eddie Quillan and Marjorie Rambeau in *Strictly Personal* (Par)
8. Syd Sayler, Edward Arnold, Wynne Gibson and Edmund Lowe in *Her Bodyguard* (Par)
9. Marlene Dietrich in *Song of Songs* (Par)
10. Ginger Rogers in *The Shriek in the Night* (AIP)
11. Frank Morgan and Al Jolson in *Hallelujah, I'm a Bum* (GB *Hallelujah I'm a Tramp*) (UA)

4

7

5

8

10

6

11

9

151

1. Kay Francis and John Halliday in *The House on 56th Street* (WB)
2. Lee Tracy and Sally Blane in *Advice to the Lovelorn* (Fox)
3. Warner Baxter and Martha Sleeper in *Penthouse* (GB *Crooks in Clover*) (MGM)
4. Lyle Talbot and Barbara Stanwyck in *Ladies They Talk About* (WB)
5. Joel McCrea and Marion Nixon in *Chance at Heaven* (RKO)
6. Barbara Stanwyck and Otto Kruger in *Ever in My Heart* (WB)
7. Henri Garat and Janet Gaynor in *Adorable* (Fox)
8. Doris Hill and Bob Steele in *Trailing North* (MoP)
9. Bing Crosby and Marion Davis in *Going Hollywood* (MGM)
10. Margaret Lindsay and William Powell in *Private Detective 62* (WB)
11. Victor Jory and Helen Twelvetrees in *My Woman* (Col)
12. Sally Eilers and James Dunn in *Sailor's Luck* (Fox)
13. Edwin Maxwell and Bill Boyd in *Emergency Call* (RKO)

9 △▽ 11

12

10 △▽ 13

1. Pat O'Brien and Bette Davis in *Bureau of Missing Persons* (FN)
2. Clark Gable and Helen Hayes in *The White Sister* (MGM)
3. Victor McLaglen and Edmund Lowe in *Hot Pepper* (Fox)
4. Lee Tracy and Jean Harlow in *Bombshell* (GB *Blonde Bombshell*) (MGM)
5. Aline MacMahon, Joan Blondell, Dick Powell and Ruby Keeler in *Gold Diggers of 1933* (WB)
6. Una Merkel and Ernest Truex in *Whistling in the Dark* (MGM)
7. Una Merkel and Charles Grapewin in *Beauty for Sale* (MGM)
8. Ruth Chatterton and George Brent in *Lilly Turner* (FN)
9. Loretta Young and Warren William in *Employees' Entrance* (FN)
10. George Raft
11. Elisabeth Bergner
12. Genevieve Tobin and Chester Morris in *Infernal Machine* (Fox)
13. Gloria Swanson and John Halliday in *Perfect Understanding* (GSBP)
14. Jean Muir and Johnny Mack Brown in *Son of a Sailor* (FN)

6 7

8 △ ▽ 14

9 △ ▽ 12   10

11 △ ▽ 13

1

2

3

4

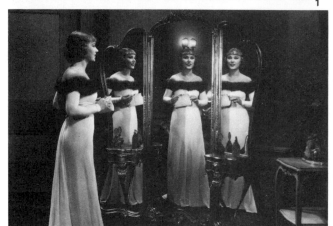

5

6

7

1. Walter Connolly and Barbara Stanwyck in *The Bitter Tea of General Yen* (Col)

2. Ralph Forbes and Adrienne Ames in *The Avenger* (MoP)

3. Fay Wray in *The Big Brain* (GB *Enemies of Society*) (AdP)

4. Robert Armstrong and Roland Young in *Blind Adventure* (RKO)

5. Raquel Torres, Bert Wheeler and Robert Woolsey in *So This is Africa* (Col)

6. Noel Madison and Noel Francis in *The Important Witness* (Tow)

7. Herbert Rawlinson and Mary Brian in *Moonlight and Pretzels* (Univ)

8. Ralph Bellamy and June Collyer in *Before Midnight* (Col)

9. Fay Wray and Paul Page in *Below the Sea* (Col)

10. Fay Wray and Jack Holt in *Master of Men* (Col)

11. Chester Morris and Genevieve Tobin in *Golden Harvest* (Par)

12. Ginger Rogers, Joan Blondell and Louise Dresser in *Broadway Bad* (Fox)

13. Noel Francis and Skeets Gallagher in *Reform Girl* (Tow)

14. Ken Maynard in *Between Fighting Men* (WW)

15. El Brendel and George O'Brien in *The Last Trail* (Fox)

16. Rex Bell and Robert Kortman in *Rainbow Ranch* (MoP)

8

9

10

11

12

13

14

15

16

1

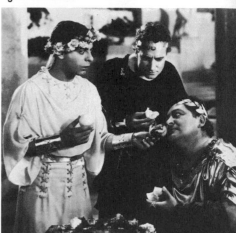

2

4

5

6 △ ▽ 9

7

8 △ ▽ 10

1. Gene Raymond, Bette Davis and Monroe Owsley in *Ex-Lady* (WB)
2. Una Merkel and Stuart Erwin in *Day of Reckoning* (MGM)
3. Helen Mack and Buck Jones in *The California Trail* (Col)
4. Ronald Colman in a dual role in *The Masquerader* (SG)
5. Eddie Cantor, Alan Mowbray and Edward Arnold in *Roman Scandals* (Par)
6. Lillian Gish and Roland Young in *His Double Life* (Par)
7. Edmund Lowe and Nancy Carroll in *I Love That Man* (Par)
8. George Blackwood and Kay Francis in *I Loved a Woman* (DZ/Fox)
9. Norma Shearer
10. Frances Drake

1. Lionel Barrymore and Lewis Stone in *Looking Forward* (MGM)
2. Loretta Young, Victor Jory and Vivienne Osborne in *Devils in Love* (Fox)
3. Joan Blondell
4. Charles Starrett and Anita Page in *Jungle Bride* (MoP)
5. Leo Carrillo and Lois Wilson in *Obey the Law* (Col)
6. George Bancroft and Judith Anderson in *Blood Money* (Fox)
7. Franciska Gaal
8. Virginia Bruce

4 △ ▽ 7

5

6 △ ▽ 8

1

2

3

4

5

6

7

1. Una Merkel, Ruby Keeler, George E Stone, Warner Baxter and Ginger Rogers in *42nd Street* (WB)
2. Oliver Hardy and Stan Laurel
3. Victor Jory
4. Ricardo Cortez
5. Una Merkel
6. Reginald Denny
7. W C Fields and Alison Skipworth in *Tillie and Gus* (Par)
8. Tala Birell and Melvyn Douglas in *Nagana* (Univ)
9. Leslie Banks in *The Fire Raisers* (Gau)
10. Bob Livingston
11. Junior Durkin and Charlotte Henry in *Man Hunt* (RKO)

8

9

10

11

1. Richard Barthelmess and Sally Eilers in *Central Airport* (FN)
2. Loretta Young and Gene Raymond in *Zoo in Budapest* (Fox)
3. Frank McHugh and Ginger Rogers in *Professional Sweetheart* (GB *Imaginary Sweetheart*) (RKO)
4. Margaret Sullavan
5. Andy Devine
6. Margaret Lindsay
7. Ned Sparks
8. Robert Armstrong, Mae Clarke and John Gilbert in *Fast Workers* (MGM)
9. Paul Cavanagh and Claudette Colbert in *Tonight is Ours* (Par)
10. Franchot Tone and Loretta Young in *Midnight Mary* (MGM)
11. Hardie Albright
12. Reginald Owen in *A Study in Scarlet* (KBS/ WW)

159

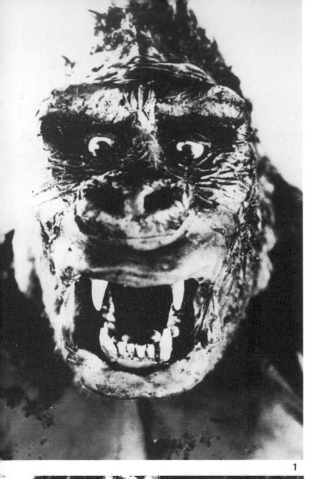

1. The monster in *King Kong* (RKO)
2. Clara Bow
3. The monster and Fay Wray in *King Kong* (RKO)
4. Greta Garbo and John Gilbert in *Queen Christina* (MGM)
5. Marie Dressler and Wallace Beery in *Tugboat Annie* (MGM)
6. Gary Cooper and Charlotte Henry in *Alice in Wonderland* (Par)
7. Bruce Cabot, Fay Wray and Robert Armstrong in *King Kong* (RKO)
8. C Aubrey Smith, Greta Garbo and John Gilbert in *Queen Christina* (MGM)
9. Greta Garbo, Elizabeth Young and C Aubrey Smith in *Queen Christina* (MGM)

2

4

3 △ ▽ 7

8

6 △ ▽ 9

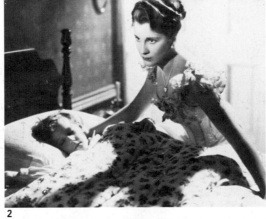

Cavalcade (Fox) was the movie version of yet another Noel Coward play. It covers the story of a well-to-do English family from the outbreak of the Boer War at the turn of the century to World War I. It was not only a cavalcade of domestic history, it was also a cavalcade of incidents with a splendid cast of stars. Hollywood film critic Louella Parsons went so far as to write 'Greater than Birth of a Nation' although it lacked the vast panoply of battle scenes and spectacle of the D W Griffiths' masterpiece.

1. Herbert Mundin and Una O'Connor
2. Diana Wynyard and Douglas Scott
3. Herbert Mundin and Bonita Granville
4. Clive Brook and Diana Wynyard
5. Clive Brook and Frank Lawton
6. John Warburton, Billy Bevan, Una O'Connor, Diana Wynyard and Bonita Granville
7. Dick Henderson Jr, Diana Wynyard, Douglas Scott and Clive Brook
8. Herbert Mundin and Una O'Connor
9. Frank Lawton and Ursula Jeans
10. Frank Lawton and Ursula Jeans

7△ ▽9

8△ ▽10

1. Rochelle Hudson
2. Paul Robeson in *The Emperor Jones* (UA)
3. Peter Lorre in *M* (Nero), a 1931 film released in the USA in 1933
4. Ken Maynard and Frances Dade in *Phantom Thunderbolt* (KBS/WW)
5. Una O'Connor and Claude Rains in *The Invisible Man* (Univ)
6. Buck Jones in *Sundown Rider* (Col)
7. Buster Keaton and Jimmy Durante in *What! No Beer?* (MGM)
8. Yvonne Arnaud
9. Isabel Jewell
10. Jean Harlow (r) in *Hold Your Man* (MGM)

162

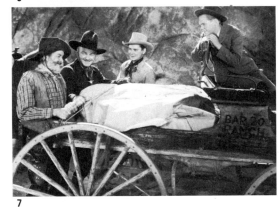

1. Jane Darwell, Ray Walter and Virginia Cherrill in *He Couldn't Take It* (MOP)
2. Sam Hardy and Lili Damita in *Goldie Gets Along* (RKO)
3. Connee Boswell
4. George Arliss and Doris Kenyon in *Voltaire* (WB)
5. Carole Lombard and Donald Cook (r) in *Brief Moment* (Col)
6. Hugh Herbert, Ann Dvorak and Lyle Talbot in *College Coach* (GB *Football Coach*) (WB)
7. Gabby Hayes, William Boyd, Russell Hayden and Billy King in *Heart of Arizona* (Par)
8. Benita Hume and Adolphe Menjou in *Worst Woman in Paris* (Lasky/Fox)
9. Verree Teasdale
10. John Barrymore

163

1 2

3

5

4

6 △ ▽9   7 △ ▽10   8 △

11   12

14   15

16   17

18 △ ▽ 20   19 △ ▽ 21

22

1. Otis Harlan (l) and William V Mong in *Women Won't Tell* (Che)
2. Edmund Breese and W C Fields in *International House* (Par)
3. Emlyn Williams, Frank Lawton and Leonora Corbett in *Friday the Thirteenth* (G'boro)
4. Marian Marsh, J Carrol Naish in *Notorious But Nice* (Che)
5. Evalyn Knapp and Reginald Barlow in *His Private Secretary* (ShP)
6. Fred Kohler Jr (l) and Preston Foster in *Corruption (XX)*
7. Pat Paterson
8. Dorothy Hyson and Anthony Bushell in *The Ghoul* (Gau)
9. Mickey Rooney in *The Big Chance* (AG)
10. Natalie Moorhead (s), Selma Jackson and Leon Ames in *Forgotten* (Inv)
11. Louise Closser Hale, Robert Montgomery and Helen Hayes in *Another Language* (MGM)
12. Buster Crabbe and Frances Dee in *Tarzan the Fearless* (Pri)
13. Herbert Marshall, Elizabeth Allen and May Robson in *The Solitaire Man* (MGM)
14. Lilian Harvey and John Boles in *My Lips Betray* (Fox)
15. Ernest Truex and Marjorie Rambeau in *The Warrior's Husband* (Fox)
16. Carole Lombard and Fredric March in *The Eagle and the Hawk* (Par)
17. Joe Girard and Monte Blue in *Officer 13* (FD)
18. Sylvia Sidney, Louise Carter and H B Warner in *Jennie Gerhardt* (Par)
19. Cicely Courtneidge in *Aunt Sally* (G'boro)
20. Pat O'Brien (r) in *The World Gone Mad* (Maj)
21. Robert Montgomery and Walter Huston in *Hell Below* (MGM)
22. Gus McNaughton, Constance Cummings and Frank Lawton in *The Charming Deceiver* (Maj)

11

12 13

14 15

1. Will Rogers and Vera Allen in *Doctor Bull* (Fox)
2. Marguerite Churchill in *Girl Without a Room* (Par)
3. Charles Bickford and Irene Dunne in *No Other Woman* (RKO)
4. Carl Esmond
5. Leslie Fenton and George Merritt in *F P 1* (Gau/Ufa)
6. Clive Brook and Ann Harding in *Gallant Lady* (Fox)
7. Herbert Mundin, James Dunn and Joan Bennett in *Arizona to Broadway* (Fox)
8. Warner Baxter and Elissa Landi in *I Loved you Wednesday* (Fox)
9. Betty Compson and Pat O'Brien in *Destination Unknown* (Univ)
10. Rex Bell in *Lucky Larrigan* (MoP)
11. Joan Crawford and Fred Astaire in *Dancing Lady* (MGM)
12. Dorothea Wieck
13. Preston Foster and Zita Johann in *The Man Who Dared* (Fox)
14. Eugene Pallette, William Powell, Jack La Rue and Helen Vinson in *The Kennel Murder Case* (WB)
15. Robert Armstrong and Frank Albertson in *The Billion Dollar Scandal* (Par)
16. Guy Kibbee and Adolphe Menjou in *Convention City* (FN)
17. Oliver Hardy and Stan Laurel in *The Devil's Brother* (G B *Fra Diavolo*) (MGM/HR)
18. Lilian Harvey
19. Diane Sinclair and Buck Jones in *Fighting Code* (Col)

16 17

18 19

167

1

2

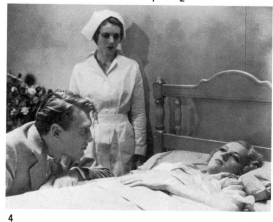

3

4

5

6 △ ▽ 10

7

8 △ ▽ 9

11   12

1. Randolph Scott in *Wild Horse Mesa* (Par)
2. Lillian Roth, Charles 'Buddy' Rogers, James Dunn and Cliff Edwards in *Take A Chance* (Par)
3. Barbara Stanwyck and John Wayne in *Baby Face* (WB)
4. Ralph Bellamy and Sally Eilers in *Second Hand Wife* (Fox)
5. Wynne Gibson, Edward Arnold and Edmund Lowe in *Her Bodyguard* (Par)
6. John Wayne and Cecilia Parker in *Riders of Destiny* (LS/MoP)
7. Buddy Rogers and Marian Nixon in *Best of Enemies* (Fox)
8. Carole Lombard in *Supernatural* (Par)
9. Evalyn Knapp and Tim McCoy in *Police Car 17* (Col)
10. Harry Woods, John Wayne, Erville Alderson and Otto Hoffman in *Haunted Gold* (WB)
11. James Dunn, Claire Trevor and Matt McHugh in *Jimmy and Sally* (Fox)
12. Skeets Gallagher, Bing Crosby, Judith Allen, Jack Oakie and Harry Green in *Too Much Harmony* (Par)
13. Matthew Betz, J Carrol Naish and Tim McCoy in *Silent Men* (Col)
14. Leslie Howard and Heather Angel in *Berkeley Square* (Fox)
15. Constance Cummings and Frank Lawton in *Heads We Go* (BiP)
16. Kent Taylor, Carole Lombard and Charles Laughton in *White Woman* (Par)
17. Fredric March, Miriam Hopkins and Gary Cooper in *Design for Living* (Par)
18. Richard Arlen and Judith Allen in *Hell and High Water* (Par)
19. Randolph Scott, Sidney Blackmer and Bebe Daniels in *Cocktail Hour* (Col)

13   14

15 △ ▽ 17   16 △ ▽ 18   19

1. Harvey Stephens, Margaret Lindsay and Janet Gaynor in *Paddy the Next Best Thing* (Fox)

2. Bill Robbins, Marceline Day, Hoot Gibson and Ethel Wales in *The Fighting Parson* (AIP)

3. James Cagney and Alice White in *Picture Snatcher* (WB)

4. Joe E Brown in *Elmer, the Great* (WB)

5. Ken Maynard and Muriel Gordon in *The Lone Avenger* (WW)

6. Clyde Beatty in *The Big Cage* (Univ)

7. Esther Muir and Lionel Barrymore in *Sweepings* (RKO)

8. Patricia Ellis, Dick Powell and George Arliss in *The King's Vacation* (WB)

9. Sari Maritza

10. Warner Baxter, Miriam Jordan and Herbert Mundin in *Dangerously Yours* (Fox)

11. Spencer Tracy and Fay Wray in *Shanghai Madness* (Fox)

12. Marie Dressler, George Coulouris and Lionel Barrymore in *Christopher Bean* (MGM)

13. Willie Fung, Douglas Fairbanks Jr and Dudley Digges in *The Narrow Corner* (WB)

14. Henry Kendall

15. James Cagney and Madge Evans in *The Mayor of Hell* (WB)

16. Mae Clarke and James Cagney in *Lady Killer* (WB)

17. James Murray, Ruth Chatterton and Robert Emmett O'Connor in *Frisco Jenny* (FN)

18. Ned Sparks and Warren William in *Lady for a Day* (Col)

19. Toby Wing

20. Kent Taylor

6 △ ▽8   7 △ ▽9

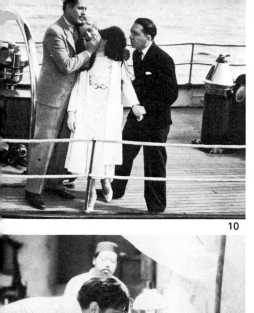
10

11

12

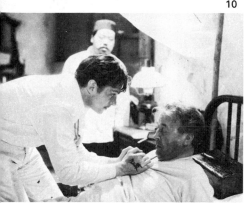
13

14

15

▽18   16 △ ▽ 19   17 △

20 ▽

1. Anita Page
2. Jack Holt and Jean Arthur in *The Whirlpool* (Col)
3. Stuart Erwin
4. Fatty Layman, Chic Sale and Billy Boyd in *Men of America* (RKO)
5. Matt Moore and Sidney Blackmer in *The Deluge* (RKO)
6. Maureen O'Sullivan
7. Ken Maynard and Charles King in *Strawberry Roan* (Univ)
8. Fay Wray and Melvyn Douglas in *Vampire Bat* (Maj)

1

2

3

4 △ ▽ 6

5

7

8

1. Sterling Holloway
2. Zita Johann and Paul Cavanagh in *The Sin of Norma Moran* (Maj)
3. Claude Allister
4. Betty Compson and Noel Madison in *West of Singapore* (MoP)
5. Tim McCoy in *Cornered* (Col)
6. John Barrymore and Lionel Barrymore in *Night Flight* (MGM)
7. Ruth Chatterton and Ferdinand Gottschalk in *Female* (FN)
8. Joan Marsh

5 △ ▽ 8

1 2

3 4 5

6 △ ▽9   7 △   8 △ ▽10

11   12

13   14

15   16

1. Purnell Pratt, Ed Wynn, William 'Stage' Boyd and Dorothy Mackaill in *The Chief* (GB *My Old Man's a Fireman*) (MGM)
2. George Weekes (l), Ann Harding, William Powell (c), Lucile Browne, Kay Hammond and Henry Stephenson (r) in *Double Harness* (RKO)
3. Gilbert Roland, Mae West and Rafaela Ottiano in *She Done Him Wrong* (Par)
4. Bill Boyd and Dorothy Wilson in *Lucky Devils* (DS/RKO)
5. Fred Astaire and Gene Raymond in *Flying Down to Rio* (RKO)
6. Richard Barthelmess, Robert Barrat, Loretta Young and Aline MacMahon in *Heroes for Sale* (FN)
7. Kate Campbell and Ken Maynard in *Come On, Tarzan* (WW)
8. Greta Nissen, Phil Harris and Charles Ruggles in *Melody Cruise* (MC/RKO)
9. Harold Huber (l), Douglas Fairbanks Jr (c), John Wayne and George Chandler in *Life of Jimmy Dolan* (GB *The Kid's Last Fight*) (WB)
10. George Raft, Helen Vinson, Alison Skipworth and Clive Brook in *Midnight Club* (Par)
11. Arthur Pierson and Fay Wray in *Ann Carver's Profession* (Col)
12. Larry 'Buster' Crabbe and Philo McCullough in *Tarzan The Fearless* (Pri)
13. Mary Boland and Charles Ruggles in *Mama Loves Papa* (Par)
14. Jimmy Durante and Jack Pearl in *Meet the Baron* (MGM)
15. Katharine Hepburn in *Christopher Strong* (RKO)
16. Purnell Pratt and Claudette Colbert in *Torch Singer* (Par)
17. Elizabeth Young and Richard Bennett in *Big Executive* (Par)
18. Irene Dunne and Frances Dee in *Silver Cord* (RKO)
19. Frances Dee, Mabel Colcord, Joan Bennett, Jean Parker and Katharine Hepburn in *Little Women* (RKO)
20. Cary Grant and Benita Hume in *Gambling Ship* (Par)

17 △ ▽ 19   18 △ ▽ 20

13

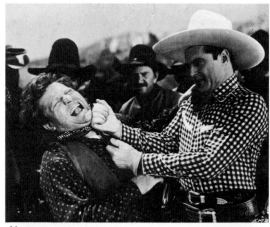

14

15

16

17

18

19

20

21

1. Lee Tracy, Mae Clarke, Peggy Shannon and C Henry Gordon in *Turn Back the Clock* (MGM)
2. Alexander Kirkland and Dorothy Jordan in *Bondage* (Fox)
3. Maurice Chevalier, Nydia Westman and Edward Everett Horton in *The Way to Love* (Par)
4. Judith Allen and Richard Arlen in *Cap'n Jericho* (Par)
5. Tom Brown, Wallace Ford, Richard Arlen and Claudette Colbert in *Three Cornered Moon* (Par)
6. Warner Oland and John Warburton in *Charlie Chan's Greatest Case* (Fox)
7. Robert Young, Ann Harding and Nils Asther in *The Right to Romance* (RKO)
8. Gloria Stuart and James Dunn in *The Girl in 419* (Par)
9. Marceline Day and John Wayne in *The Telegraph Trail* (WB)
10. Bruce Cabot and Helen Twelvetrees in *Disgraced!* (Par)
11. Randolph Scott and Tom Kennedy in *Man of the Forest* (Par)
12. Kent Taylor and Lona Andre in *The Mysterious Rider* (Par)
13. George O'Brien and Betsy King Ross in *Smoke Lightning* (Fox)
14. Fred Kohler and Ken Maynard in *Fiddlin' Buckaroo* (Univ)
15. Susan Fleming, Stuart Erwin and Alison Skipworth in *He Learned About Women* (Par)
16. Eric Linden and Arline Judge in *Flying Devils* (GB *The Flying Circus*) (RKO)
17. Boots Mallory, Alexander Kirkland and Ralph Morgan in *Humanity* (Fox)
18. Lew Ayres and Ginger Rogers in *Dont Bet on Love* (Univ)
19. Jack Oakie and Vivienne Osborne in *Sailor be Good* (RKO)
20. Una Merkel, Lee Tracy and James Gleason in *Clear All Wires* (MGM)
21. Regis Toomey in *Soldiers of the Storm* (Col)

Edward Everett Horton and Betty Grable in *The Gay Divorcee* (GB *The Gay Divorce*) (RKO)

William Powell and Myrna Loy in the first of a six-film series of *The Thin Man* (MGM)

CHAPTER FIVE
1934
GREAT PLAYERS IN GREAT ROLES

During 1934 the film industry generally enjoyed a period of prosperity and the number of films being made was on the increase.

In the USA there were, in addition, some major box-office successes. These brought bigger profits, some of which could be used to finance better pictures. One of the hits of the year was *The Gay Divorcee* (GB: *The Gay Divorce*).

It is said that Fred Astaire and Ginger Rogers never made a bad picture. *The Gay Divorcee*, the first picture in which they shared the starring roles, gave them a very good start. Their appeal was immediate and they were able to dance their way into the hearts of cinema audiences through another seven pictures before their immensely successful partnership ended.

The vivacious Ginger Rogers was every man's dream of what a girl should be. The shy, reticent style of Fred Astaire with his gaunt features, slight frame and bashful grin, won him a huge following among women the world over. Astaire and Rogers were the perfect combination.

The film was the first of several Astaire-Rogers musicals directed by Mark Sandrich.

The story is slight but offers a number of comic situations which are used to the full by the stars and a supporting cast which includes such imposing names as Edward Everett Horton, Eric Blore, Erik Rhodes and Alice Brady. Some of the cast popped up time and time again in later Astaire-Rogers films.

The musical sequences are the highlights of the film, especially the Oscar-winning 'The Continental', a catchy tune that provides splendid opportunities for one of the exciting dance routines. 'Night and Day', the Cole Porter classic, was another of the songs featured in the film. A young actress playing a small part as a hotel guest is Betty Grable; her own rise to stardom was only a little while away.

Two more of Hollywood's stars rose to a new prominence this year. Their names were William Powell and Myrna Loy, and the film was *The Thin Man*.

The story-line comes from a series of detective stories

written by Dashiell Hammett. Powell and Loy play the detectives Nick and Nora Charles.

The Thin Man was superbly scripted by Frances Goodrich and Albert Hackett and directed with delightful style and pace by W.S. Van Dyke – with so much pace that it only took him about 12 days to shoot. His nickname, very aptly, was 'One-take Woody'.

So popular did the film prove to be that it spawned five sequels – three of them filmed by Van Dyke, and all of them starring Powell and Loy, who thereby firmly established themselves as leading comedy, as well as dramatic stars.

If anyone was going to offend the Hays Office then the director Josef von Sternberg was the man to do so. He managed to avoid trouble with *The Scarlet Empress* – but only just. It was timing that saved him. The Hays Office tightened its moral code drastically in 1934, but the film was released two months in advance of this move and so got passed for screening.

The picture is based on the diary of Catherine the Great of Russia, the outrageous Empress – who was also introduced to cinemagoers by Alexander Korda through his production of *Catherine the Great* in the same year. Sternberg's version has his protegée Marlene Dietrich playing the Empress, and he ensured that every sexual fantasy is combined with the macabre to excite and horrify.

The Scarlet Empress is not thought by everyone to be a great film, but it is for Dietrich a spectacular showcase. Sam Jaffe plays the demented bridegroom, the Grand Duke Peter, and Louise Dressler is his mother, the Empress Elizabeth. Other members of the cast are John Lodge, C. Aubrey Smith, Gavin Gordon and Jameson Thomas.

One of the most successful pictures of 1934 was undoubtedly *It Happened One Night* which was taken from a short story by Samuel Hopkins Adams that had appeared in *Cosmopolitan* magazine.

It was a picture that a number of stars didn't want to know about. Robert Montgomery was offered the male lead which he refused as he had recently filmed a similar story. The role was given to a reluctant Clark Gable. The female lead was refused by Miriam Hopkins, Margaret Sullavan, Myrna Loy and Constance Bennett. Although the film was being made by Columbia, Claudette Colbert, a Paramount contract player, was approached. Because she was on holiday from her studio, and because she was able to demand double her usual salary, she accepted.

There must have been a number of disappointed stars when they realized the missed opportunity, for both Clark Gable and Claudette Colbert won Oscars. And so did director Frank Capra and the scriptwriter Robert Riskin. The film itself also won an Oscar as the Best Film of the year. It was the first time that a picture had won as many as five Oscars – and a great many years were to pass before this triumph was surpassed.

Joan Gardner and Douglas Fairbanks Jr in *Catherine the Great* (AK)

Above: Marlene Dietrich in *The Scarlet Empress* (Par)
Below: Clark Gable and Claudette Colbert in *It Happened One Night* (Col)

Conrad Veidt in *Jew Suss* (GB *Power*) (Gau)

Conrad Veidt and Frank Vosper in *Jew Suss* (GB *Power*) (Gau)

Jessie Matthews in *Evergreen* (Gau)

Benita Hume in *The Private Life of Don Juan* (LF)

When the film was first released it was not acclaimed with 'smash hit' reviews by the critics. They obviously failed to appreciate that they had witnessed one of the best light-hearted romantic film frolics ever made. The public loved it.

One of the most controversial British films of 1934 was *Jew Süss* (*US: Power*). It cost £120,000 to produce which at the time was the highest budget ever allocated to a British movie. It was made for the international market but some of the subject matter offended members of the Jewish community. On the other hand, Goebbels banned the film in Germany.

It starred Conrad Veidt as Josef Süss Oppenheimer, an ambitious Jew who leaves the ghetto to look after the financial affairs of Duke Karl Alexander (Frank Vosper) of Wurtemberg. It is basically the story of Süss Oppenheimer's rise and fall, the latter brought about by his stubborn pride.

The film, which shows a fascinating glimpse of German life at court during the eighteenth century, was produced by Michael Balcon and directed by Lothar Mendes. Besides Conrad Veidt and Frank Vosper, others in the cast are Benita Hume, Cedric Hardwicke and Pamela Ostrer.

Britain was clearly in high spirits in 1934 for that year saw the creation of what is still widely regarded as Britain's best-ever musical: *Evergreen*. Its star, Jessie Matthews, was described in the Thirties by *The New York Times* as 'the feminine equivalent of Fred Astaire' and, indeed, the director Victor Saville had hopes of that star partnering Jessie but Astaire was caught up at the time in the play *The Gay Divorce* (which, as we know, he filmed as *The Gay Divorcée* later in the year).

The story for *Evergreen* was freely adapted from the Rodgers and Hart stage show, in which Jessie had starred.

As well as such Rodgers and Hart classics as 'Dancing on the Ceiling', the film featured that lovely Harry Woods song 'Over My Shoulder'.

The Private Life of Don Juan was the last film made by Douglas Fairbanks Snr. He had had a long career and for some considerable time was the King of Hollywood, a crown eventually taken over by Clark Gable. That Fairbanks consented to make a film in England says much for the persuasive power of Alexander Korda who directed the picture.

Fairbanks plays the part of an ageing rake who had at one time been a great lover, but is now having what can only be described as a last fling. It was not a happy film for Fairbanks who by 1934 had lost much of his magic. As with all Korda pictures, detailed attention was given to the background sets, the costumes and the music. With Fairbanks were Merle Oberon, Owen Nares and Benita Hume.

It was not often that Korda made mistakes in casting and his flair for giving the right role to the most suitable person was again evident when he managed to cast Leslie Howard as the lead in *The Scarlet Pimpernel*. It was a film that Korda hoped would put him back in the American market where he had had little success since *The Private Life of Henry VIII.*

Leslie Howard is just right as the outwardly foppish Sir Percy Blakeney who, during the French revolution secretly helps members of the French aristocracy escape the guillotine. He gives a brilliant performance as he assists the underground movement with all the casualness of an upper-class Englishman. Merle Oberon portrays Lady Blakeney. The villain of the piece, Citizen Chauvelin, is played by Raymond Massey, and Nigel Bruce is the Prince Regent. Again, Korda furnished his cast with wonderful costumes. The music is by Arthur Benjamin, and to Harold Young goes the credit for directing this delightful 'swashbuckler'.

The Man Who Knew Too Much was one of the most successful British pictures of 1934, and it was the first of those back-chilling thrillers that was to make the director Alfred Hitchcock's name famous world-wide for those Hitchcock 'specials' that still attract audiences like pins to a magnet, and keep them gripped in their seats.

The story begins as a family on holiday in St. Moritz find themselves witnessing the assassination of a secret agent – who lives long enough to speak of a plan to murder a foreign diplomat in London. The agent's assassins, knowing he 'talked', kidnap the couple's little girl. The hunt for their daughter takes the couple (Leslie Banks and Edna Best) back to London where they are involved in one of Hitchcock's superb suspense scenes, this one set in the Albert Hall.

Peter Lorre (as the heartless assassin) and Nova Pilbeam are also members of the cast, and the film was produced by Michael Balcon.

Hitchcock himself enjoyed the story so much he filmed it again in 1956, this time starring Doris Day.

Toni is usually referred to as the 'neglected masterpiece' of the French director Jean Renoir. The story of the film was based on a real crime of passion that took place in Les Martigues, near Marseille.

Toni, one of the many migrants who have come to work in the region, falls for Josefa, a local farmer's daughter. However, Josefa decides that the much-wealthier Albert, foreman of the local quarry, is a better match and agrees to marry him. Toni in turn decides to marry Marie, his landlady, who has been very kind to him.

Events worsen rapidly. A jealous Marie attempts suicide, while Albert proves himself drunken, unreliable and unfaithful. Josefa takes some of his money in order to run away (with another young man) but is caught and beaten ferociously by Albert – whereupon Josefa shoots him. Toni arrives and hides Albert's body, but is arrested in the process and condemned. And although Josefa confesses, Toni is shot while trying to escape from prison.

Renoir broke with many traditions in injecting his own brand of realism into *Toni*. He shot it on location, with mainly naturally recorded sound. He used unknown actors

Leslie Howard in *The Scarlet Pimpernel* (LF)

Leslie Banks, Nova Pilbeam and Edna Best in *The Man Who Knew Too Much* (Gau)

Edward Delmont and Celia Montalvan in *Toni* (Films d'aujourd'hui)

Francoise Rosay and Pierre-Richard Willm in *Le Grand Jeu* (*The Great Game*) (FrF)

Le Grand Jeu (The Great Game) (FrF) was directed by the brilliant Jacques Feyder, husband of Francoise Rosay.
Here are Marie Bell and Pierre-Richard Wilm in the film.

Jean Vigo was one of France's greatest film-makers. He was a fore-runner in the poetic-realism of the French films of the decade. Jean Daste and Dita Parlo are seen here in his masterpiece 'L'Atalante (JN)

Luis Trenker who specialised in the popular mountaineering films of Germany in the mid-Thirties.

for his lead roles and a supporting cast of local people doing their real jobs. He portrays with a grim clarity the harsh lot of the poor immigrant worker – his often miserable conditions, his exploitation, his loneliness. The realistic style he employed for *Toni* was much admired by the eminent Italian neo-realist directors of the Forties; indeed Renoir's production assistant on *Toni* was Luchino Visconti.

Le Grand Jeu was written by Charles Spaak and Jacques Feyder who also directed. Belgian-born Feyder had first come to France in 1919 to train as an actor but rapidly showed his talents as a director. Now he was back after a few years in the USA making films for MGM.

The story is about a legionnaire who meets a girl in North Africa where he is stationed. She looks very like the girl he has left behind. They have an affair but his love can only surface when he thinks of her as the other girl in his life. It is all very touching and the tender love scenes have a realism that owes much to Feyder's direction. Both girls are played by Marie Bell, and the soldier is Pierre-Richard Willm. Feyder's own wife, Francoise Rosay, plays the wife of Charles Vanel, the owner of the down-trodden hotel in which the love-affair takes place.

Shortly after completing his last picture, *L'Atalante*, in 1934 Jean Vigo died in France at the age of 29. It is a magnificent film that serves as a fitting memorial to his work.

The story tells of a young bride who becomes the wife of a bargee travelling up and down France's rivers and canals. (Indeed, one of the picture's attractions was the enjoyable tour it gave of the French waterways.) At first she is thrilled at what promises to be a marvelous adventure, but as boredom sets in – and she also has to cope with a jealous husband – life on the barge loses its appeal.

The young couple are played by Jean Daste and Dita Parlo, but the star of film is Michel Simon who gives one of his most masterly performances as Pere Jules, the elderly, eccentric bargee's mate – surrounded by a large family of cats.

Luis Trenker, the director of *Berge in Flammen* (1931), *(The Doomed Battalion),* began his working life as a mountain guide. In 1921 he found himself guiding a film unit headed by Dr. Arnold Fanck, one of the leading directors of 'mountain films' – those propaganda films that used awesome scenery and the courage needed to conquer their heights as reflections of Germany's National Socialism.

Trenker became the lead actor in that film, and many others, before progressing to directing them himself.

In 1934 he made one of his best – *Der verlorene Sohn (The Prodigal Son).* The story is of a young Tyrolean guide (played by Trenker – all his films starred himself) who journeys to America to search for his girl-friend. He does not find her, but he has the compensation of leaving behind the arid skyscrapers of New York for the mountain magnificence of his homeland.

Leni Riefenstahl is the name that will be most widely remembered in connection with Nazi propaganda films of the Thirties.

However, one feels about her politics and principles she was, in the context of the films she was making, a brilliant director.

She began her film career as an actress starring in 'mountain films' – in many of them opposite Luis Trenker! She moved on to directing such films, and in 1934 was commissioned by Hitler to make a propaganda film for him. The setting was to be the 1934 Congress Party Rally at Nuremburg. Riefenstahl armed herself with a team of 30 cameramen – and began filming *Triumph des Willens (Triumph of the Will)*.

Hitler is shown arriving out of the sky in his airplane. Hundreds of thousands of people greet him with outstretched arms, and he moves among them, arm raised, in his open automobile. He is seen making speech after speech – to the SA, to the SS, to the Hitler Youth. Everywhere are rapt faces, rippling banners, and calm, vast displays of military might.

Nazi banners at the Congress Party Rally at Nuremberg in *Triumph des Willens* (*Triumph of the Will*) (LR/NP)

All these scenes are intercut – moving from awestruck close ups to shots of massed bands and thousands of marching soldiers – to Wagnerian music and Nazi anthems. With music, movement and a seemingly endless stream of powerful images *Triumph of the Will* generates patriotic emotion, Hitler-worship and scenes of national harmony on a phenomenal scale.

However, although Hitler was obviously delighted, Goebbels never recovered from the fact that Riefenstahl had been commissioned by the Fuhrer 'over his head' and she later had to pay the price of his displeasure.

One of the great classic films of Russian cinema appeared in 1934. This was *Chapayev*, directed by a pair of unrelated young men called Sergei Vasiliev and Georgi Vasiliev.

The film is based on the life of a commander in the Red Army who is leading a group of partisans against the White Army in 1919 at the height of the Civil War. The Party sends Commissar Furmanov to keep a check on Chapayev whose style of leadership is known to be unorthodox. At first the men are wary of one another, but gradually a remarkable friendship is formed.

Hilter on his rostrum addresses the Rally in *Triumph des Willens* (*Triumph of the Will*) :LR/NP)

Chapayev was a departure in Russian cinema in that it portrays heroic characters who are far from perfect; they are shown as having weaknesses as well as strengths, and of often being afraid while performing acts of great courage. It was not afraid to reveal, often with much humour, that great leaders and heroes are still human beings. All this combined to make *Chapayev* a film that meant as much to the people as it did to the Party.

Commissar Furmanov had written his battle experiences with Chapayev into a novel, and it was from this book that the film took its story. Chapayev was played by Boris Babochkin and Furmanov by Boris Blinov.

Boris Babochkin (top) in *Chapayev* (Len)

In American and British studios it was romance all the way. Costly costume films abounded but a modern low-budget movie – *It Happened One Night* – outstripped them all. Meanwhile Germany's super-star was Adolf Hitler.

Clark Gable and Elizabeth Allan in *Men in White* (MGM)

Carole Lombard and May Robson in *Lady by Choice* (Col)

Kay Francis and Leslie Howard in *British Agent* (FN)

Merle Oberon in *The Scarlet Pimpernel* (LF)

Right: Joan Bennett in *The Pursuit of Happiness* (Par)
Far Right: Phillips Holmes and Loretta Young in *Caravan* (Fox)

Robert Donat and Elissa Landi in *The Count of Monte Cristo* (ES/Rce)

Ann Sothern and Edmund Lowe in *Let's Fall in Love* (Col)

Jane Wyatt and Phillips Holmes in *Great Expectations* (Univ)

Ralph Bellamy and Katharine Hepburn in *Spitfire* (RKO)

Fredric March and Norma Shearer in *The Barretts of Wimpole Street* (MGM)

Dolores Del Rio in *Madame Dubarry* (WB)

Right: Dolores Del Rio, Reginald Owen and Verree Teasdale in *Madame Dubarry* (WB)

Evelyn Laye in *Evensong* (Gau)   Franchot Tone in *Gentlemen are Born* (FN)   Cedric Hardwicke in *Nell Gwyn* (B&D)

Warren William in *Cleopatra* (Par/CdeM)

Shirley Temple and James Dunn in *Bright Eyes* (Fox)   Irene Dunne and Richard Dix in *Stingaree* (RKO)

Margaret Lockwood and Roger Livesey in *Lorna Doone* (ATP)

Right: Brian Ahearne and Helen Hayes in *What Every Woman Knows* (MGM)

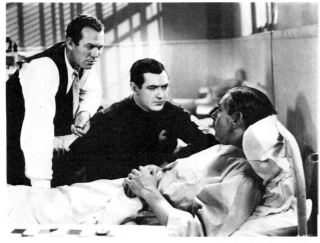

Ward Bond, Johnny Mack Brown and Arthur Hohl in *Against The Law* (Col)

Robert Taylor, Dick Winslow, Maurice Murphy, Louise Latimer and Frank Morgan in *There's Always Tomorrow* (MGM)

Donald Cook in *Fury of the Jungle* (Col)

Charles Judels

William Powell and Myrna Loy in *Evelyn Prentice* (MGM)

Edward Arnold and Joan Crawford in *Sadie McKee* (MGM)

Adrienne Ames and Jimmy 'Schnozzle' Durante in *George White's Scandals of 1934* (Fox)

Janet Gaynor and Lionel Barrymore in *Carolina* (GB *House of Connelly*) (Fox)

Ann Sothern and Neil Hamilton in *Blind Date* (Col)

187

Picture Gallery for 1934

1

2

3

4

1. Diana Wynyard and Colin Clive in *One More River* (Univ)
2. Noah Beery Jr
3. Ricardo Cortez, Edward G Robinson, Mary Astor, John Eldredge and Mae Clarke in *The Man with Two Faces* (FN)
4. Alan Dinehart, Onslow Stevens, 'Skeets' Gallagher and William Collier Snr, in *The Crosby Case* (Univ)
5. Gloria Stuart and John Boles in *Beloved* (BZ/Univ)
6. Shirley Temple, Gary Cooper, Carole Lombard, Charlotte Granville and Sir Guy Standing in *Now and Forever* (Par)
7. Wallace Beery, Katherine DeMille and Stuart Erwin in *Viva Villa* (MGM)
8. Berton Churchill, Gertrude Michael, Ray Milland and Paul Cavanagh in *Menace* (Par)
9. Joel McCrea and Miriam Hopkins in *The Richest Girl in the World* (RKO)
10. Brian Aherne

5

6 △ ▽ 10

8 △ ▽ 9

7

1

2

1 2

3 4 5

6 7 8

9 △ ▽ 11

10 △ ▽ 12

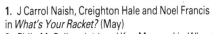

1. J Carrol Naish, Creighton Hale and Noel Francis in *What's Your Racket?* (May)

2. Philo McCullough (c) and Ken Maynard in *Wheels of Destiny* (Univ)

3. Gloria Stuart and Edmund Lowe in *Gift of Gab* (Univ)

4. Shirley Grey, Edmund Lowe and Onslow Stevens in *Bombay Mail* (Univ)

5. Lee Tracy and Roger Pryor in *I'll Tell the World* (Univ)

6. Hal Le Roy and Rochelle Hudson in *Harold Teen* (GB *Dancing Fool*) (WB)

7. Veree Teasdale, Jean Muir and George Brent in *Desirable* (WB)

8. Preston Foster, Lyle Talbot and Ann Dvorak in *Heat Lightning* (WB)

9. Barbara Stanwyck and Pat O'Brien in *Gambling Lady* (WB)

10. Elissa Landi and Paul Lukas in *By Candlelight* (Univ)

11. Phillips Holmes and Jane Wyatt in *Great Expectations* (Univ)

12. Hugh Herbert

189

The Private Life of Don Juan (LF) was the third in a series of 'Private Life' films directed by Alexander Korda. The first two, The Private Life of Helen of Troy and The Private Life of Henry the Eighth were both very successful. Regrettably, The Private life of Don Juan which was Douglas Fairbanks Snr's last costume movie, was a box office failure. Nevertheless, even at the age of 50, Doug's exuberant personality was still to the fore, as can be seen in this array of stills.

1. Merle Oberon and Douglas Fairbanks
2 - 5. Douglas Fairbanks
6. Douglas Fairbanks and Hindle Edgar
7. Douglas Fairbanks and Benita Hume
8. Benita Hume, Merle Oberon, Douglas Fairbanks, Joan Gardner and Elsa Lanchester (s)
9. Douglas Fairbanks and Toto Koopman
10. Douglas Fairbanks
11. Douglas Fairbanks and Merle Oberon
12 - 14. Douglas Fairbanks
15. Merle Oberon and Douglas Fairbanks
16. Douglas Fairbanks

1

2

3 △ ▽6

4

5 △ ▽7

8   9   10

11 △ ▽ 14   12 △ ▽ 15   13 △ ▽ 16

1

2

1. Jean Muir and Donald Woods in *As the Earth Turns* (WB)
2. Lenore Ulric
3. Edna May Oliver, Janet Beecher, George Arliss, Ralph Morgan, Harry C Bradley and Donald Meek in *The Last Gentleman* (Fox)
4. Neil Hamilton and Marion Nixon in *Once to Every Bachelor* (Lib)
5. William Farnum, Hardie Albright and Sally Blane in *Silver Streak* (RKO)
6. Mae Clarke and Pat O'Brien in *Flaming Gold* (RKO)
7. Alice Faye and Harry Green (r) in *She Learned About Sailors* (JSt/Fox)
8. Francis Lederer and Steffi Duna in *Man of Two Worlds* (RKO)
9. Ralph Morgan and Ann Harding in *Their Big Moment* (GB *Afterwards*) (RKO)
10. Pert Kelton and James Gleason in *The Meanest Gal in Town* (RKO)
11. Erin O'Brien Moore, Dorothy Wilson and Richard Dix in *His Greatest Gamble* (RKO)
12. Pert Kelton, Stuart Erwin and Rochelle Hudson in *Bachelor Bait* (RKO)
13. Jean Parker, William Henry and Robert Taylor in *A Wicked Woman* (MGM)

3

4

5

6

7

8 △ ▽ 11

9 △ ▽ 12

10 △ ▽ 13

1

2

1. George Murphy
2. Tom Brown, Mary Carlisle, Lionel Barrymore, Mae Clarke and Fay Bainter in *This Side of Heaven* (MGM)
3. Karen Morley and Tom Keene in *Our Daily Bread* (V/KV)
4. Dick Winslow, Robert Taylor, Elizabeth Young, Louis Latimer, Binnie Barnes and Maurice Murphy in *There's always Tomorrow* (Univ)
5. Alice Brady, Edward Everett Horton, Erik Rhodes, Ginger Rogers and Fred Astaire in *The Gay Divorcée* (GB *The Gay Divorce*) (RKO)
6. Bela Lugosi, Boris Karloff, David Manners, Henry Armetta and Albert Conti in *The Black Cat* (GB *House of Doom*) (Univ)
7. Will Rogers and Kent Taylor in *David Harum* (Fox)
8. Jean Parker in *Sequoia* (MGM)
9. Miriam Hopkins, Fredric March and Nella Walka in *All of Me* (Par)
10. Ann Sothern and Neil Hamilton in *Blind Date* (Col)
11. Jimmy Butler, Francis Lederer and Ginger Rogers in *Romance in Manhattan* (RKO)
12. Billie Burke and Alan Mowbray in *Where Sinners Meet* (GB *The Dover Road*)
13. Ida Lupino, Richard Arlen and Toby Wing in *Come on, Marines!* (Par)

3

4

5

6

7

8 △ ▽ 11

9 △ ▽ 12

10 △ ▽ 13

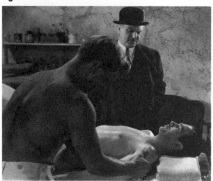

1. David Manners and Phyllis Barry in *The Moonstone* (MoP)
2. Pat O'Brien and Joan Blondell in *I've Got Your Number* (WB)
3. Monroe Owsley and Claire Trevor in *Wild Gold* (Fox)
4. Kent Taylor and Evelyn Venable in *Death Takes a Holiday* (Par)
5. Douglas Fairbanks Jr and Frank Morgan in *Success At Any Price* (RKO)
6. Leo G Carroll and Norma Shearer in *The Barretts of Wimpole Street* (MGM)
7. Evalyn Knapp and Tim McCoy in *A Man's Game* (Col)
8. Warren William and Kay Francis in *Doctor Monica* (WB)
9. Connie Gilchrist and Ann Sothern in *Let's Fall in Love* (Col)
10. Robert Armstrong and Dixie Lee in *Manhattan Love Song* (MoP)
11. Raymond Griffith
12. Margaret Sullavan, Catherine Doucet and Douglass Montgomery in *Little Man, What Now?* (Univ)

194

1. Carole Lombard, Roscoe Karns and Walter Connolly in *Twentieth Century* (Col)
2. Guy Kibbee (l) and Alan Hale (r) in *Babbit* (FN)
3. Spencer Tracy and Paul Harvey in *Looking for Trouble* (DZ/UA)
4. Robert Young and George Arliss in *The House of Rothschild* (Fox)
5. Roger Imhof and Warner Baxter in *Grand Canary* (Lasky/Fox)
6. William Haines and Conrad Nagel in *The Marines Are Coming* (MaP)
7. Robert Young and Madge Evans in *Paris Interlude* (MGM)
8. Mickey Rooney (l) in *Manhattan Melodrama* (MGM)
9. Dewey Robinson
10. Matheson Lang in *Channel Crossing* (Gau)
11. Neil Hamilton and Florence Rice in *Fugitive Lady* (Col)
12. Ann Dvorak and Charles Ruggles in *Friends of Mr Sweeney* (WB)
13. Jack Holt and Jean Arthur in *The Defense Rests* (Col)

195

1. Sig Rumann, Spencer Tracy and Ketti Gallian in *Marie Galante* (Fox)
2. Guy Kibbee and Aline MacMahon in *Big Hearted Herbert* (WB)
3. Claude Rains in *Crime Without Passion* (Par)
4. Ralph Morgan (rear), Frankie Darro and Erin O'Brien-Moore in *Little Men* (MaP)
5. Evelyn Laye and Edward Everett Horton in *The Night is Young* (MGM)
6. Adolphe Menjou and Genevieve Tobin in *Easy to Love* (WB)
7. O P Heggie and Jackie Cooper in *Peck's Bad Boy* (SL/Fox)
8. Janet Gaynor and Lionel Barrymore in *Carolina* (GB *House of Connelly*) (Fox)
9. Leslie Banks, Gene Raymond and Lilian Harvey in *I am Suzanne* (Fox)
10. Roger Pryor and Heather Angel in *Romance in the Rain* (Univ)

2

3

4 △ ▽ 7

5

6 △ ▽ 10

8 △ ▽ 9

196

1

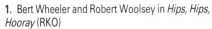

3

2

5 △ ▽ 8

6 △ ▽ 9

1. Bert Wheeler and Robert Woolsey in *Hips, Hips, Hooray* (RKO)
2. Joe Penner and Lyda Roberti in *College Rhythm* (Par)
3. Donald Woods and Warner Oland in *Charlie Chan's Courage* (Fox)
4. E E Clive and Warner Oland in *Charlie Chan in London* (Fox)
5. Virginia Bruce and Conrad Nagel in *Dangerous Corner* (RKO)
6. Will Rogers and Stepin Fetchit in *Judge Priest* (Fox)
7. Sally Blane and Charles Starrett in *Stolen Sweets* (Che)
8. Una Merkel and Charles Ruggles in *Murder in the Private Car* (MGM)
9. James Murray and Merle Oberon in *Broken Melody* (OIP)
10. Rosemary Ames and Warner Baxter in *Such Women Are Dangerous* (Fox)

7 △ ▽ 10

197

1 2

3 4

5 6 7

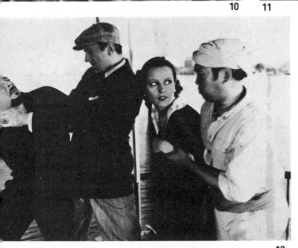

1. Stan Laurel, Oliver Hardy and Mae Busch in *Sons of the Desert* (GB *Fraternally Yours*) (HR)
2. Genevieve Tobin and Edward G Robinson in *Dark Hazard* (FN)
3. Jeanne De Casalis and Anna Neagle in *Nell Gwyn* (B&D)
4. Reginald Denny, Boris Karloff, Billy Bevan, Howard Wilson, Alan Hale, Paul Hurst, Wallace Ford, Victor McLaglen and J M Kerrigan in *The Lost Patrol* (RKO)
5. William Cagney (c) in *Flirting with Danger* (MoP)
6. Evelyn Laye and George Graves in *Princess Charming* (Gau)
7. Marian Nixon and Chester Morris in *Embarrassing Moments* (Univ)
8. Maude Eburne, Raymond Hatton and Jean Parker in *Lazy River* (Univ)
9. Clarence Muse, Walter Connolly, Myrna Loy and Warner Baxter in *Broadway Bill* (GB *Strictly Confidential*) (Col)
10. Paul Cavanagh, Neil Hamilton, Maureen O'Sullivan and Johnny Weissmuller in *Tarzan and His Mate* (MGM)
11. Gail Patrick in *Wagon Wheels* (Par)
12. Gladys George
13. Lucien Prival, Bela Lugosi and Maria Alba in *Return of Chandu* (Pri)
14. Gladys Cooper
15. Edward Arnold
16. George E Stone, George O'Brien, Irene Bentley and Alan Edwards in *Frontier Marshal* (Fox)
17. Joan Gardner

1

2

1. John Boles, Loretta Young and Joyce Compton in *The White Parade* (Lasky/Fox)
2. Ann Sothern and Robert Armstrong in *The Hellcat* (Col)
3. Roger Pryor, Andy Devine and Russ Columbo in *Wake Up and Dream* (Univ)
4. George Burns, Gracie Allen and Guy Lombardo in *Many Happy Returns* (Par)
5. Sally Blane, Edmund Lowe and Victor McLaglen in *No More Women* (Par)
6. Tom Brown and Jean Parker in *Two Alone* (RKO)
7. William Gargan, Herbert Marshall and Claudette Colbert in *Four Frightened People* (Par/CdeM)
8. Eddie Quillan and June Clyde in *Hollywood Party* (MGM)
9. Sylvia Sidney and Fredric March in *Good Dame* (GB *Good Girl*) (Par)
10. George Bancroft and Frances Fuller in *Elmer and Elsie* (Par)

3

5 △ ▽8

6 △ ▽9

7 △ ▽10

1

2

3

1. Gertrude Michael and 'Buster' Crabbe in *Search for Beauty* (Par)
2. Jimmy Durante
3. Victor Jory, Leslie Fenton, William Demarest, Walter Connolly and Fay Wray in *White Lies* (Col)
4. Margaret Lindsay and Bette Davis in *Fog over Frisco* (FN)
5. W C Fields, Mary Boland and Charles Ruggles in *Six of a Kind* (Par)
6. William Powell, Bette Davis and Verree Teasdale in *Fashions of 1934* (FN)
7. Walter Gilbert, George M Cohan and Dorothy Burgess in *Gambling* (Fox)
8. George Raft and William Frawley in *Bolero* (Par)
9. Ricardo Cortez and Barbara Robbins in *Hat, Coat and Glove* (RKO)
10. Robert Young, Ruth Channing, Jean Parker and Maude Eburne in *Lazy River* (MGM)
11. Bruce Cabot and Grant Mitchell in *Shadows of Sing Sing* (Col)
12. Conchita Montenegro and Warner Baxter in *Hell in the Heavens* (Fox)

5

8 △ ▽ 11

9 △ ▽ 12

7 △ ▽ 10

1

2

3

4

1. Cary Grant
2. Johnny Downs
3. Clark Gable
4. Pat O'Brien and Claire Dodd in
I Sell Anything (FN)
5. William Haines and Judith Allen in
Young and Beautiful (MaP)
6. Arthur Hohl and Carole Lombard
in Lady By Choice (Col)
7. Dick Powell and Ruby Keeler in
Flirtation Walk (FN)
8. Judith Allen and Minna Gombell
in Marrying Widows (Tow)
9. Eddie Cantor in Kid Millions (SG)
10. Eddie Cantor in Kid Millions (SG)
11. George Brent

5

8

6

7

9

10

11

1. Dorothy Dell
2. William Gargan
3. Roscoe Karns and Arline Judge in *Shoot the Works* (GB *Thank Your Lucky Stars*) (Par)
4. John Boles and Irene Dunne in *Age of Innocence* (RKO)
5. Paul Page and Fay Wray in *Countess of Monte Cristo* (Univ)
6. Janet Gaynor
7. Helen Twelvetrees and Hugh Williams in *All Men Are Enemies* (Roc/Fox)
8. Anita Louise and Tom Brown in *Bachelor of Arts* (Fox)
9. Donald Woods and Helen Twelvetrees in *She Was a Lady* (Fox)

1

2

3

1. Warner Baxter and Helen Vinson in *As Husbands Go* (Fox)
2. Kitty Carlisle and Bing Crosby in *Here is my Heart* (Par)
3. Robert Donat
4. Joan Crawford and Esther Ralston in *Sadie McKee* (MGM)
5. Dorothy Dell, Alison Skipworth and Victor McLaglen in *Wharf Angel* (Par)
6. Bing Crosby, Carole Lombard and Ethel Merman in *We're Not Dressing* (Par)
7. Sylvia Sidney and Cary Grant in *Thirty Day Princess* (Par)
8. Margaret Lindsay and Franchot Tone in *Gentlemen Are Born* (FN)
9. Charles Ruggles, Robert Young, Francis Lederer, Mary Boland and Joan Bennett in *The Pursuit of Happiness* (Par)

4 △ ▽ 7

5

6

8 △ ▽ 9

1. Marie Wilson, Lorimer Johnson and Alice Moore in *Down to their Last Yacht* (GB *Hawaiian Nights*) (RKO)
2. Allen Jenkins, Patricia Ellis, James Cagney and Hobart Cavanaugh in *The St. Louis Kid* (GB *A Perfect Weekend*) (WB)
3. Cary Grant and Loretta Young in *Born to be Bad* (Fox)
4. Sig Rumann, Fay Wray and Jack Holt in *Black Moon* (col)
5. Fredric March in *The Affairs of Cellini* (Fox)
6. Jackie Cooper and Wallace Beery in *Treasure Island* (MGM)
7. Eddie Nugent, June Collyer and William Cagney in *Lost in the Stratosphere* (MoP)
8. Charles Middleton and Richard Cromwell in *When Strangers Meet* (Lib)
9. Luise Rainer
10. Lila Lee, Russell Gleason and Onslow Stevens in *I Can't Escape* (Bea)
11. Gladys George and Franchot Tone in *Straight is the Way* (MGM)

7 △ ▽ 10

8 △ ▽ 11

9

1. William Powell and Myrna Loy in
Evelyn Prentice (MGM)
2. Rudy Vallee and Alice Faye in
*George White's Scandals of
1934* (Fox)
3. Hobart Cavanaugh, Ann Dvorak,
John Halliday and George Brent in
Housewife (WB)
4. Frank Vosper and Fay Compton in
Waltzes from Vienna (TA)
5. Frances Dee in *Coming Out Party*
(Fox)
6. Carole Lombard in *The Gay Bride*
(MGM)
7. David Holt, Helen Mack and Arthur
Pierson in *You Belong to Me* (LL/Par)
8. Evelyn Laye in *Evensong* (Gau)
9. Dick Powell and Ted Fiorito in
Twenty Million Sweethearts (FN)
10. Marion Burns and Kane Richmond
in *Devil Tiger* (Fox)

1

6

4 △ ▽ 7

5 △ ▽ 8

9 △ ▽ 10

1

2

3

4

5

1. Warren William, Joan Blondell and Edward Everett Horton in *Smarty* (GB *Hit Me Again*) (WB)
2. Effie Ellsier, James Dunn and Claire Trevor in *Hold That Girl* (Fox)
3. Robert Montgomery, Joan Crawford and Clark Gable in *Forsaking All Others* (MGM)
4. Ricardo Cortez, Dick Powell, Al Jolson and Dolores Del Rio in *Wonder Bar* (FN)
5. Otto Kruger, Joan Crawford and Clark Gable in *Chained* (MGM)
6. Alice White, Joe E Brown and Hobart Cavanaugh in *A Very Honorable Guy* (FN)
7. Stuart Erwin, Ann Sothern, Catherine Doucet, Chick Chandler, Arline Judge, Henry Travers and William Bakewell in *The Party's Over* (Col)
8. Chester Morris in *Let's Talk It Over* (Univ)
9. Paul Muni, Donald Meek and Douglas Dumbrille in *Hi Nellie* (WB)
10. Warren William, Rochelle Hudson and Claudette Colbert in *Imitation of Life* (Univ)
11. Frank McHugh, Isabel Jewell and Lew Ayres in *Let's Be Ritzy* (Univ)

6   7

8 △ ▽ 10   9 △ ▽ 11

1

2

3

4

6

1. Spencer Tracy and Madge Evans in *Show Off* (MGM)
2. Richard Dix in *Stingaree* (RKO)
3. Herbert Marshall and Norma Shearer in *Riptide* (MGM)
4. Jean Rogers
5. Brian Aherne and Helen Hayes in *What Every Woman Knows* (MGM)
6. Russell Hicks and Lyle Talbot in *Murder in the Clouds* (FN)
7. Myrna Loy and George Brent in *Stamboul Quest* (MGM)
8. Charles Boyer in *Caravan* (Fox)
9. Warren William and Claudette Colbert in *Cleopatra* (Par/CdeM)
10. Maurice Chevalier and Jeanette MacDonald in *The Merry Widow* (MGM)
11. Matheson Lang
12. Joan Blondell and Dick Powell in *Dames* (WB)

8

7 △ ▽ 10

9 △ ▽ 11

▽ 12

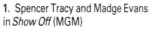

1. Loretta Young and Warner Oland in *Bulldog Drummond Strikes Back* (UA/Fox)
2. Greta Garbo and George Brent in *The Painted Veil* (MGM)
3. Norma Shearer and Robert Montgomery in *Private Lives* (MGM)
4. Jeanette MacDonald and Ramon Novarro in *The Cat and the Fiddle* (MGM)
5. Dick Powell and John Halliday in *Happiness Ahead* (FN)
6. Bette Davis and Charles Farrell in *The Big Shakedown* (FN)
7. William Bakewell and Barbara Bedford in *The Quitter* (Che)
8. Lewis Stone and Jean Parker in *You Can't Buy Everything* (MGM)
9. Ricardo Cortez and Kay Francis in *Mandalay* (FN)
10. Bette Davis and Leslie Howard in *Of Human Bondage* (RKO)
11. Mary Astor and Lyle Talbot in *Return of the Terror* (FN)

4 △ ▽ 9

5

6

7 △ ▽ 10

8 △ ▽ 11

1. Richard Arlen and Sally Eilers in *She Made Her Bed* (Par)
2. Buck Jones and Ward Bond in *The Fighting Code* (Col)
3. John Wayne, Noah Beery Jr and Eddie Parker in *The Trail Beyond* (Col)
4. Buck Jones, Ward Bond and Dorothy Revier in *The Fighting Ranger* (Col)
5. Bob Steele in *Brand of Hate* (Sup/WS)
6. Ken Maynard with Tarzan
7. Barton MacLane, Richard Carle and Randolph Scott in *The Last Roundup* (Par)

1

2

3

4 △ ▽ 7

5 △ ▽ 6

1

2

3

5

6

8 △ ▽ 9

7 △ ▽ 10

1. Ken Maynard in *Smoking Guns* (Univ)
2. Dorothy Revier and Buck Jones in *When a Man Sees Red* (Univ)
3. Cecilia Parker and Ken Maynard in *The Trail Drive* (KM)
4. Martha Sleeper and Richard Dix in *West of the Pecos* (RKO)
5. Sheila Terry, Silver and Buck Jones in *Rocky Rhodes* (Univ)
6. George 'Gabby' Hayes and John Wayne in *Blue Steel* (LS/MoP)
7. Johnny Mack Brown
8. Ken Maynard, Kenneth Thomson and Evalyn Knapp in *In Old Santa Fe* (MoP)
9. Ann Dvorak and Richard Barthelmess in *Massacre* (FN)
10. Roberta Gale, Charles 'Slim' Whitaker and Tom Tyler in *The Terror of the Plains* (Rel/WS)
11. Sam Hardy

11

1. Katharine Hepburn in *The Little Minister* (RKO)
2. Leon Errol
3. George Murphy and Nancy Carroll in *Jealousy* (Col)
4. Edna May Oliver and Edward Everett Horton in *The Poor Rich* (Univ)
5. William Farnum and Anita Louise in *Are We Civilised?* (RaP)
6. James Dunn and Shirley Temple in *Bright Eyes* (Fox)
7. Charles Laughton and Wallace Beery in *The Mighty Barnum* (DZ)
8. Claire Trevor and Shirley Temple in *Baby Take a Bow* (Fox)
9. Constance Bennett and Russ Columbo in *Moulin Rouge* (DZ)
10. Heather Angel and Victor Jory in *Murder in Trinidad* (Fox)

1

2

3

5

6 △ ▽ 8

▽ 9

7 △ ▽ 10

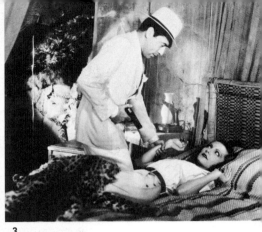

1. El Brendel and John Arledge in *Olsen's Big Moment* (Fox)
2. Boots Mallory and John Darrow in *The Big Race* (ShP)
3. Harold Huber and Peggy Shannon in *Fury of the Jungle* (Col)
4. Larry 'Buster' Crabbe in *Badge of Honor* (May)
5. Otto Kruger and Ethel Wales in *Crime Doctor* (RKO)
6. Alice Faye, Jack Durant, John Bradford and Frank Mitchell in *365 Nights in Hollywood* (SW/Fox)
7. Paul Cavanagh and Gertrude Michael in *The Notorious Sophie Lang* (Par)
8. Vince Barnett
9. Marlene Dietrich in *The Scarlet Empress* (Par)
10. Marlene Dietrich and John Lodge in *The Scarlet Empress* (Par)
11. Russell Hopton and Gail Patrick in *Take the Stand* (Lib)

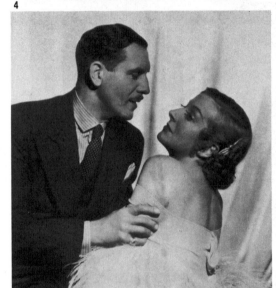

8 △ ▽ 11

7 △ ▽ 10

6 △ ▽ 9

213

1

2

3

4

6

7

5

8

9

12

10

11

214

13

14

15

16

17

18

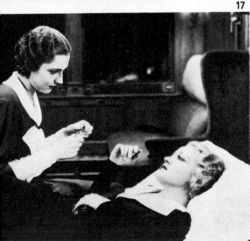

19

20

21

22

1. Bert Wheeler and Robert Woolsey in *Cockeyed Cavaliers* (RKO)
2. Dorothea Wieck and Baby Le Roy in *Miss Fane's Baby is Stolen* (Par)
3. Billy Seward, Henrietta Crosman, Richard Cromwell and Paul Hurst in *Among the Missing* (Col)
4. Warren Willam and Mary Astor in *Upper World* (FN)
5. Aline MacMahon and Ann Dvorak in *Side Streets* (GB *A Woman in her Thirties*) (FN)
6. Addison Richards, Shirley Grey and Tim McCoy in *Special Agent* (WB)
7. The Three Stooges and Ted Healey in *Beer and Pretzels* (MGM)
8. Barbara Stanwyck and Lyle Talbot in *A Lost lady* (GB *Courageous*) (FN)
9. George Meeker, Mary Brian and Peggy Blythe in *Ever Since Eve* (Fox)
10. Stan Laurel and Oliver Hardy in *Babes in Toyland* (HR)
11. Will Rogers and Peggy Wood in *Handy Andy* (Fox)
12. Helen Trenholme and Warren William in *The Case of the Howling Dog* (WB)
13. Fredric March and Anna Sten in *We Live Again* (SG)
14. Merle Oberon, Charles Boyer and John Loder in *The Battle* (Gau) ·
15. Colin Tapley, Kent Taylor and Evelyn Venable in *Double Door* (Par)
16. James Cagney and Arthur Hohl in *Jimmy the Gent* (WB)
17. Victor McLaglen, John Wray and Wynne Gibson in *The Captain Hates the Sea* (Col)
18. Ann Harding and Paul Lukas in *The Fountain* (RKO)
19. Frances Dee and Bruce Cabot in *Finishing School* (RKO)
20. Mona Barrie and Wynne Gibson in *Sleepers East* (Fox)
21. Roger Pryor and Mae West in *Belle of the Nineties* (Par)
22. Irene Hervey and Clive Brook in *Let's Try Again* (RKO)

12

13

14

15

1. Charles Starrett and Pat Paterson in *Call it Luck* (Fox)
2. Charles Farrell, Janet Gaynor and James Dunn in *Change of Heart* (Fox)
3. Verree Teasdale, Charles Ruggles and Sidney Blackmer in *Goodbye Love* (RKO)
4. Peter Lorre and Leslie Banks in *The Man Who Knew Too Much* (Gau)
5. Jean Muir, Warren William and Kathryn Sergava in *Bedside* (FN)
6. Adolphe Menjou and Doris Kenyon in *The Human Side* (Univ)
7. Frank Albertson and Betty Furness in *The Life of Vergie Winters* (RKO)
8. Dewey Robinson, Charles Butterworth and Jimmy Durante in *Student Tour* (MGM)
9. Bradley Page, Arthur Hohl and Johnny Mack Brown in *Against the Law* (Col)
10. James Cagney, Frank McHugh, Gloria Stuart and Pat O'Brian in *Here Comes the Navy* (WB)
11. Arthur Hohl, J Carrol Naish and Ward Bond in *Crime of Helen Stanley* (Col)
12. Robert Montgomery, Henry Stephenson and Lewis Stone in *The Mystery of Mr X* (MGM)
13. Donald Cook, Genevieve Tobin and Hardie Albright in *The Ninth Guest* (Col)
14. Joe E Brown, Donald Dillaway and Patricia Ellis in *The Circus Clown* (FN)
15. Frank McHugh, Joe E Brown and Maxine Doyle in *6 Day Bike Rider* (FN)
16. ZaSu Pitts and W C Fields in *Mrs Wiggs of the Cabbage Patch* (Par)
17. Paul Kelly, Janet Beecher and Paul Harvey in *The President Vanishes* (GB *Strange Conspiracy*) (WW)
18. Robert Montgomery and Maureen O'Sullivan in *Hide Out* (MGM)
19. W C Fields and Clarence Wilson in *The Old Fashioned Way* (Par)
20. Ann Sothern and Lanny Ross in *Melody of Spring* (Par)

16

17

18

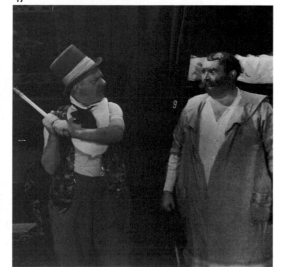

19

20

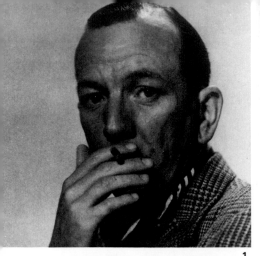

1. Noel Coward
2. Madge Evans
3. Richard Whorf
4. Alice Faye
5. Mona Maris
6. Frankie Thomas
7. Rudy Vallee
8. Warner Baxter
9. Charles Farrell
10. Valerie Hobson
11. Jeanette MacDonald
12. Harold Huth
13. Judith Allen
14. May Robson

218

1

2

3

4

5

6

7

8   9

10 △ ▽ 13

11 △ ▽ 14

12

1. Aline MacMahon
2. Leonora Corbett
3. Edith Fellows
4. Ralph Forbes
5. Ramon Novarro
6. Marjorie Main
7. Harold Lloyd
8. Colin Clive
9. Lew Cody
10. Gertrude Lawrence
11. Conway Tearle
12. Alfred Drayton
13. Dolores Del Rio
14. Louise Brooks

219

1

2 3

4

5 6

7 △ ▽10

8 △ ▽11 9 △

12

13 14

1. Donald Cook, Mary Brian and Reginald Denny in *Fog* (Col)
2. Aline MacMahon and Ivan Lebedeff in *The Merry Frinks* (GB *Happy Family*) (FN)
3. Helen Chandler and Hans Jaray in *Lover Divine* (Gau)
4. Donald Woods and Margaret Lindsay in *Merry Wives of Reno* (WB)
5. Gloria Shea and Wallace Ford in *Money Means Nothing* (MoP)
6. Douglas Fairbanks Jr and Elisabeth Bergner in *Catherine the Great* (AK)
7. Una Merkel, Stuart Erwin and James Dunn in *Have a Heart* (MGM)
8. George Arliss (s) in *The Iron Duke* (Gau)
9. Fay Wray and Nils Asther in *Madame Spy* (Univ)
10. Jack Oakie and Victor McLaglen in *Murder at the Vanities* (Par)
11. Lafe McKee, Lillian Bond and Tim McCoy in *Hell Bent for Love* (Col)
12. Jane Baxter in *Blossom Time* (BIP)
13. Carl Esmond in *Blossom Time* (BIP)
14. Richard Tauber in *Blossom Time* (BIP)
15. Dorothy Hyson
16. Miriam Hopkins
17. Esmond Knight in *Girls Will Be Boys* (BIP)
18. Nelson Eddy
19. Franchot Tone and Madeleine Carroll in *The World Moves On* (Fox)
20. Judith Allen and Bruce Cabot in *Men of the Night* (Col)
21. Conway Tearle, Noel Francis and Ralf Harolde in *Fifteen Wives* (Inv)

15

16

17 △ ▽ 19 20 ▽ 18 △ ▽ 21

1

2

3

4

5

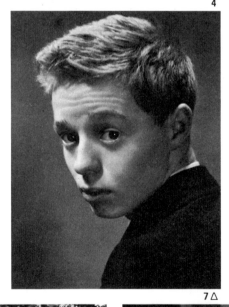

6 △ ▽ 9

7 △

8 △ ▽ 10

11   12

13   14

15   16

17 △ ▽ 19   18 △ ▽ 20

1. Harold Lloyd, Vince Barnett and Dewey Robinson (fr) in *The Cat's-Paw* (Fox)

2. Henry O'Neill, Pat O'Brien and Clarence Muse in *The Personality Kid* (WB)

3. Paul Cavanagh and Natalie Moorhead in *Curtain at Eight* (Maj)

4. Rosemary Ames and Victor Jory in *I Believed In You* (Fox)

5. Bruce Cabot and Grace Bradley in *Redhead* (MoP)

6. Frank Morgan and Genevieve Tobin in *By Your Leave* (RKO)

7. Jimmy Hanley

8. Bela Lugosi and Boris Karloff

9. Lafe McKee, Roberta Gale, Tom Tyler, Louise Gabo and Jack Perrin in *Mystery Ranch* (Rel/WS)

10. Regis Toomey in *Big Time or Bust* (Tow)

11. Doris Lloyd, Ralph Morgan, Elissa Landi and Joseph Schildkraut in *Sisters under the Skin* (Col)

12. Mary Nash, Genevieve Tobin, George Meeker, Renee Gadd (r) and Edward Everett Horton in *Uncertain Lady* (Univ)

13. Buck Jones and Arthur Vinton in *The Man Trailer* (Col)

14. Lupe Velez, Stuart Erwin and Jimmie 'Schnozzle Durante' in *Palooka* (UA)

15. Lillian Bond, Edward Nugent and Mary Carlisle in *Girl o' my Dreams* (MoP)

16. Stanley Fields, Jimmy 'Schnozzle' Durante and Lupe Velez in *Strictly Dynamite* (RKO)

17. Leila Hyams and Paul Lukas in *Affairs of a Gentleman* (Univ)

18. George Robey and Fedor Chaliapin in *Don Quixote (Va/N/W)*

19. *Gracie Fields (l) in Sing as We Go* (ATP)

20. Sterling Holloway and Marie Wilson in *My Girl Sally* (Univ)

223

1

2 3

4 5 6

7 8 △ ▽ 11 9 10 △ ▽ 12

1. Dorothy Jordan
2. Olympe Bradna
3. Una O'Connor
4. Tom Tyler
5. Lois Moran
6. Thomas Mitchell
7. Margaret Hamilton
8. George E Stone
9. H B Walthall
10. Rex Harrison
11. Max Baer
12. Anna Neagle

224

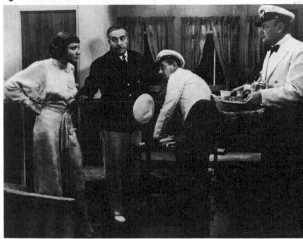

1

2

3

4 5

6

7 △ ▽ 10 8

9

It Happened One Night (Col) was a winner all the way. It won in one fell swoop five Oscars — best picture, actor, actress, director and screenplay. It is a record no other film has ever surpassed.

1. 2. 3. 5. 7. and **10.** Clark Gable and Claudette Colbert
4. Clark Gable
6. Claudette Colbert and Walter Connolly
8. Walter Connolly and Claudette Colbert
9. Clark Gable, Claudette Colbert and Roscoe Karns

225

1

4

7

2

5

3

6

8

9

10

11

Chu Chin Chow (Gau/G'boro) was a musical stage production that regaled audiences and enjoyed a record run in London during World War 1. Anna May Wong and George Robey headed the cast of the film adaptation in 1934.

1. Pearl Argyle
2. George Robey
3. Lawrence Hanray
4. Gibb McLaughlin, Francis Sullivan and George Robey (k)
5. Pearl Argyle and John Garrick
6. George Robey
7. George Robey and his donkey Jasmin
8. Sydney Fairbrother
9. Fritz Kortner
10. John Garrick
11. George Robey and John Garrick
12. Sydney Fairbrother
13. Anna May Wong
14. Fritz Kortner
15. Anna May Wong (f)
16. Dennis Hoey (l) and Fritz Kortner (r)
17. Dennis Hoey and Fritz Kortner
18. Fritz Kortner
19. Fritz Kortner
20. Fritz Kortner

226

12 13 14

15

16 17

18 19 20

1   2   3

4   5   6   7

8   9 10 11

12 △ ▽ 15   13 △ ▽ 16   14 △ ▽ 17

18 19

20 21 22 23

24 25 26

27 △ ▽ 29 28 △ ▽ 30

1. Edward Arnold in *Unknown Blonde* (Maj)
2. Helen Westley in *Anne of Green Gables* (RKO)
3. Ed Wynn
4. Shirley Grey and Ralph Bellamy in *Girl in Danger* (Col)
5. John Eldredge
6. Jan Kiepura
7. Karen Morley and David Durand in *Wednesday's Child* (RKO)
8. Grace Moore, Lyle Talbot and Tullio Carminati in *One Night of Love* (Col)
9. John Mills
10. Carroll Nye
11. Dorothy Wilson and Douglass Montgomery in *Eight Girls in a Boat* (Par)
12. Tom Tyler (c) and Lafe McKee (r) in *Mystery Ranch* (Rel/WS)
13. Edna May Oliver and James Gleason in *Murder on the Blackboard* (RKO)
14. Griffith Jones
15. John Wayne, Lloyd Whitlock and Virginia Brown Faire in *West of the Divide* (LS/MoP)
16. Barbara Sheldon and John Wayne in *Lucky Texan* (LS/MoP)
17. Philo McCullough, Lafe McKee and Tom Tyler in *Ridin' Thru* (Rel/WS)
18. Jimmy Aubrey (k) and Bill Cody (c) in *The Border Menace* (Ayw)
19. Ken Maynard (c), William Gould and Hank Bell in *Gun Justice* (Univ)
20. Constance Cummings and Philip Reed in *Glamour* (Univ)
21. Bruce Cabot
22. Merle Oberon
23. O P Heggie and Ann Shirley in *Anne of Green Gables* (RKO)
24. Frank Buck in *Wild Cargo* (RKO)
25. Duncan Renaldo
26. Ernest Thesiger
27. Noel Francis, John Miljan, Paul Hurst, Joseph Crehan and William Gargan in *Line Up* (Col)
28. Buffalo Bill Jr in *Rawhide Romance* (Spr)
29. Ken Maynard and Frank Hagney (s) in *Honor of the Range* (Univ)
30. Jackie Cooper in *The Lone Cowboy* (Par)

229

Errol Flynn in *Captain Blood* (FN)

Above: Ross Alexander in *Captain Blood* (FN)
Below: Basil Rathbone in *Captain Blood* (FN)

CHAPTER SIX
1935
THE YEAR OF THE CLASSICS

A little-known actor from Australia who had arrived in Hollywood via Britain saved the day when Warner Brothers were left without a star for Captain Blood. His name was Errol Flynn and he stepped into the shoes that were to have been worn by Robert Donat, but contract difficulties got in his way.

Flynn proved himself a brave, all-action swashbuckling star in the Douglas Fairbanks Snr tradition. As Captain Blood he is a surgeon-turned-pirate exiled to Barbados by Judge Jeffries of the Bloody Assizes for attending to the wounds of a rebel in the Duke of Monmouth's insurgent army. Olivia de Havilland has the role of Arabella Bishop, the niece of a Caribbean plantation owner. The villain of the piece is Basil Rathbone whose energetic and exciting duel with Flynn provides one of the film's many highlights.

Much credit must go to the director Michael Curtiz who filled his screen with billowing galleon sails and clashing swords, and was as responsible as any for displaying the talents of two great stars. Among the cast were Lionel Atwill, Ross Alexander, Guy Kibbee and Henry Stephenson.

Whenever *The Informer* is talked about, it is always coupled with the name of the director, John Ford. It was his film, he made it, and he made it an Oscar winner. All this in spite of the RKO bosses' reluctance to back him. They grudgingly did so eventually, but insisted on a tight budget of under 300,000 dollars and a short shooting schedule. The film was completed in three weeks, well under budget.

The story is set in Dublin during the Irish Rebellion of 1922. Ford was a student of Irish life and literature and in spite of the meagreness of the budget, cheap backdrops and low-key lighting, he brilliantly captured the Dublin of the story.

Gypo Nolan (Victor McLaglen), seen as a lumbering, impoverished labourer, reveals to the police the secret whereabouts of his friend Frankie McPhillip (Wallace Ford), an IRA man wanted for murder. He does it for a reward of £20; he wants the money to emigrate to America. The film ends with Gypo, mortally wounded, forgiven for his betrayal of Frankie McPhillip by Frankie's widow.

As the informer, Victor McLaglen enacted the blustering, beer-sodden, despicable Gypo to perfection, and his performance won him the Best Actor Academy Award for 1935. The film also won John Ford the first of his four Oscars; and Dudley Nichols received one for his screenplay and Max Steiner another for his musical score.

To go and see *Mutiny on the Bounty* is in itself an adventure. Charles Laughton, as the notorious Captain Bligh, is still able to persuade audiences they are on the high seas witnessing the life of sea-dogs under the most brutal commander (according to the film) ever to set foot on a ship.

In addition there is Clark Gable as Fletcher Christian, the man who challenges Bligh and leads the famous mutiny.

The third member of the leading trio is Franchot Tone. He plays Roger Byam, the foppish, aristocratic, English midshipman whose part in the mutiny eventually leads to his court-martial.

The action starts in 1787. On the high seas, Captain Bligh treats the men brutally and the merest offence earns a flogging or being put in chains – sometimes both.

Eventually the ship reaches Tahiti where the crew is allowed to indulge in the delights of the land – including the beautiful native girls.

It is on the return trip that the final confrontation between Bligh and Christian reaches its climax. Mutiny led by Christian follows and Bligh and a few loyal seamen are set adrift in an open boat.

It is then that Bligh's true worth as a seaman reveals itself. He navigates the open boat across the 3,000 miles to a Dutch settlement at Timor in the East Indies and becomes a national hero. Later, he sets sail in another ship to bring the mutineers back to England for court-martial. But he is only able to locate Byam and a couple of the crew. Christian and the rest have settled on Pitcairn Island with their Tahitian families. Back in England Byam is convicted of mutiny – but is pardoned by the king after the conditions on the 'Bounty' are revealed. In the film Bligh becomes discredited in the public eye, but in truth the real Bligh was much maligned by the film.

Charles Laughton, Clark Gable and Franchot Tone were all nominated for the Oscar that was won by Victor McLaglen for *The Informer*.

However, *Mutiny on the Bounty* (directed by Frank Lloyd and produced by Irving Thalberg) did win the Academy Award for the year's best film.

It seems incredible that the man who plays the obliging butler in *Ruggles of Red Gap* should go on to become the ruthless tyrant of *Mutiny on the Bounty*. But Charles Laughton masters both roles with credit. What a great actor he was.

Ruggles of Red Gap has become a comedy classic and

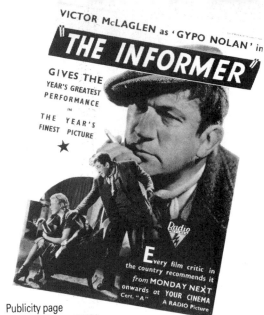

Publicity page
for *The Informer* (RKO)

Above: Clark Gable and Movita in *Mutiny on the Bounty* (MGM)
Below: Charles Laughton in *Ruggles of Red Gap* (Par)

Groucho Marx and Margaret Dumont in *A Night At The Opera* (MGM)

Chico and Groucho Marx in *A Night At The Opera* (MGM)

Above: Frank Lawton as *David Copperfield* (MGM)
Below: W C Fields in *David Copperfield* (MGM)

earned high praise for its director Leo McCarey who guided the cast through a host of hilarious situations.

When Paramount dropped the Marx Brothers it appeared that their number was up as a film team, but MGM's production chief Irving Thalberg had other ideas. He invited them to his studio but on the way there they lost Zeppo, the brother who acted as a straight man. He retired.

The studio did not rush them into a film immediately but first sent them on a tour to test the gags they would use in *A Night at the Opera*. It was a good move and the film profited from it. The result – a tremendously successful comedy.

The brothers divide their time between causing havoc among the passengers and crew of a transatlantic liner and creating chaos at the New York Opera House.

There is the unforgettable scene where innumerable people are crammed into a ship's tiny cabin. There is the wonderful sketch with Chico and Groucho treading a tortuous path through a legal contract; they find a way to simplify it – tearing out the clauses they don't like. And the climax has the brothers at their most anarchic when, at first innocently enough, but then with growing demonic glee, they destroy the premiere of the opera 'Il Trovatore.'

Margaret Dumont was the foil of much of their humour, and Sig Ruman played the man unfortunate enough to have the Marx Brothers helping him put on an opera.

Charles Dickens' stories have always been popular film subjects, and 1935 saw the appearance of two filmed versions of his work that have comfortably stood the test of time: *David Copperfield* and *A Tale of Two Cities*.

The first to be released was *David Copperfield*, directed by George Cukor. Many delightful stories surround this film. There is the tale of how Freddie Bartholomew was manoeuvered into the part of Copperfield by an ambitious aunt, and of how after a few days of filming Charles Laughton gave up the part of Mr Micawber, insisting that the only man to play it was W C Fields, and of how along came Fields – 'he of the bulbous nose, the love of gin and the general hatred of mankind' – who, in spite of refusing to make any concessions toward an English accent *and* trying to sneak in a bit of his famous juggling, produced one of those all-time memorable performances.

MGM put all its lavish production capabilities into the film and did a formidable casting job. Basil Rathbone is the sadistic Mr Murdstone, Elizabeth Allan is Mrs Copperfield, Roland Young the repulsive Uriah Heep, Edna May Oliver is Aunt Betsey, Maureen O'Sullivan the gentle Dora, and Lionel Barrymore plays Dan Peggotty.

Just as *David Copperfield* was a top-ten box-office draw and an Academy Award nominee for 1935, so *A Tale of Two Cities* (directed by Jack Conway), released later that year, earned the same accolades for 1936. Once again David O Selznick produced for MGM, and again the studio spared no expense. Some 17,000 extras were employed for the Paris mob scenes, and one of Hollywood's largest sets was needed for the storming of the Bastille.

The story is set during the French Revolution. Ronald Colman (here without his famous moustache) as Sydney Carton, the English lawyer who makes the noble self-sacrifice of taking the place of an innocent French aristocrat, Charles Darnay (Donald Woods), when he is about to face the guillotine. Colman's calm dignity in assuming the place of a convicted man with death staring him in the face is most moving.

As for the rest of the starring cast, Elizabeth Allan, Edna May Oliver and Basil Rathbone, all fresh from their practice run on *David Copperfield*, were but a few of the famous names that helped to make the 1935 version of *A Tale of Two Cities* a film to remember.

Will Rogers was a Wild-West-show performer with a special line in lassoing tricks. He was an actor, a wit, a raconteur and a very, very influential man. His fans included Franklin D Roosevelt, and he played a big part in getting Roosevelt elected in 1933. From 1930 till his death in a plane crash in 1935 his films were never out of the top-box-office lists. The last film that he made was *Steamboat Round the Bend*.

The film was the third in a trilogy that the director John Ford made with Rogers about small-town American life and recounted the adventures of a steamboat captain on the Mississippi.

When Will Rogers died all America mourned, and a statue to him was placed in the White House's Hall of Fame.

Two of Hollywood's eternal superstars, Garbo and Dietrich, could be seen by fans in peak form this year.

Anna Karenina was the second time Greta Garbo had played Tolstoy's tragic heroine. The setting is nineteenth-century Russia. Anna asks Karenin, her cold, wealthy husband (Basil Rathbone), for a divorce after falling passionately in love with the young Count Vronsky (Fredric March), but Karenin will not let her take her adored son Sergei (Freddie Bartholomew) with her if she goes. Garbo's heartbroken loveliness is superbly captured on camera by William Daniels under the direction of Clarence Brown, with the film's visual splendour further enriched by glorious costumes (Adrian) and period settings (Cedric Gibbons).

The Devil Is a Woman is the last of the films Marlene Dietrich made with director Joseph von Sternberg. This time the setting is Spain in the 1890s. Conchita (Dietrich) is beautiful, alluring, heartless – the true *femme fatale*.

Sternberg makes marvellous use of camera and lighting in creating the perfect atmosphere in which his lovely witch can weave her wicked spells.

One of the biggest box-office successes of 1935 was *Top Hat*, with Fred Astaire and Ginger Rogers dancing their way through a mass of plot complications from London to Venice. The couple here are at their most sophisticated – indeed, they never seem to be out of evening dress. The

Elizabeth Allan in *A Tale of Two Cities* (MGM)

Above: Sterling Holloway and Will Rogers in *Steamboat Round The Bend* (Fox)
Below: Greta Garbo in *Anna Karenina* (MGM)

Edward Everett Horton

Miriam Hopkins

William Stack and Alison Skipworth in *Becky Sharp*
(RKO)

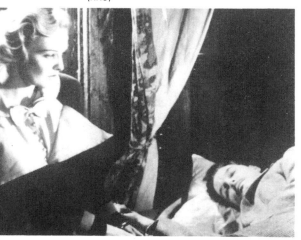

Robert Donat and Madeleine Carroll in *The 39
Steps* (Gau)

film has a marvellous score: 'Cheek to Cheek', with Rogers in that famous ostrich-feather dress, 'Isn't It a Lovely Day to Be Caught in the Rain' and 'Top Hat, White Tie and Tails' (more or less Astaire's theme song after this) are all there, plus the best of comic support from Edward Everett Horton and Eric Blore.

Worthy of mention is *Becky Sharp* (based on Thackeray's novel *Vanity Fair*). It was the first three-colour Technicolor feature film, directed by Rouben Mamoulian and featured the lovely Miriam Hopkins as the scheming heroine.

One of the best-known, and indeed the best, of Alfred Hitchcock's British-made films is *The Thirty-Nine Steps*. Not only did it do well in Britain, but it put Hitchcock on the map as far as American audiences were concerned.

Richard Hannay (Robert Donat) meets a young woman under dramatic circumstances. She tells him she is a spy. She reappears later in his hotel bedroom only to fall across the bed murmuring 'They'll get you, too' before she dies – stabbed in the back.

From then on the film is a non-stop chase with the innocent Hannay hotly pursued by both police and foreign agents, trying to clear his name by finding the murderer. The 'master' never allows excitement to waver, with one ever more suspenseful scene following another.

This was the year, too, when Jacques Feyder directed one of the great classic comedies of French cinema: *La Kermesse Héroïque*. The film starred Françoise Rosay (Feyder's wife) – a superb actress with a special gift for comedy.

The story, set in seventeenth-century Flanders, begins as the peaceful, prosperous little town of Boom awakes one sunny morning. The Burgomaster bustles his well-upholstered way through the market place to the town hall. (The settings and costumes throughout are a mingling of every favourite Flemish painting.)

A message arrives; the Duke of Olivares, the much-feared Governor of the Low Countries (currently under Spanish domination) is heading towards Boom with a sizeable army.

The town councillors are terrified. The town will expect them to do something courageous! They have a brilliant idea. The Burgomaster will pretend to be dead, and all the men of the town will gather in mourning at the town hall. The ladies, headed by Madame Burgomaster (Françoise Rosay) will go to meet the army and say 'Please respect our grief and be on your way.'

The ladies comply but the troops are very tired and are ordered to rest in the town for several days. The ladies – with, of course, no husbands to protect them – manage to make the soldiers so comfortable that they feel no need to loot and pillage!

Our heroine, now in charge of Boom, conducts the whole incident with great skill. She even manages to reinstate her husband, with his dignity, when the troops have gone.

The Youth of Maxim, the first (and usually voted the best) part of an excellent trilogy of Russian films, was released in 1935. These films, always referred to as *The Maxim Trilogy*, were directed by two young but very experienced film-makers called Grigori Kozintsev and Leonid Trauberg and were further blessed by a fine musical score from Dmitri Shostakovich.

The Maxim Trilogy is the story of the development, ideological and professional, of a young Communist who progresses from being a labourer in St. Petersberg to being Minister of Finance.

The Youth of Maxim opens on New Year's Eve in 1909. It is a joyous start to both the year and the film. Sleighbells and laughter can be heard everywhere. And Maxim carries this sense of exuberance with him right through the trilogy: through his early years as a very innocent youth; through his training as a party worker; through the dangerous years he spends as a fully-fledged revolutionary working 'underground' *(The Return of Maxim*, 1937); and even into his more sober and dignified life after he has been appointed a commissar *(The Vyborg Side*, 1939).

This warm humour did much to bring an element of vitality and humanity to Maxim – a factor too often missing from the traditional heroes of Russian revolutionary films.

It is interesting to realise that, unlike the classic *Chapayev* (1934) which is modelled on a real hero, Maxim is a fictional character. However, like Sherlock Holmes he generated a life of his own and went on later to 'star' in other films.

Long before the work of Italian directors such as Luchino Visconti and Roberto Rossellini made the expression 'neo-realism' famous, film-makers from a very different part of the world were already making films featuring this kind of realism. These were the Japanese, one of the most prominent of whom in the Thirties was Mikio Naruse.

Naruse was, it seems, a very gloomy man. He was orphaned very young; perhaps that was the reason. Naruse's films usually revolved around family life – although they often featured characters who were very independent women. One of his most constant themes concerned 'the question of living without love and in service to something else' – a question which featured strongly in his (far from gloomy) film *Wife, Be Like a Rose*. The story centres on a young girl who lives with her poetess mother. Father, however, has wandered off to live with his mistress in the country. The daughter now wants to get married, and she wants both her parents – reconciled – at her wedding. But when she goes out to the country to persuade him to come back, she finds, in addition to a very poor home quite over-run with children, love of a quality and a quantity she never saw in her own home.

Father does indeed come to the wedding, but then he goes back to the country – where he truly belongs.

This was Naruse's first sound film. It was deemed to be sophisticated enough and 'international' enough to be shown in New York – and was well-received there.

Robert Donat in *The 39 Steps* (Gau)

Francoise Rosay in *La Kermesse Heroique* (XX)

Francoise Rosay

Film Favourites 1935

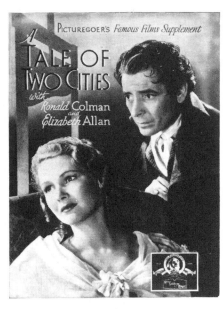

Newcomer Errol Flynn proved to be the sensational new Find of the Year. From comparative obscurity he sprang into prominence with *Captain Blood* (FN). British studios were coming to the fore in the field of farce with Will Hay and the inimitable twosome of Tom Walls and Ralph Lynn.

Above: Cover of a special supplement devoted to *A Tale of Two Cities* (MGM) which was given away with Picturegoer Weekly

Left: Henry Hull in *Werewolf of London* (Univ)

Brian Donlevy and Sylvia Sidney in *Mary Burns – Fugitive* (Par)

Ann Sothern and Ralph Bellamy in *Eight Bells* (Col)

Bette Davis and Wini Shaw in *Front Page Woman* (WB)

Hoot Gibson and Buddy Roosevelt in *Rainbow's End* (FD)

236

Errol Flynn in *Captain Blood* (FN)

Joe E Brown in *Alibi Ike* (WB)

Tom Walls and Ralph Lynn in *Fighting Stock* (G'boro)

Gertrude Lawrence in *Mimi* (BIP)

Will Hay in *Boys will be Boys* (G'boro)

Tim McCoy, Bob Allen and Alan Sears in *The Revenge Rider* (Col)

Colin Clive, Elsa Lanchester, Boris Karloff and Ernest Thesiger in *The Bride of Frankenstein* (Univ)

Walter Abel, Onslow Stevens, Moroni Olsen, Paul Lukas and Heather Angel in *The Three Musketeers* (RKO)

Fredric March and Rochelle Hudson in *Les Miserables* (Fox)

Bette Davis and Alison Skipworth in *The Girl from 10th Avenue* (GB *Men on Her Mind*) (FN)

Bill Boyd and Joan Woodbury in *The Eagle's Brood* (Par)

Clark Gable and Constance Bennett in *After Office Hours* (MGM)

Helen Morgan and Rudy Vallee in *Sweet Music* (WB)

Top left Greta Garbo, Reginald Denny and Fredric March in *Anna Karenina* (MGM)
Above Henry Wilcoxon and Loretta Young in *The Crusades* (Par/CdeM)
Left Miriam Hopkins, Nigel Bruce and Frances Dee in *Becky Sharp* (RKO)

Jan Kiepura and Marta Eggerth in *My Heart is Calling* (Gau/CAT)

Charlotte Granville (s), Laura Hope Crews (st)
H B Warner and Sylvia Sidney in *Behold My Wife* (Par)

Paula Stone, Charles Middleton (in boots) and Robert Warwick (r) in *Hopalong Cassidy* (Par)

Stan Laurel and Oliver Hardy in
Bonnie Scotland (MGM/HR)

Nydia Westman and Clive Brook in *Dressed to Thrill* (Fox)

George Barbier. Gracie Allen, George Burns and
Betty Furness in *Here Comes Cookie* (WLB/Par)

Helen Vinson and Minor Watson in *Age of Indiscretion* (MGM)

Mickey Rooney in *A Midsummer Night's Dream* (WB)

Olivia de Havilland in *A Midsummer Night's Dream* (WB)

Far left: Nelson Eddy in *Naughty Marietta* (MGM)

Randolph Scott and Helen Gahagan in *She* (RKO)

Picture Gallery

for 1935

1. Phil Regan and Wini Shaw in *Broadway Hostess* (FN)
2. Marion Burns and John Wayne in *The Dawn Rider* (LS/MoP)
3. John Elliott (sl) and Hoot Gibson (sr) in *Sunset Range* (FD)
4. Ken Maynard in *Western Frontier* (Col)
5. Bob Steele, Guinn 'Big Boy' Williams, Hoot Gibson, Harry Carey and Tom Tyler in *Powdersmoke Range* (RKO)
6. Tim McCoy (c) in *The Outlaw Deputy* (Pur)
7. Dewey Robinson, Joan Blondell and Glenda Farrell in *We're in the Money* (WB)
8. Jane Withers in *Ginger* (Fox)
9. Karen Morley and Edward Everett Horton in *$10 Raise* (Fox)
10. Charles Bickford (c) and Raquel Torres in *Red Wagon* (All)
11. Charles Delaney, Bobby Nelson and Marion Shilling in *Captured in Chinatown* (Spr)
12. Ann Carol, Bobby Nelson (c) and Rex Lease in *The Ghost Rider* (Arg/Spr)

7 △ ▽ 10

8 △ ▽ 11

9 △ ▽ 12

1
2

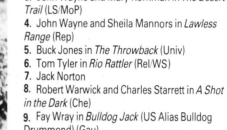

3
4

1. John Wayne in *The New Frontier* (Rep)
2. John Wayne in *Texas Terror* (LS/MoP)
3. John Wayne and Mary Kornman in *The Desert Trail* (LS/MoP)
4. John Wayne and Sheila Mannors in *Lawless Range* (Rep)
5. Buck Jones in *The Throwback* (Univ)
6. Tom Tyler in *Rio Rattler* (Rel/WS)
7. Jack Norton
8. Robert Warwick and Charles Starrett in *A Shot in the Dark* (Che)
9. Fay Wray in *Bulldog Jack* (US Alias Bulldog Drummond) (Gau)
10. Evelyn Venable , Kent Taylor, Charles Middleton, Will Rogers in *The County Chairman* (Fox)
11. George O'Brien, Dorothy Wilson and Harry Woods in *When a Man's a Man* (Fox)
12. Herbert Marshall, Ann Harding, Louis Hayward and Henry Stephenson in *The Flame Within* (MGM)
13. Arline Judge, James Dunn and Rosina Lawrence in *Welcome Home* (Fox)

5
6
7

8 △ ▽ 11
9 △ ▽ 12
10 △ ▽ 13

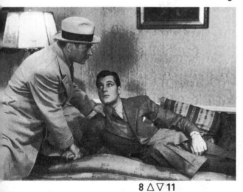

1. Joan Bennett in *The Man who Broke the Bank at Monte Carlo* (Fox)
2. Merle Oberon in *The Scarlet Pimpernel* (LF)
3. Preston Foster, Barbara Stanwyck and Melvyn Douglas in *Annie Oakley* (RKO)
4. Leslie Banks
5. Clark Gable, Constance Bennett and Henry Travers in *After Office Hours* (MGM)
6. Preston Foster, Barbara Stanwyck and Moroni Olsen in *Annie Oakley* (RKO)
7. Ivan Lebedeff, Mae West and Paul Cavanagh in *Goin' to Town* (Par)
8. Chief Thunderbird and Barbara Stanwyck in *Annie Oakley* (RKO)
9. Jean Arthur and Edward G Robinson in *The Whole Town's Talking* (GB *Passport to Fame*) (Col)
10. Donald Woods and Paul Muni in *The Story of Louis Pasteur* (WB)

1   2

3   4

5

6 △▽8   7△▽9   ▽10

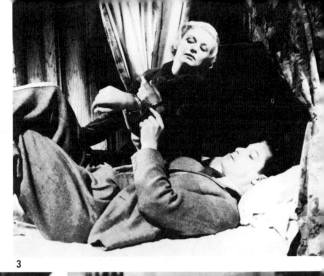

1. Kathleen Burke and Jack Holt in *Awakening of Jim Burke* (Col)
2. Gene Gerrard and Wendy Barrie in *Scandals of Paris* (Reg)
3. Madeleine Carroll and Robert Donat in *The 39 Steps* (Gau)
4. Clark Gable in *China Seas* (MGM)
5. John McGuire and Jane Withers in *This is the Life* (Fox)
6. Joe E Brown and Ann Dvorak in *Bright Lights* (GB *Funny Face*) (FN)
7. Charles Winninger
8. Ian Hunter
9. Patricia Ellis
10. Fred MacMurray and Katharine Hepburn in *Alice Adams* (RKO)
11. Gilbert Roland in *Ladies Love Danger* (Fox)
12. Richard Cromwell
13. Flora Robson
14. Harry Stockwell and Virginia Bruce in *Here Comes the Band* (MGM)

7 △ ▽ 11

9 △ ▽ 12

13

10 △ ▽ 14

1   2

3   4

5   6   7

1. Joan Blondell and Hugh Herbert in *Traveling Saleslady* (FN)
2. Barbara Stanwyck in *The Secret Bride* (GB *Concealment*) (WB)
3. Bela Lugosi in *Mysterious Mr Wong* (MoP)
4. Bette Davis and George Brent in *Front Page Woman* (WB)
5. Franklin Pangborn
6. Mary Astor, Ricardo Cortez, Irving Pichel and Robert Barrat in *I am a Thief* (WB)
7. Donald Woods, Irene Dunne and Louis Calhern in *Sweet Adeline* (WB)
8. Margot Grahame
9. Sonnie Hale and Jessie Matthews in *First a Girl* (Gau)
10. Ginger Rogers and Fred Astaire in *Top Hat* (RKO)

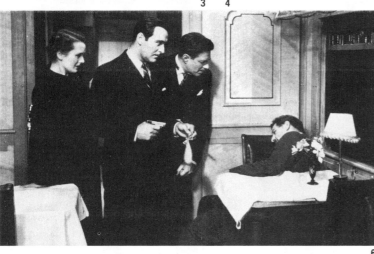

1

2

3

1. Valerie Hobson in *Chinatown Squad* (Univ)
2. John Boles, Karen Morley and Shirley Temple in *The Littlest Rebel* (Fox)
3. Gene Raymond and Barbara Stanwyck in *The Woman in Red* (WB)
4. Rosemary Ames, Lyle Talbot and Joel McCrea in *Our Little Girl* (Fox)
5. Helen Westley and Josephine Hutchinson in *The Melody Lingers On* (ES)
6. Ruth Mix
7. Rosemary Ames, Shirley Temple and Joel McCrea in *Our Little Girl* (Fox)
8. Lionel Barrymore, Lionel Atwill and Jean Hersholt in *Mark of the Vampire* (MGM)
9. Colin Clive, Elsa Lanchester and Boris Karloff in *The Bride of Frankenstein* (Univ)
10. Una O'Connor and Boris Karloff in *The Bride of Frankenstein* (Univ)
11. Leon Errol

4

5

6 △ ▽ 9

7 △ ▽ 10

8 △ ▽ 11

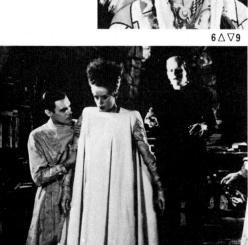

1 and **2** Marlene Dietrich in *The Devil is a Woman* (Par)
3. Marlene Dietrich and Lionel Atwill in *The Devil is a Woman* (Par)
4. Randolph Scott and Helen Mack in *She* (RKO)
5. Tullio Carminati
6. Jack Oakie, Clark Gable and Loretta Young in *Call of the Wild* (Fox)
7. Bill Boyd in *Bar 20 Rides Again* (HS)
8. Rex Bell
9. Basil Rathbone, Jessie Ralph, Freddie Bartholomew and Elizabeth Allan in *David Copperfield* (MGM)
10. George Brent and Kay Francis in *Living on Velvet* (WB)
11. Sally Eilers, Chester Morris and Scotty Beckett in *Pursuit* (MGM)

6 △ ▽ 9   7 △ ▽ 10   8 △ ▽ 11

1

2

1. Basil Rathbone, Pauline Lord and Nydia Westman in *A Feather in Her Hat* (Col)
2. Edmund Lowe in *The Great Impersonation* (Univ)
3. Edward G Robinson and J M Kerrigan in *Barbary Coast* (SG)
4. Robert Taylor and Helen Twelvetrees in *Times Square Lady* (MGM)
5. Walter Connolly and Paul Lukas in *Father Brown, Detective* (Par)
6. **and 16**. Peter Lorre in *Mad Love* (GB *The Hands of Orlac*) (MGM)
7. Ian Hunter and Bette Davis in *The Girl from Tenth Avenue* (GB *Men on Her Mind*) (WB)
8. Charles Coleman, Frank Orth and Ralph Forbes in *The Goose and the Gander* (FN)
9. Bill Boyd and George 'Gabby' Hayes in *Eagle's Brood* (Par)
10. Merle Oberon and Herbert Marshall in *The Dark Angel* (SG)
11. Robert Cummings, Eleanore Whitney and Benny Baker in *Millions in the Air* (Par)
12. Joan Crawford and Gail Patrick in *No More Ladies* (MGM)
13. Dudley Digges, Basil Rathbone and Murray Kinnell in *Kind Lady* (MGM)
14. Kay Francis and Paul Lukas in *I Found Stella Parish* (FN)
15. Gene Autry and Barbara Pepper in *The Sagebrush Troubadour* (Rep)
17. Eleanor Powell, Buddy and Vilma Ebsen and Una Merkel in *Broadway Melody of 1936* (MGM)

3

5 △ ▽ 8

6

7 △ ▽ 9

10 11 12

13

14 △ ▽ 17

15 △ ▽ 16

1

3

4

5

6

8

7

9

10

I. Clive Brook and Madeleine Carroll in *The Dictator* (aka For Love of a Queen; The Loves of a Dictator)

2. Ronald Colman and Francis Lister in *Clive of India* (Fox)

3. Dick Powell and Gloria Stuart in *Gold Diggers of 1935* (WB)

4. Maurice Chevalier and Merle Oberon in *Folies Bergere* (Fox)

5. Kay Francis in *Living on Velvet* (WB)

6. Paul Robeson and Nina Mae McKinney in *Sanders of the River* (LF) (US Bosambo)

7. Kay Francis and Donald Woods in *Stranded* (WB)

8. Leslie Banks and Paul Robeson in *Sanders of the River* (LF) (US Bosambo)

9. Melvyn Douglas and Claudette Colbert in *She Married Her Boss* (Col)

10. Joan Crawford and Brian Aherne in *I Live My Life* (MGM)

1. Miles Mander, Francis Lister, Katherine Alexander, Douglas Dumbrille, Violet Cooper and Cesar Romero in *Cardinal Richelieu* (Fox)
2. Alan Mowbray and Peggy Shannon in *Night Life of the Gods* (Univ)
3. Richard Cromwell, (c) C Aubrey Smith and Sir Guy Standing in *Lives of a Bengal Lancer* (Par)
4. John Buckler and Ann Sothern in *Eight Bells* (Col)
5. Roland Young, Charles Ruggles and Charles Laughton in *Ruggles of Red Gap* (Par)
6. Ann Rutherford
7. Fredric March and Charles Laughton in *Les Miserables* (Fox)
8. John Qualen and Paul Muni in *Black Fury* (WB)
9. Pat O'Brien, Jean Muir and James Melton in *Stars Over Broadway* (WB)
10. Ann Dvorak and Barton MacLane in *Dr Socrates* (WB)
11. Anita Louise and Nino Martini in *Here's to Romance* (Fox)

1 2

3

4 5

▽8

6△▽9

7△▽10

11 12

13

A Tale of Two Cities (MGM) proved that another of Dickens' novels could be transferred successfully to the screen. Much was made at the time of Ronald Colman having shaved his famous moustache for his role of Sydney Carton. As usual, with or without moustache, Colman was superb.

1. Elizabeth Allan
2. Blanche Yurka
3. Elizabeth Allan and Claude Gillingwater
4. Walter Catlett, Donald Woods and Ronald Colman
5. Elizabeth Allan and Ronald Colman
6. Reginald Owen, Ronald Colman, Lawrence Grant and Walter Catlett
7. Claude Gillingwater, Henry B Walthall, Elizabeth Allan and Ronald Colman
8. Elizabeth Allan
9. Ronald Colman
10. Basil Rathbone
11. Reginald Owen and Ronald Colman
12. Elizabeth Allan and Ronald Colman
13. Ronald Colman
14. Basil Rathbone and John Davidson
15. Reginald Owen and Ronald Colman
16. Claude Gillingwater, Ronald Colman and Donald Woods
17. Elizabeth Allan
18. Reginald Owen, Ronald Colman, Lawrence Grant, Walter Catlett, Edna May Oliver, Elizabeth Allan, Henry B Walthall, Claude Gillingwater and Donald Woods

15

14 △ ▽ 17

16 △ ▽ 18

1

2   3

4 △ ▽ 6

5 △ ▽ 7

8 **9 10**

Captain Blood was Errol Flynn's first starring role. He leaped to the occasion physically as well as figuratively. Thereafter he was one of Hollywood's top-ranking stars. In *Captain Blood* he was supported by a brilliant cast.

1. Olivia de Havilland and Errol Flynn
2. Errol Flynn and Lionel Atwill
3. Ross Alexander
4. Lionel Atwill, Forrester Harvey, Robert Barrat and Errol Flynn
5. Errol Flynn
6. George Hassell, Mary Forbes, Olivia de Havilland and Lionel Atwill
7. Henry Stephenson
8. J Carrol Naish
9. Lionel Atwill
10. Olivia de Havilland
11. Henry Stephenson, Olivia de Havilland and Errol Flynn
12. Olivia de Havilland and Errol Flynn
13. Errol Flynn, Basil Rathbone and Yola D'Avril
14. J. Carrol Naish, Errol Flynn and Basil Rathbone

12 △ ▽ 14

11 △ ▽ 13

1. Warren William, Claire Dodd and Guy Kibbee in *Don't Bet on Blondes* (WB)

2. Jean Muir and Pat O'Brien in *Oil For The Lamps Of China* (Cos/FN)

3. Dick Powell and Ann Dvorak in *Thanks a Million* (Fox)

4. Miriam Hopkins and Joel McCrea in *Splendor* (SG)

5. Donald Woods and Margaret Lindsay in *The Case Of The Curious Bride* (FN)

6. Ian Hunter and Kay Johnson in *Jalna* (RKO)

7. Ginger Rogers and William Powell in *Star of Midnight* (RKO)

8. Arline Judge and Ray Walker in *Million Dollar Baby* (MoP)

9. Dolores Del Rio, Pat O'Brien and Leo Carrillo in *In Caliente* (FN)

10. Judith Allen and Regis Toomey in *Reckless Roads* (Maj)

11. Pat O'Brien, Mary Gordon and James Cagney in *The Irish In Us* (FN)

12. George Raft and Carole Lombard in *Rumba* (Par)

13. Ken Maynard and Geneva Mitchell in *Western Courage* (Col)

14. Alison Skipworth, Louise Henry and Donald Cook in *The Casino Murder Case* (MGM)

15. Will Rogers and Billie Burke in *Doubting Thomas* (Fox)

12 △ ▽ 14   13 △ ▽ 15

The Three Musketeers (RKO). This was Hollywood's second filming of the Alexandre Dumas' classic. Walter Abel was an import from the New York stage.

1. Ralph Forbes and Rosamond Pinchot
2. John Qualen, Paul Lukas, Walter Abel and Heather Angel
3. Paul Lukas and Margot Grahame
4. Walter Abel and Heather Angel
5. Heather Angel and Rosamond Pinchot
6. Heather Angel and Murray Kinnell
7. Walter Abel and Margot Grahame

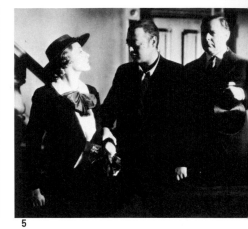

1. John Boles and Dixie Lee in *Redheads on Parade* (Fox)
2. Charles Farrell and Ann Sheridan in *Fighting Youth* (Univ)
3. Ned Sparks, Ann Dvorak and Rudy Vallee in *Sweet Music* (WB)
4. Barbara Stanwyck and Robert Young in *Red Salute* (GB *Arms and the Girl*) (ES)
5. Tala Birell, Peter Lorre and Gene Lockhart in *Crime and Punishment* (Col)
6. Constance Cummings
7. Martha Eggerth
8. John Wayne in *Westward Ho* (Rep)
9. Herbert Marshall, Sylvia Sidney and Philip Reed in *Accent on Youth* (Par)

6 △ ▽8 9 ▽ 7 △

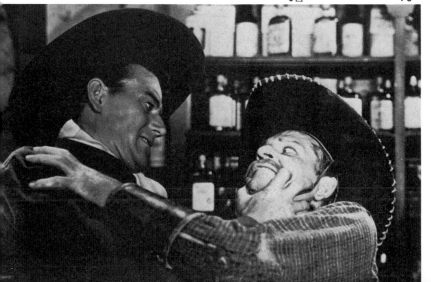

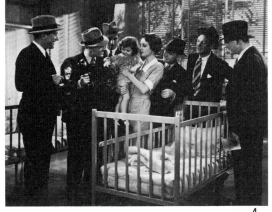

1. Evalyn Knapp and Warren Hymer in *Confidential* (MaP)

2. Don Alvarado, Everett Marshall and Dolores Del Rio in *I Live for Love* (GB *I Live for You*) (WB)

3. Mary Astor and Roger Pryor in *Straight from the Heart* (Univ)

4. Baby Jane Quigley and Mary Astor in *Straight from the Heart* (Univ)

5. Pat Paterson, Rita Hayworth and Warner Oland in *Charlie Chan in Egypt* (Fox)

6. Henry Fonda

7. Basil Rathbone

8. Eugene Pallette, Bette Davis and Paul Muni in *Bordertown* (WB)

9. Ann Sothern and Gene Raymond in *Hooray for Love* (RKO)

△ 6   ▽ 8   9 ▽   7 △

1. Roger Pryor and Heather Angel in *The Headline Woman* (MoP)
2. Lola Lane and Russell Hopton in *Death from a Distance* (Inv)
3. Marta Eggerth in *My Heart is Calling* (Gau)
4. Herbert Marshall and Jean Arthur in *If You Could Only Cook* (Col)
5. Paul Cavanagh
6. Frank McHugh, Helen Lowell, Ruth Donnelly, Henry Travers, Gloria Stuart and Ross Alexander in *Maybe It's Love* (FN)
7. Buck Jones and Polly Ann Young in *Crimson Trail* (Univ)
8. Joel McCrea and Claudette Colbert in *Private Worlds* (Par)
9. Madge Evans and Fred MacMurray in *Men Without Names* (Par)
10. Edna May Oliver
11. (l) Jason Robards, Francis McDonald and Jack Mulhall (c) in *Burn 'Em up Barnes* (MaP)
12. Russell Hopton, Leroy Mason and Frankie Darro in *Valley of Wanted Men* (CoP)

1

2

5

4

8

6 △ ▽ 9

7 △ ▽ 10

11 △ ▽ 12

1

1. Pert Kelton and Walter Catlett in *Lightning Strikes Twice* (RKO)
2. Warner Baxter (I) in *Under the Pampas Moon* (Fox)
3. Hugh Sinclair and Elisabeth Bergner in *Escape Me Never* (UA)
4. Mayo Methot
5. John Loder and Anna May Wong in *Java Head* (FD)
6. Fred MacMurray, Ann Sheridan and William Frawley in *Car No 99* (Par)
7. Harry Woods and Ken Maynard in *Heir to Trouble* (Col)
8. Claire Trevor and Edmund Lowe in *Black Sheep* (Fox)
9. Tim McCoy in *The Westerner* (Col)
10. Henri Garat
11. Helen Westley, James Barton and Helen Mack in *Captain Hurricane* (RKO)

2

3

4

5

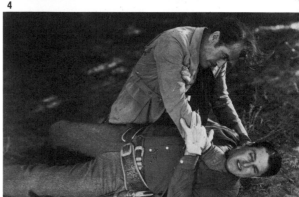

6 △ ▽ 10

7 △ ▽ 11

8 △ ▽ 9

1

2

4

5

3

6

1. Jean Muir
2. Gene Autry
3. Warner Baxter and Janet Gaynor in *One More Spring* (Fox)
4. Leslie Perrin
5. Richard Talmadge in *Now or Never* (Aja)
6. Sidney Toler, James Dunn and Warren Hymer in *The Daring Young Man* (Fox)
7. John Wayne
8. Florence Rice, Victor McLaglen, Charles Bickford and Edmund Lowe in *Under Pressure* (Fox)
9. O P Heggie and Frankie Thomas in *A Dog of Flanders* (RKO)
10. Steve Clark, Buck Connors and Bob Steele in *No Man's Range* (Sup/WS)
11. Hattie McDaniel
12. Tutta Rolf and Clive Brook in *Dressed to Thrill* (Fox)
13. Natalie Paley, Edmund Gwenn and Brian Aherne in *Sylvia Scarlett* (RKO)

7

8

9 △ ▽ 12

10 △ ▽ 13

11

1

2

3

4 5

6

7

8

1. George O'Brien and Edgar Kennedy in *The Cowboy Millionaire* (Ath/Fox)
2. Chester Morris and Rochelle Hudson in *I've Been Around* (Univ)
3. Melvyn Douglas and Preston Foster in *The People's Enemy* (SeP)
4. Jane Baxter, Athene Seyler and Matheson Lang in *Drake of England* (US *Drake the Pirate; Elizabeth of England*) (War)
5. Irene Ware and George O'Brien in *Whispering Smith Speaks* (Fox)
6. Buck Jones and Lona Andre in *Border Brigands* (Univ)
7. Betty Balfour and John Mills in *Forever England* (Gau)
8. Conrad Veidt
9. Jack Benny
10. Warner Oland and Keye Luke in *Charlie Chan in Shanghai* (Fox)
11. Gertrude Michael
12. Virginia Field
13. George Barbier
14. Virginia Weidler

9 △ ▽ 14

10 △ ▽ 12

▽ 13

11

263

1 2

1. Mary Carlisle, Norman Foster and Florine McKinney in *Superspeed* (Col)
2. Henry Stephenson and Robert Montgomery in *Vanessa, Her Love Story* (MGM)
3. Ben Lyon, Helen Twelvetrees and Rod La Rocque in *Frisco Waterfront* (Rep)
4. Sheila Mannors and William Bakewell in *Together We Live* (Col)
5. Gloria Stuart
6. Ann Sothern
7. Suzanne Aaren and Preston Foster in *Strangers All* (RKO)
8. Leo Carrillo and Louise Fazenda in *Winning Ticket* (Par)
9. Fred MacMurray and Claudette Colbert in *The Bride Comes Home* (Par)
10. O P Heggie and Anne Shirley in *Chasing Yesterday* (RKO)
11. Owen Moore
12. Edward Underdown
13. Carl Brisson and Mary Ellis in *All The King's Horses* (Par)
14. Edward Pawley, Dorothy Page and Pinky Tomlin in *King Solomon of Broadway* (Univ)

3

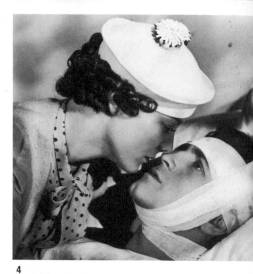

4

6

7

5

8 △ ▽ 11

▽ 12

9 △ ▽ 13

10 △ ▽ 14

1

3

4

1. George E Stone, Dickie Jones, Dick Foran and Glenn Strange in *Moonlight on the Prairie* (WB)
2. Godfrey Tearle (c) in *Wolves of the Underworld* (Reg)
3. Ken Maynard and Geneva Mitchell in *Lawless Riders* (Col)
4. Aline MacMahon and Guy Kibbee in *While the Patient Slept* (FN)
5. Jack Holt, Florence Rice and Edmund Lowe in *The Best Man Wins* (Col)
6. Frances Dee
7. Polly Walters
8. Tim McCody (I) and Billie Seward in *Law Beyond The Range* (Col)
9. Joe E Brown and Ruth Donnelly in *Alibi Ike* (WB)
10. Mona Barrie and Warner Baxter in *King of Burlesque* (Fox)
11. Tom Dugan, Paul Guilfoyle, George McKay, Roger Pryor and Joan Perry in *Case of the Missing Man* (Col)
12. Jackie Cooper and Jimmy Butler in *Dinky* (WB)
13. Fred Kohler
14. Arturo de Cordoba

5

6

7

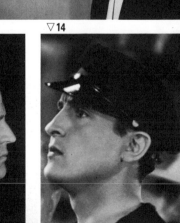

8△ ▽11

9△ ▽12

10△ ▽13

▽14

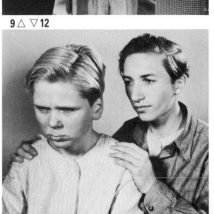

1

2

3

1. Nelson Eddy and Jeanette MacDonald in
Naughty Marietta (MGM)
2. John Wayne and Sheila Terry in *The Lawless
Frontier* (MoP)
3. James Dunn in *Bad Boy* (Fox)
4. Helen Twelvetrees and Joe Morrison in *One
Hour Late* (Par)
5. ZaSu Pitts and Guy Kibbee in *Going High Brow*
(WB)
6. Aline MacMahon and Guy Kibbee in *Mary
Jane's Pa* (GB *Wanderlust*) (FN)
7. Alan Hale, Phyllis Brooks and James Dunn in
Another Face (RKO)
8. Cary Grant, Roscoe Karns and Myrna Loy in
Wings in the Dark (Par)
9. Ray Corrigan
10. Will Rogers and Dorothy Wilson in *In Old
Kentucky* (Fox)
11. Cesar Romero, Edward Norris and Rochelle
Hudson in *Show Them No Mercy* (GB *Tainted
Money*) (Fox)
12. Mona Barrie and Gilbert Roland in *Mystery
Woman* (Fox)
13. Paul Kelly, Claire Trevor and Kent Taylor in *My
Marriage* (Fox)

4

5

6

7

8 △ ▽ 11

9 △ ▽ 12

10 △ ▽ 13

1 (top left)

2 (top centre)

3 (top right)

4

1. Henry Fonda and Janet Gaynor in *The Farmer Takes a Wife* (Fox)
2. Wendy Barrie, Spencer Tracy and Raymond Walburn in *It's a Small World* (Fox)
3. Charles Bickford and Helen Vinson in *A Notorious Gentleman* (Univ)
4. James Dunn and Claire Dodd in *The Payoff* (FN)
5. Fred MacMurray and Carole Lombard in *Hands Across the Table* (Par)
6. J Farrell MacDonald, Spencer Tracy, Jean Harlow and Joseph Calleia in *Riff-Raff* (MGM)
7. Benita Humé, Hugh Wakefield, Katherine Sergava and John Loder in *Eighteen Minutes* (AIP)
8. W C Fields and Kathleen Howard in *The Man on the Flying Trapeze* (GB *The Memory Expert*) (Par)
9. Syd Saylor
10. Sig Rumann and Anna Sten in *The Wedding Night* (SG)
11. Frankie Darro and Lyle Talbot in *Red Hot Tires* (GB *Racing Luck*) (FN)
12. Donald Crisp and John Beal in *Laddie* (PB/RKO)
13. Eddie Acuff, Dick Powell and Ruby Keeler in *Shipmates Forever* (FN)

5

7

6

8 △ ▽ **11**

9 △ ▽ **12**

10 △ ▽ **13**

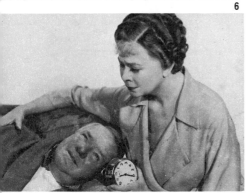

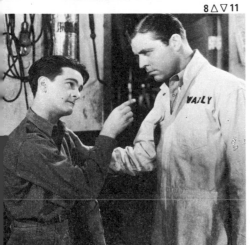

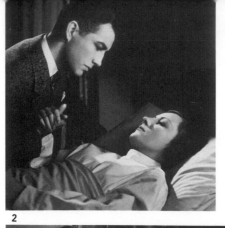

1. Bing Crosby

2. Robert Taylor and Irene Dunne in *Magnificent Obsession* (Univ)

3. Dorothy Peterson and Barton MacLane in *Man of Iron* (FN)

4. Lawrence Tibbett, Virginia Bruce, Cesar Romero and Luis Alberni in *Metropolitan* (Fox)

5. Robert Kortman and Harry Carey (c) in *Wild Mustang* (Aja)

6. Mae Clarke and Alison Skipworth in *Hitch-hike Lady* (Rep)

7. Lola Lane, Edna May Oliver and James Gleason in *Murder on a Honeymoon* (RKO)

8. Ralph Forbes, Frank Morgan and Ann Harding in *Enchanted April* (RKO)

9. Frank Albertson and Anita Louise in *Personal Maid's Secret* (WB)

10. Florence Rice and Conrad Nagel in *Death Flies East* (Col)

11. Kane Richmond (c) in *Silent Code* (FD)

12. Paul Kelly

9 △ ▽ 11

10 △ ▽ 12

1 2

3 4

5

6 7

8

9 △ ▽ 11

10 △ ▽ 12

1. Richard Cromwell and Tom Brown in *Annapolis Farewell* (Par)

2. Jean Parker and Chester Morris in *Princess O'Hara* (Univ)

3. Jack La Rue (r) in *Calling All Cars* (Emp)

4. Hay Petrie and Anna Neagle in *Peg of Old Drury* (HW/B&D)

5. Betty Grable

6. Lyle Talbot and Heather Angel in *It Happened in New York* (Univ)

7. Francis Lederer and Frances Dee in *The Gay Deception* (Fox)

8. Charles Bickford, Elizabeth Young, Clarence Muse, Sig Rumann and Leslie Fenton in *East of Java* (Univ)

9. Wendy Barrie, William Stack and Arline Judge in *College Scandal* (Par)

10. Gene Raymond and Sylvia Sidney in *Behold My Wife* (Par)

11. Robert Cummings, Marsha Hunt and Johnny Downs in *The Virginia Judge* (Par)

12. Wallace Ford

1. Noel Coward and Julie Haydon in *The Scoundrel* (Par)
2. Mary Boland and Charlie Ruggles in *People Will Talk* (Par)
3. Clifford Heatherley, Laura La Plante and John Batten in *The Church Mouse* (FN)
4. Will Rogers, Francis Ford and Berton Churchill in *Steamboat Round the Bend* (Fox)
5. James Ellison, Gabby Hayes and William Boyd in *Hopalong Cassidy* (Par)
6. Allan Jones and the Marx Brothers in *A Night at the Opera* (MGM)
7. Dickie Moore and John Miljan in *Tomorrow's Youth* (MoP)
8. Robert Armstrong and Donald Cook in *Gigolette* (GB: *Night Club*) (RKO)
9. Robert McWade, J Farrell MacDonald and Ralph Bellamy in *The Healer* (Mop)
10. Victor McLaglen in *Professional Soldier* (Fox)
11. Ben Lyon and Claire Trevor in *Navy Wife* (Fox)
12. Yakima Canutt and John Wayne in *Paradise Canyon* (MoP)
13. George O'Brien (r) in *Thunder Mountain* (Fox)

8 △ ▽ 11   9 △ ▽ 12   10 △ ▽ 13

1

2

3

1. Mary Ellis and Tullio Carminati in *Paris in Spring* (GB:*Paris Love Song*) (Par)

2. Dean Jagger (r) in *Wanderer of the Wasteland* (Par)

3. Jack Haley, Sig Rumann, Lew Ayres, Walter Woolf King and Claire Trevor in *Spring Tonic* (Fox)

4. Geneva Mitchell and Ralph Bellamy in *Air Fury* (Col)

5. Patricia Ellis, George E Stone, Andy Devine, William Frawley and Warren Hymer in *Hold 'Em Yale* (Par)

6. Erich Von Stroheim and Harriet Russell in *The Crime of Dr. Crespi* (Rep)

7. Warren Hymer, George E Stone, Cesar Romero, Patricia Ellis, Andy Devine, William Frawley, Larry 'Buster' Crabbe and George Barbier in *Hold 'Em Yale* (Par)

8. Ann Sothern, Jack Haley and Roger Pryor in *The Girl Friend* (Col)

9. Pat Paterson, Lew Ayres and Alan Dinehart in *Lottery Lover* (Fox)

10. Will Rogers and Alison Skipworth in *Doubting Thomas* (Fox)

11. George Raft, Claire Dodd and Rosalind Keith in *The Glass Key* (Par)

12. Ann Sothern and Edmund Lowe in *Grand Exit* (Col)

13. Tim McCoy and Billie Seward in *Riding Wild* (Col)

4

5

7

6

8 △ ▽ 11

9 △ ▽ 12

10 △ ▽ 13

1

2

5

6

7

8

9 △ ▽ 12

10 △ ▽ 13

11 △ ▽ 14

1. Ian Keith, Loretta Young and Henry Wilcoxon in *The Crusades* (CdeM/Par)

2. Henry Wilcoxon in *The Crusades* (CdeM/Par)

3. Betty Burgess and Johnny Downs in *Coronado* (Par)

4. Robert Young and Evelyn Venable in *Vagabond Lady* (MGM)

5. Henry Fonda and Rochelle Hudson in *Way Down East* (Fox)

6. Cornelius Keefe, Nancy Carroll and Lloyd Nolan in *Atlantic Adventure* (Col)

7. Addison Randall in *His Family Tree* (RKO)

8. Maureen O'Sullivan, Wallace Beery, Robert Young, Richard Tucker, Rosalind Russell and Russell Hardie in *West Point of the Air* (MGM)

9. Claude Rains and Joan Bennett in *The Man Who Reclaimed His Head* (Univ)

10. Sylvia Sidney and Alan Baxter in *Mary Burns, Fugitive* (Par)

11. Glenda Farrell and Sybil Jason in *Little Big Shot* (WB)

12. William Gargan and Joy Hodges in *Personal Secretary* (Univ)

13. Charles Butterworth and Una Merkel in *Baby Face Harrington* (MGM)

14. June Clayworth and Roger Pryor in *Strange Wives* (Univ)

15. Henry Kendall and Eve Gray in *Death on the Set* (TFS)

16. Eleanore Whitney

17. Jean Gillie, Mackenzie Ward and Enid Stamp Taylor in *While Parents Sleep* (TFC)

18. Boris Karloff and Bela Lugosi in *The Raven* (Univ)

19. Niles Welch, Marion Shilling and Buck Jones in *Stone of Silver Creek* (Univ)

20. Lewis Stone, Louis Calhern and William B Davidson in *Woman Wanted* (MGM)

21. Maureen O'Sullivan and Joel McCrea in *Woman Wanted* (MGM)

22. Herbert Marshall and Margaret Sullavan in *The Good Fairy* (Univ)

23. Sally Eilers, Constance Cummings and Robert Young in *Remember Last Night* (Univ)

15   16

17   18

19

20 △ ▽ 22   21 △ ▽ 23

1. May Robson, William Benedict, Frankie Darro, Charlotte Henry and Billy Burrud in *Three Kids and a Queen* (Univ)
2. Shirley Grey (c) and Sidney Blackmer in *The Girl Who Came Back* (Che)
3. Edward Nugent and Patricia Scott in *Kentucky Blue Streak* (Pur)
4. John Miljan, Warner Oland, Henry Kolker and Murray Kinnell in *Charlie Chan in Paris* (Fox)
5. Douglass Montgomery and Evelyn Venable in *Harmony Lane* (MaP/CC)
6. Sally Eilers and Chick Chandler in *Alias Mary Dow* (Univ)
7. Robert Montgomery, Ann Harding and Edward Everett Horton in *Biography of a Bachelor Girl* (MGM)
8. George Murphy and Jean Arthur in *The Public Menace* (Col)
9. Lucile Watson, Maureen O'Sullivan and Edmund Gwenn in *The Bishop Misbehaves* (MGM)
10. Charles Boyer and Katharine Hepburn in *Break of Hearts* (RKO)
11. Jack Holt and Mona Barrie in *Unwelcome Stranger* (Col)

274

1

2

3

4

5

6

1. Lyle Talbot and Patricia Ellis in *The Case of the Lucky Legs* (FN)
2. Bob Steele and Julian Rivero in *Western Justice* (Sup/WS)
3. Lee Tracy and Jimmy Durante in *Carnival* (Col)
4. Bela Lugosi in *Murder by Television* (Cam)
5. Luis Alberni, Lilian Harvey and Tullio Carminati in *Let's Live Tonight* (Col)
6. George Burns, Dixie Lee, Gracie Allen and Joe Morrison in *Love in Bloom* (Par)
7. Jane Darwell and Walter C Kelly in *McFadden's Flats* (Par)
8. Wyrley Birch, Jack Dean, George Murphy and Nancy Carroll in *After the Dance* (Col)
9. William Benedict, Rosina Lawrence, Marjorie Gateson and Edward Everett Horton in *Your Uncle Dudley* (Fox)
10. Pat O'Brien and Margaret Lindsay in *Devil Dogs of the Air* (Cos)
11. ZaSu Pitts and Margaret Callahan in *Hot Tip* (RKO)

7

8

9

10

11

1   2

3

4

5

6 △ ▽ 9

7 △ ▽ 10

8 △ ▽ 11

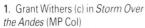

1. Grant Withers (c) in *Storm Over the Andes* (MP Col)
2. Florine McKinney and Ray Walker in *Cappy Ricks Returns* (Rep)
3. Virginia Bruce, Ricardo Cortez and Regis Toomey in *Shadow of Doubt* (MGM)
4. Patric Knowles in *The Student's Romance* (BIP)
5. Bill Cody (k) in *The Vanishing Riders* (Spe)
6. Norman Foster in *Behind the Green Lights* (MaP)
7. Ronald Colman
8. Ginger Rogers, Joan Breslau and George Brent in *In Person* (RKO)
9. Shirley Temple and John Boles in *Curly Top* (Fox)
10. Lilian Harvey in *Invitation to the Waltz* (BIP)
11. Luise Rainer and William Powell in *Escapade* (MGM)
12. Ralph Bellamy and Valerie Hobson in *Rendezvous at Midnight* (Univ)
13. Irene Ware and Russell Hopton in *The Cheers of the Crowd* (Rep)
14. Gail Patrick and Kent Taylor in *Smart Girl* (Par)
15. Edward Everett Horton in *His Night Out* (Univ)
16. Edwin Maxwell
17. Ernest Truex
18. Anne Revere
19. Lawrence Gray and Bryant Washburn (r) in *Danger Ahead* (Vic)
20. Ted Healey
21. Ralph Forbes, Evelyn Venable and Victor Jory in *Streamline Express* (MaP)
22. Sheila Terry (l) and Regis Toomey (r) in *Bars of Hate* (Vic)

12 **13**

14 **15**

16 **17**

18

19 △ ▽ 21   20 △ ▽ 22

1. Ginger Rogers, Fred Astaire and Irene Dunne in *Roberta* (RKO)
2. Monte Blue in *On Probation* (Pee)
3. Richard Cromwell and Wallace Ford in *Men of the Hour* (Col)
4. Noel Madison, Edward Pawley and Barton MacLane, in *G Men* (WB)
5. Spring Byington and Wallace Beery in *Ah, Wilderness* (MGM)
6. Patsy Kelly, Frances Langford, George Raft and Alice Faye in *Every Night at Eight* (Par)
7. Ann Harding and Gary Cooper in *Peter Ibbetson* (Par)
8. Benita Hume and Gregory Ratoff in *This Woman is Mine* (Par)
9. Russell Hopton in *The World Accuses* (Che)
10. Raymond Walburn, Jean Dixon, George Murphy and Nancy Carroll in *I'll Love You Always* (Col)

1

2

3

1.George Raft, Grace Bradley and Ben Bernie in *Stolen Harmony* (Par)
2. Bill Robinson and Shirley Temple in *The Little Colonel* (Fox)
3. Lionel Barrymore and Shirley Temple in *The Little Colonel* (Fox)
4. Pedro De Cordova, Ralph Morgan and Russell Gleason in *Condemned to Live* (Che)
5. Wallace Ford, George Raft and Joan Bennett in *She Couldn't Take It* (Col)
6. Mickey Rooney and Lionel Barrymore in *Ah, Wilderness* (MGM)
7. Wallace Ford in *The Nut Farm* (MoP)
8. Nancy DeShon, Tom Tyler and Charles King in *Silent Valley* (Com)
9. Margaret Lindsay, George E Stone and James Cagney in *Frisco Kid* (WB)
10. Patricia Ellis and William Gargan in *A Night at the Ritz* (WB)
11. Laura La Plante and Douglas Fairbanks Jr in *Man of the Moment* (FN)

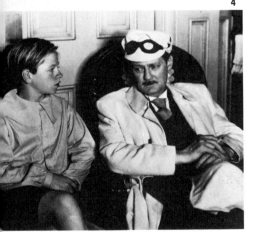

4

5

6

7

8

9

10

11

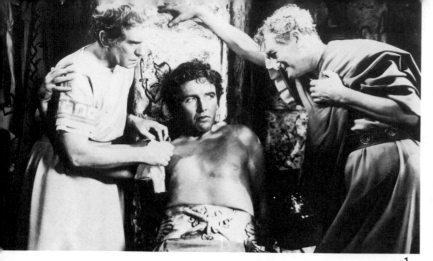

1　2

3　　　　4　5

6△ ▽8　7△

1. Gene Autry in *Tumbling Tumbleweeds* (Rep)
2. Lily Pons and Henry Fonda in *I Dream Too Much* (RKO)
3. Henry Travers, Clive Tell, Charles Wilson, Joe Morrison and Paul Harvey in *Four Hours to Kill* (Par)
4. Ken Maynard and Lucile Browne in *Western Frontier* (Col)
5. Richard Cromwell, Henry Armetta and Marian Marsh in *Unknown Woman* (Col)
6. Preston Foster, Francis Ford and Richard Dix *The Arizonian* (RKO)
7. Roger Pryor and Leila Hyams in *Thousand Dollars a Minute* (RKO)
8. Sally O'Neill, Victor Jory and James Millican in *Too Tough to Kill* (Col)
9. Boris Karloff and Marian Marsh in *The Black Room* (Col)

Facing page *The Last Days of Pompeii* (RKO) borrowed only the title from Lord Lytton's famous book. It was the familiar Hollywood-cum-Ancient Rome opus with Basil Rathbone in his element as Pontius Pilate

1. John Wood, Preston Foster and William V Mong
2. Dorothy Wilson and Preston Foster
3. Preston Foster
4. Preston Foster, John Wood and David Holt
5. Preston Foster and Louis Calhern
6. The Christians die in the Arena.
7. Basil Rathbone and Preston Foster
8. The earthquake in the Bay of Naples

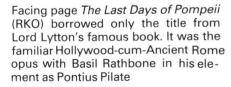

6 △ ▽ 8

7 △ ▽ 9

1

2

3   4

5   6

7 △ ▽ 9

8 △ ▽ 10

11

The Informer (RKO) is probably the film for which Victor McLaglen will always be remembered. His portrayal as Gypo the informer won him the Academy Award for Best Actor.

1. Margot Grahame
2. Margot Grahame and Victor McLaglen
3. Wallace Ford and Heather Angel
4. Preston Foster, Joe Sawyer and Victor McLaglen
5. Victor McLaglen
6. Victor McLaglen and D'Arcy Corrigan
7. Victor McLaglen
8. Victor McLaglen, J M Kerrigan and Wallace Ford
9. Margot Grahame and Victor McLaglen
10. Margot Grahame and Victor McLaglen
11. Margot Grahame and Heather Angel

1

2

3

4

5

1. O P Heggie
2. Cora Sue Collins
3. Jack Haley
4. Bill Boyd
5. Marjorie Weaver
6. Mary Ellis
7. Gracie Fields
8. Alan Hale
9. Beulah Bondi
10. Virginia Field
11. George 'Gabby' Hayes
12. Allen Jenkins

6 △ ▽ 10

7 △ ▽ 11

8

9 △ ▽ 12

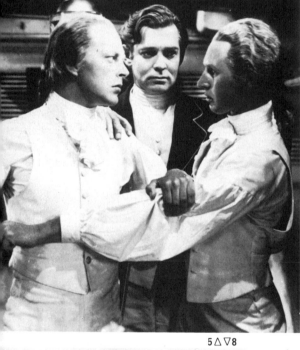

1

2

3

4

5 △ ▽8

6 △ ▽9

7 △

10

11

12

13

Mutiny on the Bounty (MGM) was accorded the motion picture Academy Award for Best Picture in 1935. Today, though, the film is probably better remembered for Charles Laughton's magnificent portrayal of Captain William Bligh RN who was in fact unfairly treated.

1. Doris Lloyd and Clark Gable
2. Clark Gable and De Witt Jennings
3. Spring Byington and Franchot Tone
4. Clark Gable
5. Douglas Walton, Clark Gable and Vernon Downing
6. De Witt Jennings, Dudley Digges, Charles Laughton, Herbert Mundin, Clark Gable and Franchot Tone
7 and 8. Movita and Clark Gable
9. Clark Gable, Dudley Digges, Charles Laughton and Donald Crisp
10. Charles Laughton and Clark Gable
11. Charles Laughton
12. Franchot Tone and Doris Lloyd (r)
13. Franchot Tone
14. Franchot Tone, Vernon Downing, Clark Gable and Douglas Walton
15. Clark Gable
16. Clark Gable, De Witt Jennings and Charles Laughton
17. Dudley Digges (c) and Ian Wolfe
18. Movita, Clark Gable, Douglas Walton, Franchot Tone, Mamo Clark and Richard Skinner

14

16 △ ▽ 18

15 △ ▽ 17

1

2

3

4

5

6

7

8

9 10

11

12 13

14

15 △ ▽ 18

16 △ ▽ 19

17 △ ▽ 20

21   22   23

24   25   26

27   28

29   30   31

32 △ ▽ 35   33 △ ▽ 36   34 △

1. Molly O'Day and Bill Cody in *Lawless Borders* (Spe)
2. Spencer Tracy (s) and William Demarest (rc) in *The Murder Man* (MGM)
3. Reed Howes, William Farnum and Tarzan the Police Dog in *Million Dollar Haul* (FD)
4. Fred Kohler, Jean Rogers and Noah Beery Jr in *Stormy* (Univ)
5. William Boyd in *Racing Luck* (Rep)
6. James Cagney and Pat O'Brien in *Ceiling Zero* (WB)
7. Toby Wing, Onslow Stevens and Barbara Pepper in *Forced Landing* (Rep)
8. Regis Toomey, Rafaela Ottiano, Mary Carlisle, Wallace Ford, Lucien Littlefield and Clarence Wilson in *One Frightened Night* (MaP)
9. Otto Kruger in *Two Sinners* (Rep)
10. Guinn 'Big Boy' Williams (c) in *Big Boy Rides Again* (Bea/FD)
11. Esther Ralston, Edmund Lowe and Jean Dixon in *Mr Dynamite* (Univ)
12. Donald Cook and Sheila Mannors in *Behind the Evidence* (Col)
13. Tom London, June Love and John Preston in *Courage of the North* (FD)
14. Richard Talmadge in *Never Too Late* (Rel)
15. Bert Wheeler and Robert Woolsey in *Nitwits* (RKO)
16. Norman Foster, Charlotte Henry and Fred Kohler Jr in *The Hoosier Schoolmaster* (GB *The Schoolmaster*) (MoP)
17. Gloria Stuart in *Secrets of Chinatown* (NF)
18. Louise Fazenda and Joan Blondell in *Broadway Gondolier* (WB)
19. Johnny Mack Brown and Jeanette Loff in *St Louis Woman* (ShP)
20. Benny Corbett, Rex Lease, Janet Morgan and Alphonse Martel in *The Cowboy and the Bandit* (Int/Spr)
21. Rochelle Hudson, Richard Cromwell and Will Rogers in *Life Begins at 40* (Fox)
22. Norman Foster and Victor Jory in *Escape from Devil's Island* (Col)
23. Donald Cook and Helen Twelvetrees in *Spanish Cape Mystery* (Rep)
24. Lionel Barrymore and Helen Mack in *The Return of Peter Grimm* (RKO)
25. Louis Alberni and Grace Moore in *Love Me Forever* (GB *On Wings of Song*) (Col)
26. Robert Young and Madge Evans in *Calm Yourself* (MGM)
27. Norman Foster, Eric Linden and Syd Saylor in *Ladies Crave Excitement* (MaP)
28. Kay Hammond (l) and Madeleine Carroll in *Sleeping Car* (Gau)
29. Ralph Forbes in *Rescue Squad* (Emp)
30. Maria Ouspenskaya
31. Diana Churchill in *Foreign Affairs* (G'boro)
32. Jack Hylton, Freddie Schweitzer and June Clyde in *She Shall Have Music* (TFS)
33. Hardie Albright and Minna Gombell in *Women Must Dress* (MoP)
34. Bernadine Hayes and Conway Tearle in *The Judgement Book* (Bet)
35. Steven Geray, Charles 'Buddy' Rogers and Magda Kun in *Dance Band* (All)
36. Tim McCoy in *Bulldog Courage* (Pur)

287

Gary Cooper

CHAPTER SEVEN
1936
FILMS FOR EVERYONE

Was there ever a time in the Thirties when Gary Cooper was not in front of the cameras? In 1936 alone, he appeared in several major films and his roles could not have been more diverse. It seemed that whenever a reliable, good-looking male star was needed for a major film someone would call for 'Coop.' And Gary Cooper would appear on the set. Moreover, whatever the role, he never let a studio down.

Frank Capra called for 'Coop' to play the title role in his social comedy, *Mr Deeds Goes to Town*. It proved to be an excellent choice, as it led to Capra walking off with his second Oscar, having won his first two years earlier with *It Happened One Night*.

Mr Deeds Goes To Town was adapted from a *Saturday Evening Post* short story. Its plot is not entirely original; the originality lies in Robert Riskin's script and its treatment by Capra.

Cooper is seen as Longfellow Deeds, a tuba-playing country boy, a decent, ordinary and simple man who is suddenly left a huge fortune by a relative. His New York cousin is disgusted at not receiving a single dollar from the uncle's money, and plots to grab the inheritance. When Deeds arrives in New York he meets a newspaper woman (Jean Arthur), who pretends she is seeking a job, but is in fact feeding her newspaper with stories about the country millionaire who has come to town.

Deeds rapidly becomes disenchanted with New York, realizing that it is full of phonies who are only interested in his money. Instead of joining them in their crooked swindles, he decides to put his money into helping some impoverished farmers. He gives each a cow, a horse, some seed and a piece of land.

But now the newspaper woman has discovered Deeds' true worth and is there to back him in court, where the New York cousin is trying to obtain control of the money by proving that Deeds is insane. But in a brilliant court-scene speech, Deeds easily convinces everyone there that all he has done is uphold the real values of American life.

Gary Cooper and Jean Arthur in *Mr Deeds Goes to Town* (Col)

Gary Cooper again starred with Jean Arthur in Cecil B. DeMille's spectacular Western, *The Plainsman*, a film purporting to tell the story of Wild Bill Hickok.

Western films were actually in somewhat of a decline about this time. But DeMille stimulated a new interest in them by giving the film the full treatment. He used top stars, the six-acre Paramount ranch as the setting for the actions, thousands of Sioux and Cheyenne Indians as extras, and a love story that never played a part in the real life of Hickok.

Cooper discards the image he had created for 'Mr Deeds' to become Hickok, the tough, rough frontiersman who falls in love with the legendary Calamity Jane (Jean Arthur). Supporting the main stars are James Ellison as Buffalo Bill, John Miljan as Lt.Col Custer, backed by the ever-reliable Charles Bickford and Porter Hall.

In 1936 one of the greatest stars of all time, Greta Garbo, was still at the height of her illustrious career. In this year she played in *Camille*, the best of several screen versions of the famous novel by Alexandre Dumas the Younger. Because she was regarded as being little short of a goddess, it seemed incongruous that she should portray a courtesan, but she did so with a delicacy and warmth that made her performance outstanding even by her own high standards.

Robert Taylor in *Camille* plays opposite her as Armand, her lover. Somewhat overawed by acting with the superb Garbo, he is a little too stiff as the innocent young man who loves her to the end. And what an end it is! Her death from consumption, as he holds her in his arms with tears streaming down his face, provides one of the great highlights of cinema melodrama. The director George Cukor, managed to extract from Garbo one of her finest performances in this elegantly mounted production.

Modern Times is a remarkable picture for its time, inasmuch as Charles Chaplin was still refusing to succumb to sound, even though nine years had passed since the event of *The Jazz Singer*. The film had one song that was sung in incomprehensible gibberish, but that was Chaplin's sole concession to the talkies. Perhaps even more remarkable is the fact that this has not impeded the film's ultimate place in the list of all-time cinema 'greats'.

Playing his lovable tramp for the last time, Chaplin is seen as a factory hand working on a conveyer belt, spanner in hand, tightening up assembly nuts as they reach him. The monotony of the job eventually sends him crazy. In a hilarious scene, he runs amok in the factory before ending up in a mental hospital.

With his release, his troubles are still far from being over, and after unwittingly leading a protest march, he lands up in jail. Even after his release again, life is still difficult and not made much easier when he throws in his lot with an orphaned girl (Paulette Goddard) on the run from both the police and child-welfare officials. Working at the factory again, and later as a singing waiter, he still

Gary Cooper and Jean Arthur in *The Plainsman* (Par)

Robert Taylor and Greta Garbo in *Camille* (MGM)

Charles Chaplin in *Modern Times* (ChC)

Paulette Goddard in *Modern Times* (ChC)

Irene Dunne and Charles Winninger in *Showboat* (Univ)

Hattie McDaniel in *Showboat* (Univ)

Humphrey Bogart in *The Petrified Forest* (WB)

cannot avoid disaster until the very end when he walks out of the film, hand in hand with the girl.

In this film all Chaplin's many skills are put to good use as he skates, ballet dances, mimes and generally creates havoc with all his endeavours. It was a fitting end for the tramp and one that will always be remembered.

The 1936 Universal version of *Showboat* is probably not remembered today for its story but for its wonderful songs, all sung by great singing stars. There have been several film versions of the famous novel by Edna Ferber, but this one is generally considered to be the best. It was adapted by Oscar Hammerstein II from his stage musical, and Jerome Kern wrote the songs.

Could anyone better Paul Robeson singing 'Ole Man River'? In *Showboat* he renders this old favourite and 'Ah Still Suits Me' with a power and magnificence that still reaches straight into the hearts of his audience. Helen Morgan, as the doomed singer, Julie, gives a heart-stopping rendition of 'My Bill', and Allan Jones and Irene Dunne sing gloriously together as the old-time showboat cruises through the Mississippi river towns of the nineteenth century.

Nearly all the cast had appeared in the stage version of the show and were therefore well accustomed to their parts. The big surprise, however, was the man chosen to direct the film. It was James Whale, an Englishman noted for his horror films such as *Frankenstein*, *The Old Dark House* and *The Invisible Man*. The experiment, as it turned out, was a huge success.

It says a lot for the professional integrity of Leslie Howard that he insisted on dying in *The Petrified Forest* in which he shared starring honours with Bette Davis. Had the studio bosses had their way the film's ending would have differed from Robert E. Sherwood's original stage play in being less downbeat. Howard would not agree to any change from the original end – and so he dies.

It also says much for Howard that he threatened to pull out of the picture unless they also cast in the film the man who had starred opposite him in the stage show. And that is how Humphrey Bogart got his first major film role.

Bogart plays Duke Mantee, a dangerous killer on the loose after escaping from prison. Howard is a wandering poet and philosopher who falls in love with Bette Davis, a waitress in a motor restaurant. She also loves to paint and hopes that one day she will be able to study art in Paris.

The Petrified Forest, directed by Archie Mayo was a highly marketable drama in its day. It can still hold audiences, even though some of it seems somewhat dated.

In 1936 Errol Flynn's place among the Hollywood superstars was assured with his performance in Warner Brothers' *The Charge of the Light Brigade*. This was made on a larger scale than his previous movie, *Captain Blood*, and is probably the best of all his costume dramas.

The first part of the story is set in India, where Captain

Geoffrey Vickers (Errol Flynn) is serving with the 27th Lancers. While he is there he happens to save the life of a potentate named Surat Khan, during a leopard hunt, a service which the Khan vows to repay. Later, when the Khan has shifted his allegiance to the Russians, he attacks the garrison where Vickers is stationed and wipes it out almost to the last man. Captain Vickers' life, however, is spared by Surat Khan, thereby repaying his debt.

The scene shifts to the Crimean War, where Vickers is still brooding over Surat Khan's treachery. When he learns that Surat Khan is with the Russians at Sebastopol, he leads the men of the 27th on the famous Charge of the Light Brigade – a mission of vengeance – which leads to Surat Khan being killed by Captain Vickers.

The motivation for the charge may have nothing to do with history (in actual fact, it was the 17th Lancers that led the Light Brigade) but it makes one of the finest action sequences ever seen on the screen, with the cameras tracking alongside, or in front of, the charging horses, while shells from the Russian artillery fall among them. The charge on the screen lasts for approximately ten minutes and is, of course, the high spot of the film. It remains to this day one of the best examples of Hollywood hokum. Directed by Michael Curtiz, it has an excellent supporting cast which includes Olivia de Havilland, Patric Knowles, David Niven, C. Aubrey Smith, Nigel Bruce and C. Henry Gordon as the treacherous Surat Khan.

Fury, directed by Fritz Lang, which remains one of the milestones in the history of the cinema in the way that it showed how mob violence and a desire for personal vengeance can lead to a man brutally taking the law into his own hands.

The basic story is a simple one. A traveller arrives in a small town where he is mistaken for a murderer. An attempt is made to lynch him but he escapes, vowing to bring his persecutors to justice. In the unravelling of its story, the film gives us a horrifying picture of the bigotry and vicious small-mindedness that can exist in some small towns in America. As usual, when Hollywood sets out to attack some of the more unedifying aspects of the American scene, it makes a thoroughly good job of it.

Spencer Tracy is the star of this major American film, and he is supported by a strong cast which includes Sylvia Sidney, Bruce Cabot and Walter Abel.

In 1936, Alexander Korda directed *Rembrandt*, in which Charles Laughton gives a splendid portrayal of the artist during his later years.

Korda took his usual care with the historical scenes. The realistic recreation of seventeenth-century Holland is the result of much research by Vincent Korda (Alexander's brother), the designer of the sets. Everything is beautifully captured by the cameras which were controlled by Robert Krasker and Georges Perinal.

Secret Agent was taken by Alfred Hitchcock from Somer-

Leslie Howard and Bette Davis in *The Petrified Forest* (WB)

Errol Flynn in *The Charge of the Light Brigade* (WB)

Spencer Tracy and Sylvia Sidney in *Fury* (MGM)

Peter Lorre in *Secret Agent* (Gau)

Charles Boyer and Danielle Darrieux in *Mayerling* (Nero)

Mireille Ballin and Jean Gabin in *Pepe le Moko* (Paris)

set Maugham's book, *Ashenden* and turned into a gripping thriller with a dead body seated at a church organ as one of the ingredients calculated to send a chill down the spine.

The story has an innocent man being killed by mistake during a search for a spy. The spy is played by the American film star Robert Young, but the hero of the piece is John Gielgud as Edgar Brodie, the man who has been reluctantly recruited by the British to be a spy hunter, accompanied by Madeleine Carroll who has been sent with him to provide him cover as his 'wife'. The film offered John Gielgud his first major film role since his appearance in *The Good Companions* (1933), while Peter Lorre gives one of his fine snake-in-the grass performances as a professional assassin. In this film Hitchcock once more displayed his flair for extracting the maximum suspense from every situation.

France had a tremendous world-wide success with *Mayerling*, which recalls the doomed love affair between Crown Prince Rudolf of Austria and his 17-year-old mistress, Marie Vetsera. In 1889, they were found dead together in the hunting lodge at Mayerling. Rudolf had committed suicide. Marie lay dead in the same room.

Charles Boyer, who plays Rudolf, had established himself as one of the screen's greatest lovers. Millions of fans went weak at the knees at the sound of his low, sexy Gallic voice and at the sight of his soulful eyes.

Mayerling made an international star of Danielle Darrieux, who plays Marie, and it also led to a Hollywood career for director Anatole Litvak.

This year saw the completion in France of Marcel Pagnol's *Marius* trilogy, which consisted of *Marius* (1931) *Fanny* (1932) and *Cesar* (1936). The stories are set along the Marseille waterfront, and are one of the most delightful depictions of French provincial life ever created for the screen.

Cesar, played by that superb French comedian Raimu, is the pivotal character throughout the stories. Many a glorious scene takes place in his little bar around a card table with his cronies who, while they play, exchange wit and hilarious bits of homespun philosophy.

Alexander Korda directed *Marius*, Marc Allegret directed *Fanny*, and Pagnol himself directed *Cesar* – as well as producing and writing the stories for all three.

One of the top French box-office stars for over 40 years was Jean Gabin, not unlike Spencer Tracy in appearance and manner. The Thirties were his best years, and in 1936 he had a big success with *Pepe le Moko* (remade in America shortly afterwards as *Algiers* starring Charles Boyer). Pepe is a French crook living in Algeria, who cannot leave the Casbah, a den of low-life crime without being arrested – and he very much wants to leave when he meets and falls in love with a Parisian charmer (Mireille Ballin). He finally attempts to leave with fatal results to himself.

Pepe le Moko was the top box-office film that year in many parts of the world including Japan where it still retains a popularity on a par with *Casablanca*.

A crime story laced with black comedy was also made this year by Jean Renoir. It is *Le Crime de Monsieur Lange*, and tells of the staff of a failing business who, on learning of their boss's death, sets about turning it into a successful venture. In fact, the boss (Jules Berry) has absconded with his girl friend and the company funds. When he sees that the business is thriving again, he comes back to take over, at which point Monsieur Lange (Rene Lefevre), a hitherto mild little employee, decides to kill him . . .

Renoir was unquestionably one of the master directors of the Thirties, and in 1936, he clearly showed his versatility. His *Une Partie de Campagne (A Day in the Country)* is a delightful, lyrical film based on a story by Guy de Maupassant. It takes a day in 1860 when a Paris ironmonger and his wife and daughter go for a country outing. At a riverside inn they meet two young men, whereupon the daughter falls deeply in love with one of them, while the mother has an afternoon of charming flirtation with the other.

Jean Gabin (I) in *Pepe le Moko* (Paris)

The film is beautiful to look at, which is perhaps not surprising considering the director's father was the world-famous artist Auguste Renoir. *Une Partie de Campagne* was never properly completed, and it was thought that all the prints had been destroyed by the Nazis. But one did survive, and the film was first shown to the public in 1946.

A typical Russian film of the day was a dramatic love story set at the outset of the Revolution called *The Last Night*. Russian film-makers also took time out from making serious films by producing some musicals, one of the most popular of them being Grigori Alexandrov's *Circus*.

An excellent Swedish film made in 1936, directed by Gustaf Molander, is *Intermezzo*. It is the intense love story of a famous – and married – violinist who has an affair with his young protegee. As a consequence of the terrific impact the film made on foreign critics, David O. Selznick decided to remake it in Hollywood with the same leading lady. Thus, English speaking-audiences were introduced to someone who would become a world favourite – Ingrid Bergman.

Rene Lefevre and Jules Berry in *Le Crime de Monsieur Lange* (Oberon)

The great Japanese director Kenji Mizoguchi was well established by the mid-Thirties. He is noted for his sympathetic treatment of the status of women in society, and two films with such a theme were made in 1936.

In *Osaka Elegy*, a young girl endures the humiliations that arise from allowing herself to be seduced by her employer, which she does in order to get the money her family needs. *Sisters of the Gion* shows two geishas: one is brought up in the old ways; the other looks at herself and her role in society through much more contemporary eyes. Both films starred Isuzu Yamada, one of Japan's most renowned actresses.

Also in 1936, Yasujiro Ozu was making his first sound film, *The Only Son*, which shows a mother's distress on discovering that her adored son is married and unemployed, but who finally comes to accept and understand his difficulties and disappointments.

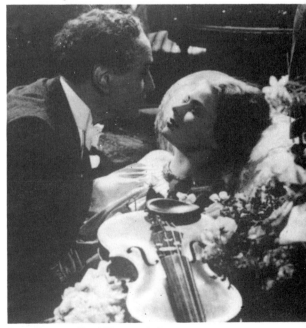
Gosta Ekman and Ingrid Bergman in *Intermezzo* (SF)

Film Favourites 1936

The war drums may have been beating in Germany but elsewhere film-making continued on its joyous way. Jeanette MacDonald and Nelson Eddy were singing their duets in *Rose Marie* (MGM) and Bing Crosby was crooning other sorts of melodies in *Pennies from Heaven* (Col) and *Rhythm on the Range* (Par)

Roy Rogers and Trigger

Boris Karloff

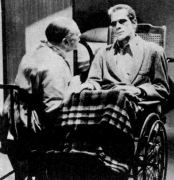

Boris Karloff in *The Walking Dead* (WB)

Charles Chaplin and Paulette Goddard in *Modern Times* (ChC)

Arline Judge and Paul Kelly in *Here Comes Trouble* (Fox)

Stan Laurel and Oliver Hardy favourites throughout the Thirities

Warner Baxter and Myrna Loy in *To Mary with Love* (Fox)

Madge Evans and Bing Crosby in *Pennies from Heaven* (Col)

Left: William Boyd, Muriel Evans and James Ellison in *Three on the Trail* (Par)

Right: William Powell and Virginia Bruce in *The Great Ziegfeld* (MGM)

Humphrey Bogart, star of *The Petrified Forest* (WB)

Norma Shearer in *Romeo and Juliet* (MGM)

Fredric March in *Anthony Adverse* (WB)

Tyrone Power and Madeleine Carroll in *Lloyds of London* (Fox)

Ian Hunter and Kay Francis in *Stolen Holiday* (WB)

Helen Wood and Brian Donlevy in *Crack Up* (Fox)

Patricia Ellis and Warren Hull in *Freshman Love* (WB)

Frank Moran, Shirley Temple and Robert Kent in *Dimples* (Fox)

Kay Francis in *White Angel* (FN)

Freddie Bartholomew in *Little Lord Fauntleroy* (DS)

Left: William Boyd, James Ellison and Gwyne Shipman in *Trail Dust* (Par)

Right: Warner Baxter and Gloria Stuart in *The Prisoner of Shark Island* (Fox)

Johnny Weismuller, Benita Hume and
Maureen O'Sullivan in *Tarzan Escapes* (MGM)

William Powell, Myrna Loy, Jean Harlow
and Spencer Tracy in *Libeled Lady* (MGM)

Ralph Reader and Anna Neagle in *Limelight* (US
Back Stage) (GFD)

Binnie Barnes and Victor McLaglen in *The
Magnificent Brute* (Univ)

Ronald Colman and Claudette Colbert in
Under Two Flags (Fox)

Fred MacMurray and Jean Parker in *The
Texas Rangers* (Par)

Left: Guinn 'Big Boy' Williams, Jack Holt,
Louise Henry in *End of the Trail* (Col)

Right: Ralph Bellamy (l) in *The Final Hour* (Col)

Michael Whalen, Claire Trevor and Paul
Kelly in *Song and Dance Man* (Fox)

Humphrey Bogart and Dick Foran in *Black
Legion* (WB)

Sonnie Hale, Jessie Matthews and Cyril
Raymond in *It's Love Again* (Gau)

Bernadine Hayes and Paul Kelly in *The Accusing Finger* (Par)

Mae Clarke and John Payne in *Hats Off* (GN)

Walter Pidgeon, John Halliday and Mary Ellis in *Fatal Lady* (WdW/Par)

Madge Evans and Bing Crosby in *Rhythm on the Range* (Par)

John Howard and Walter Connolly in *Soak the Rich* (Par)

Beverly Roberts and George Brent in *God's Country and the Woman* (WB)

Left: Ruth Chatterton and Herbert Marshall in *Girl's Dormitory* (Fox)

Right: Herbert Marshall and Gertrude Michael in *Reunion* (Fox)

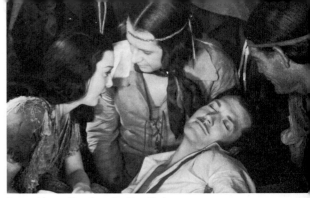

Loretta Young, Don Ameche, Kent Taylor, Pedro de Cordoba and Chief Thundercloud in *Ramona* (Fox)

Jeanette MacDonald and Nelson Eddy in *Rose Marie* (MGM)

Mickey Rooney, Jackie Cooper and Freddie Bartholomew in *The Devil is a Sissy* (MGM)

1. Lilli Palmer
2. Barton MacLane and Glenda Farrell in *Smart Blonde* (WB)
3. Heather Thatcher
4. Paul Kelly, Alan Hale and Rochelle Hudson in *The Country Beyond* (Fox)
5. Claire Trevor and Paul Kelly in *Song and Dance Man* (Fox)
6. Charles King, Earl Dwire, David Sharpe, Rex Bell, Lafe McKee and Marion Shilling in *Idaho Kid* (GN)
7. Jerry Howard (Curly of the Three Stooges)
8. Helen Vinson and Conrad Veidt in *King of the Damned* (Gau)
9. Jan Kiepura, Philip Merivale and Gladys Swarthout in *Give Us This Night* (Par)
10. George Meeker
11. Gertrude Michael and Lionel Atwill in *Till We Meet Again* (Par)
12. Eleanore Whitney and Tom Brown in *Rose Bowl* (Par)
13. Paul Cavanagh and Margot Grahame in *Crime Over London* (Cri)

Picture Gallery for 1936

9 △ ▽ 12

10 △ ▽ 13

1

2

3

4

5

6

7

8

9

1. David Niven, Virginia Field and Arthur Treacher in *Thank You, Jeeves!* (Fox)

2. Katherine DeMille and Joel McCrea in *Banjo on my Knee*

3. Gregory Ratoff, Claudette Colbert and Ronald Colman in *Under Two Flags* (Fox)

4. Robert Barratt and Dick Foran in *Trailin' West* (GB *On Secret Service*) (FN)

5. Desmond Tester

6. Alan Dinehart and Warner Oland in *Charlie Chan at the Race Track* (Fox)

7. Cecilia Parker and Russell Hopton in *Below the Deadline* (Che)

8. Lew Ayres in *Panic on the Air* (Col)

9. Harry Cording

10. Rosalind Russell and George Raft in *It Had to Happen* (GB *Lady of Secrets*) (Col)

11. Robert Armstrong and Betty Furness in *All American Chump* (MGM)

12. Cary Grant, Joan Bennett and William Demarest in *Wedding Present* (Par)

13. Randolph Scott and Frances Drake in *And Sudden Death* (Par)

14. Ann Sothern, Gene Raymond and Eric Blore in *Smartest Girl in Town* (RKO)

10

11 △ ▽ 13

12 △ ▽ 14

1

2

3

4

5

6

7

8

9

10   11

12

1. Warren Hymer, Erin O'Brien Moore, Jean Rouverol, Norman Foster and Donald Cook in *The Leavenworth Case* (Rep)
2. Loretta Young and Franchot Tone in *Unguarded Hour* (MGM)
3. Penelope Dudley Ward and Laurence Olivier in *I Stand Condemned* (UA)
4. Joel McCrea and Joan Bennett in *Two in a Crowd* (Univ)
5. Charles Starrett and Joan Perry in *The Mysterious Avenger* (Col)
6. Laurence Olivier and Elisabeth Bergner in *As You Like It* (Fox/IA)
7. Wendy Barrie and Roger Pryor in *Ticket to Paradise* (Rep)
8. Alma Lloyd and Warren Hull in *The Big Noise* (GB *Modern Madness*) (WB)
9. Jean Muir and Michael Whalen in *White Fang* (Fox)
10. Raymond Massey and Margaretta Scott in *Things to Come* (LF)
11. Raymond Massey in *Things to Come* (LF)
12. Ginger Rogers and Fred Astaire in *Follow the Fleet* (RKO)
13. Ralph Bellamy and Fay Wray in *Roaming Lady* (Col)
14. Paul Robeson and Elizabeth Welch in *Song of Freedom* (Hammer)
15. Katherine DeMille and Kent Taylor in *The Sky Parade* (Par)
16. Ray Walker, Evalyn Knapp and Regis Toomey in *Bulldog Edition* (Rep)
17. George Regas
18. Jane Darwell, Shirley Dean, Johnny Downs, and Gene Lockhart in *The First Baby* (Fox)
19. Cecilia Parker in *In His Steps* (GN)
20. Lew Ayres in *The Leathernecks Have Landed* (Rep)
21. Marguerite Churchill and William Gargan in *Man Hunt* (WB)
22. Ken Maynard and Beth Marion in *The Fugitive Sheriff* (Col)

13   14

15

16   17

18   19   20

21   22

1. Elissa Landi and Douglas Fairbanks Jr in *The Amateur Gentleman* (Cri)
2. Kay Linaker and Donald Woods in *Road Gang* (FN)
3. John Carroll and Steffi Duna in *Hi Gaucho!* (RKO)
4. George Ernest
5. Frank McHugh, Dick Powell, Joan Blondell and Warren William in *Stage Struck* (FN)
6. George O'Brien in *Daniel Boone* (RKO)
7. Gertrude Michael and Herbert Marshall in *Make Way for a Lady* (ZM/RKO)
8. William Boyd, George Hayes, Muriel Evans and James Ellison in *Call of the Prairie* (Par)
9. Mary Astor and Ricardo Cortez in *The Murder of Dr Harrigan* (FN)
10. Edmund Lowe and Constance Cummings in *Seven Sinners* (US *Doomed Cargo*) (Gau)

1

2

5

4

3

8 △ ▽ 9

6   7 △ ▽ 10

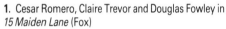

1. Cesar Romero, Claire Trevor and Douglas Fowley in
15 Maiden Lane (Fox)

2. Simone Simon and Tyrone Power in *Girls' Dormitory* (Fox)

3. Gertrude Astor and Buck Jones in *Empty Saddles* (Univ)

4. Ann Dvorak and John Beal in *We Who Are About to Die* (RKO)

5. Joel McCrea and Jean Arthur in *Adventure in Manhattan* (GB
Manhattan Madness) (Col)

6. Chester Morris, Walter Brennan and Lewis Stone in *The Three
Godfathers* (MGM/Arg)

7. Pat O'Brien, Margaret Lindsay and Robert Armstrong in *Public
Enemy's Wife* (GB *G-Man's Wife*) (WB)

8. Robert Taylor and Janet Gaynor in *Small Town Girl* (MGM)

9. Hugh Herbert, Una Merkel, Charles Butterworth, Edith
Atwater and Walter Abel in *We Went to College* (GB *The Old
School Tie*) (MGM)

10. Anne Shirley and Erik Rhodes in *Chatterbox* (RKO)

11. Raymond Walburn and Melvyn Douglas in *The Lone Wolf
Returns* (Col)

12. Fred Kohler and Fred MacMurray in *The Texas Rangers* (Par)

8 △ ▽ 10

9 △ ▽ 12

11

1

2　3

4　5

6

7 △ ▽ 10

8　9

1. Ray Walker (l) in *The Crime Patrol* (Emp)
2. Warren Hull and Margaret Lindsay in *The Law in her Hands* (FN)
3. John Boles and Rosalind Russell in *Craig's Wife* (Col)
4. Edward Ellis, Frances Drake and Clarke Williams in *Transient Lady* (Univ)
5. Claude Rains
6. Grace Bradley, Fred MacMurray and Joan Bennett in *Thirteen Hours by Air* (Par)
7. Joe E Brown and June Travis in *Earthworm Tractors* (GB *A Natural Born Salesman*) (WB)
8. Ray Corrigan
9. Mary Boland, Charles Ruggles and Gail Patrick in *Early to Bed* (Par)
10. Joe E Brown in *Earthworm Tractors* (GB *A Natural Born Salesman*) (WB)

1. Fredric March and Olivia de Havilland in *Anthony Adverse* (WB)
2. Irving Pichel
3. Richard Arlen and Norman Willis in *Secret Valley* (Fox)
4. Barbara Stanwyck and John Boles in *A Message to Garcia* (Fox)
5. Cecil B. DeMille
6. Mischa Auer
7. Jack Haley and Grace Bradley in *F Man* (Par)
8. Sybil Jason and Al Jolson in *The Singing Kid* (FN)
9. Roscoe Karns, Gertrude Michael and George Murphy in *Woman Trap* (Par)
10. Charles Laughton and Roger Livesey in *Rembrandt* (LF)
11. Warner Baxter and Myrna Loy in *To Mary – with Love* (Fox)
12. Boris Karloff and Frank Cellier in *The Man Who Lived Again* (Gau)
13. The Three Stooges in *Ants in the Pantry* (Col)
14. George Burns, Gracie Allen and Jack Benny in *College Holiday* (Par)

10 △ ▽ 12

11 △ ▽ 14

13

1. Peter Lorre and John Gielgud in *Secret Agent* (Gau)

2. Kenneth Howell and Dixie Dunbar in *Educating Father* (Fox)

3. Sylvia Sidney and Spencer Tracy in *Fury* (MGM)

4. John Gielgud and Peter Lorre in *Secret Agent* (Gau)

5. Tom London, George O'Brien and Roy Mason in *The Border Patrolman* (Fox)

6. Brian Aherne, Merle Oberon and David Niven in *Beloved Enemy* (SG)

7. Merle Oberon and Joel McCrea in *These Three* (SG)

8. Miriam Hopkins and Rex Harrison in *Men Are Not Gods* (LF)

9. Katherine Alexander, Leo Carrillo and Benita Hume in *Moonlight Murder* (MGM)

10. Lili Damita

11. Rex Bell and Joan Barclay in *West of Nevada* (Coy)

12. Bing Crosby, Ethel Merman and Charles Ruggles in *Anything Goes* (Par)

6   7

8 △ ▽ 11   9 △ ▽ 12

10

306

1

2

3

4

5

6

7

1. Hobart Bosworth and William V Mong in *The Dark Hour* (Che)
2. William Davidson, Dick Powell, Joan Blondell and Lee Dixon in *Gold Diggers of 1937* (FN)
3. Paulette Goddard and Charles Chaplin in *Modern Times* (ChC)
4. Diana Gibson and Jack Holt in *Dangerous Waters* (Univ)
5. Humphrey Bogart and Joan Blondell in *Bullets and Ballots* (FN)
6. Humphrey Bogart and Robert E Homans in *Black Legion* (WB)
7. Edward Arnold, Joan Perry, Victor Jory and Lionel Stander in *Meet Nero Wolfe* (Col)
8. Fredric March, June Lang and Warner Baxter in *Road to Glory* (Fox)
9. Joyce Compton, Nat Pendleton, Mary Astor and Lyle Talbot in *Trapped by Television* (Col)
10. Keye Luke (I), J Carrol Naish, Francis Ford and Warner Oland in *Charlie Chan at the Circus* (Fox)
11. Gloria Stuart in *The Girl on the Front Page* (Univ)

8 △ ▽ 10

9 △ ▽ 11

1

4   5   6

7

8   9

10 △ ▽ 11

1. Marian Marsh and Ruth Chatterton in *Lady of Secrets* (BPS/Col)
2. Florence Rice and William Gargan in *The Blackmailer* (Col)
3. Grady Sutton and Arline Judge in *Pigskin Parade* (GB *Harmony Parade*) (Fox)
4. Robert Cummings, Tom Keene, Marsha Hunt, Raymond Hatton and Larry 'Buster' Crabbe in *Desert Gold* (Par)
5. Clark Gable and Jeanette MacDonald in *San Francisco* (MGM)
6. Oscar Polk and Rex Ingram in *The Green Pastures* (WB)
7. Tom Keene, Marsha Hunt and Larry 'Buster' Crabbe in *Desert Gold* (Par)
8. Otto Kruger and Gloria Holden in *Dracula's Daughter* (Univ)
9. Gene Morgan, Marguerite Churchill, William Gargan, Egon Brocher, Drue Leyton, Raymond Lawrence and Romaine Callender in *Alibi for Murder* (Col)
10. William Gargan and Marguerite Churchill in *Alibi for Murder* (Col)
11. Mary Astor, Edith Fellows, Jack Moran and

Melvyn Douglas in *And So They Were Married* (Col)
12. Gene Autry, Ann Rutherford and Smiley Burnett (r) in *Comin' 'Round the Mountain* (Rep)
13. Frances Langford and Joe Penner in *Collegiate* (Par)
14. Eddie Acuff, June Travis and Craig Reynolds in *Jailbreak* (GB *Murder in the Big House*) (WB)
15. James Ellison and William Boyd in *Three on the Trail* (Par)
16. Madeleine Carroll
17. Frank McHugh, Joan Blondell and Sam Levene in *Three Men on a Horse* (FN)
18. Barton MacLane, Kathleen Lockhart, Warren William and Gene Lockhart in *Times Square Playboy* (GB *His Best Man*) (WB)
19. William Boyd and George 'Gabby' Hayes in *Trail Dust* (Par)
20. Douglass Montgomery and Constance Bennett in *Everything is Thunder* (Gau)
21. Deanna Durbin and Judy Garland in *Every Sunday* (MGM)
22. Bob Steel (r) in *Cavalry* (Rep)
23. Katharine Hepburn and John Carradine in *Mary of Scotland* (RKO)

12

13

14

16

15

18

17 △ ▽ 21

20 △ ▽ 23

19 △ ▽ 22

1

4

5

2

6

3

8

9

10

1. Paul Robeson in *Showboat* (Univ)
2. Allan Jones and Irene Dunne in *Showboat* (Univ)
3. Paul Robeson, Irene Dunne, Hattie McDaniel and Helen Morgan in *Showboat* (Univ)
4. Paul Robeson in *Showboat* (Univ)
5. Allan Jones in *Showboat* (Univ)
6. Cary Grant and Jean Harlow in *Suzy* (MGM)
7. Allan Jones and Irene Dunne in *Showboat* (Univ)
8. Rochelle Hudson, Johnny Downs and Irvin S Cobb in *Everybody's Old Man* (Fox)
9. Ann Sothern, Douglass Dumbrille and Lloyd Nolan in *You May Be Next* (Col)
10. Warren William and Bette Davis in *Satan Met a Lady* (WB)
11. Harry Jans, Bruce Cabot and Grace Bradley in *Don't Turn 'Em Loose* (RKO)
12. Freddie Bartholomew and Dolores Costello in *Little Lord Fauntleroy* (DS)
13. Barbara Stanwyck and Preston Foster in *The Plough and the Stars* (RKO)
14. C Aubrey Smith and Freddie Bartholomew in *Little Lord Fauntleroy* (DS)

11 △ ▽ 13

12 △ ▽ 14

1

2

4

5

6 △ ▽ 9

7

8

10 △ ▽ 12

11 △ ▽ 13

1. Spencer Tracy and Myrna Loy in *Whipsaw* (MGM)

2. Madeleine Carroll and Gary Cooper in *The General Died at Dawn* (Par)

3. Jameson Thomas in *Lady Luck* (Che)

4. Robert Taylor and Joan Crawford in *The Gorgeous Hussy* (MGM)

5. Chester Morris and Fay Wray in *They Met in a Taxi* (Col)

6. Patric Knowles, Viola Keats, George Arliss and Gene Gerrard in *Mr Hobo* (Gau)

7. Anita Louise, Ross Alexander and Dick Purcell in *Brides Are Like That* (FN)

8. Sharon Lynne, James Finlayson, Oliver Hardy and Stan Laurel in *Way Out West* (HR)

9. Humphrey Bogart, Leslie Howard and Bette Davis in *The Petrified Forest* (WB)

10. Patricia Ellis and Warren Hull in *Freshman Love* (GB *Rhythm on the River*) (WB)

11. Alison Skipworth, Ian Hunter and Kay Francis in *Stolen Holiday* (FN)

12. Dick Powell and Marion Davies in *Hearts Divided* (Cos/FN)

13. Reginald Owen, Myrna Loy and Robert Montgomery in *Petticoat Fever* (MGM)

311

1. Stan Laurel and Oliver Hardy in *The Bohemian Girl* (HR)
2. Fred Stone, Moroni Olsen, Jean Parker and Frank Albertson in *The Farmer in the Dell* (RKO)
3. Warner Oland, Margaret Irving and William Demarest in *Charlie Chan at the Opera* (Fox)
4. Walter Pidgeon
5. Elissa Landi and Edmund Lowe in *Mad Holiday* (MGM)
6. Jackie Cooper and Joseph Calleia in *Tough Guy* (MGM)
7. Henry O'Neill, Bette Davis and George Brent in *The Golden Arrow* (FN)
8. Richard Arlen in *Mine with the Iron Door* (Pri)
9. Edmund Gwenn in *The Walking Dead* (WB)
10. Lew Ayres in *Lady Be Careful* (Par)
11. Eleanor Powell in *Born to Dance* (MGM)

1. Shirley Temple in *Dimples* (Fox)
2. Slim Summerville, Shirley Temple, Guy Kibbee and Buddy Ebsen in *Captain January* (Fox)
3. James Stewart and Margaret Sullavan in *Next Time We Love* (GB *Next Time We Live*) (Univ)
4. Ian Hunter in *The White Angel* (FN)
5. Pat O'Brien
6. Bobby Breen, May Robson and Benita Hume in *Rainbow on the River* (SL)
7. Warner Baxter in *Prisoner of Shark Island* (Fox)
8. Spring Byington in *Hotel Haywire* (Par)
9. Irene Dunne and Melvyn Douglas in *Theodora Goes Wild* (Col)
10. Beverly Roberts, Pat O'Brien and Ross Alexander in *China Clipper* (FN)
11. Minna Gombell, Helen Wood and Paul Cavanagh in *Champagne Charlie* (Fox)

1

4   5   6

7   8   9

1. Felix Aylmer, Leslie Perrins and Cedric Hardwicke in *Tudor Rose* (US *Nine Days a Queen*) (G'boro)
2. Charles Ruggles and Mary Boland in *Wives Never Know* (Par)
3. Ann Harding and Walter Abel in *The Witness Chair* (RKO)
4. Fred MacMurray, Sylvia Sidney and Henry Fonda in *Trail of the Lonesome Pine* (Par)
5. Frances Farmer in *Too Many Parents* (Par)
6. H B Warner, Frieda Inescort, Gene Lockhart, Edmund Lowe, Kent Smith and Benita Hume in *The Garden Murder Case* (MGM)
7. Harry Carey and Gladys George in *Valiant is the Word for Carrie* (Par)
8. Edward Arnold and Frances Farmer in *Come and Get It* (SG)
9. Sheila Terry, Richard Dix and Erik Rhodes in *Special Investigator* (RKO)
10. Alan Mowbray and Janet Gaynor in *Ladies in Love* (Fox)
11. Jean Harlow, Clark Gable, May Robson and Myrna Loy in *Wife Versus Secretary* (MGM)
12. Binnie Barnes and Heather Angel in *The Last of the Mohicans* (ES)
13. Ross Alexander and Anne Nagel in *Hot Money* (WB)

10 △ ▽ 12   11 △ ▽ 13

1

2   3

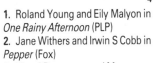

4

5   6

1. Roland Young and Eily Malyon in
One Rainy Afternoon (PLP)
2. Jane Withers and Irwin S Cobb in
Pepper (Fox)
3. Lionel Barrymore and Maureen
O'Sullivan in *The Voice of Bugle Ann*
(MGM)
4. Frances Farmer and Bing Crosby
in *Rhythm On the Range* (Par)
5. Judith Barrett, Mary Gordon and
Alan Hale in *Yellowstone* (Univ)
6. Dolores Costello and George Raft
in *Yours for the Asking* (Par)
7. Joan Woodbury (s) and Jack
Mulhall (st) in *The Rogues Tavern*
(Par)
8. Robert Montgomery, Frank
Morgan and Billie Burke in *Piccadilly
Jim* (MGM)
9. Ann Sothern and Gene Raymond
in *Walking on Air* (RKO)
10. Eddie Quillan (l) in *Gentleman
from Louisiana* (Rep)
11. Tom Tyler, Joan Barclay and
Roger Williams in *Ridin' On* (Rel/WS)
12. Henry Stephenson, Ann Sothern
and Jessie Ralph in *Walking on Air*
(RKO)
13. Loretta Young and Robert Taylor
in *Private Number* (GB *Secret
Interlude* (Fox)

7   8

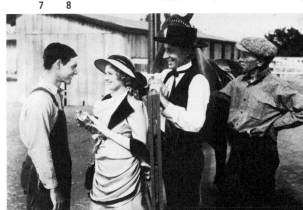

9 △ ▽ 12   10 △ ▽ 13

11

1 2

3 4 5

6 △ ▽ 9

7 △ ▽ 10

8

11 △ ▽ 12

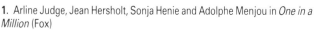

1. Arline Judge, Jean Hersholt, Sonja Henie and Adolphe Menjou in *One in a Million* (Fox)
2. Margaret Seddon and Big Boy Williams in *The Big Game* (RKO)
3. Hedda Hopper, Louise Latimer and Owen Davis Jr in *Bunker Bean* (RKO)
4. John Wayne and Jean Rogers in *Conflict* (Univ)
5. June Lang and Warner Baxter in *White Hunter* (Fox)
6. Binnie Barnes and Edward Arnold in *Sutter's Gold* (Univ)
7. Spring Byington, Tom London, Jed Prouty and Kenneth Powell in *Every Saturday Night* (Fox)
8. Jean Howard, John Dilson and Ralph Bellamy in *The Final Hour* (Col)
9. Dorothy Lamour and Ray Milland in *The Jungle Princess* (Par)
10. Derrick De Marney in *Land without Music* (Cap)
11. Barbara Stanwyck and Robert Taylor in *His Brother's Wife* (MGM)
12. William Powell, Carole Lombard and Alice Brady in *My Man Godfrey* (Univ)
13. Jack Holt, Douglass Dumbrille, Blackie Whiteford, Art Mix and 'Black Jack' Ward in *End of the Trail* (Col)
14. Gene Autry and Smiley Burnette in *Guns and Guitars* (Rep)
15. Yakima Canutt and John Wayne in *King of the Pecos* (Rep)
16. J P McGowan, Charles Starrett and Finis Barton in *Stampede* (Col)
17. Ken Maynard and John Elliot in *Avenging Waters* (Col)
18. Rex Bell in *Stormy Trails* (Coy)
19. Billy Burrud and Buck Jones in *The Cowboy and the Kid* (Univ)
20. David Holt and Andy Clyde in *Straight from the Shoulder* (Par)
21. Smiley Burnette, Gene Autry and Lois Wilde in *The Singing Cowboy* (Rep)
22. Nelson Eddy and Jeanette MacDonald in *Rose Marie* (MGM)

13

14   **15**

16   **17**

18 △ ▽ 21   **19 △ ▽ 22**   **20**

1

2

3

4 5

6

7

8

9

1. Pauline Frederick, Kent Taylor, Loretta Young, Pedro De Cordoba, Don Ameche and Chief Thundercloud in *Ramona* (Fox)
2. Dewey Robinson, Rochelle Hudson and W C Fields in *Poppy* (Par)
3. Esther Dale, George Brent, Madeleine Carroll in *The Case Against Mrs Ames* (WaW/Par)
4. ZaSu Pitts, James Melton and Patricia Ellis in *Sing Me a Love Song* (GB *Come Up Smiling*) (FN)
5. Mary Astor in *Lady from Nowhere* (Col)
6. Gene Raymond and Lily Pons in *That Girl from Paris* (RKO)
7. Frank Orth and Joe E Brown in *Polo Joe* (WB)
8. Erik Rhodes, Gertrude Michael and Walter Abel in *Second Wife* (RKO)
9. John King, Nan Grey and Jack Holt in *Crash Donovan* (Univ)
10. Jane Withers and Jackie Searl in *Gentle Julia* (Fox)
11. Marion Shilling and Fred Scott in *Romance Rides the Range* (Spe)

10 11

1. Betty Lawford, Preston Foster, Carole Lombard and Cesar Romero in *Love Before Breakfast* (Univ)
2. Jean Hersholt and J Edward Bromberg in *Reunion* (DZ/Fox)
3. Claire Trevor and Donald Woods in *Big Town Girl* (Fox)
4. Helen Vinson and Clive Brook in *Love in Exile* (Cap)
5. Myrna Loy and William Powell in *After the Thin Man* (MGM)
6. Ruth Donnelly
7. Margo and Burgess Meredith in *Winterset* (RKO)
8. Paul Kelly and Marsha Hunt in *The Accusing Finger* (Par)
9. Michael Whalen, Shirley Temple and Sara Haden in *Poor Little Rich Girl* (Fox)
10. John 'Fuzzy' Knight
11. Claire Dodd, Warren William and Wini Shaw in *Case of the Velvet Claws* (FN)
12. Alan Mowbray, Marlene Dietrich, Gary Cooper and Ernest Cossart in *Desire* (Par)

319

1. Johnny Weissmuller in *Tarzan Escapes* (MGM)
2. George Bancroft
3. Mae West and Victor McLaglen in *Klondike Annie* (Par)
4. Johnny Weissmuller and Maureen O'Sullivan in *Tarzan Escapes* (MGM)
5. Robert Young and Shirley Temple in *Stowaway* (Fox)
6. Brian Donlevy and Claire Trevor in *Human Cargo* (Fox)
7. Doris Nolan, Skeets Gallagher, Michael Whalen and Cliff Edwards in *The Man I Marry* (Univ)
8. Mickey Rooney and Patricia Ellis in *Down the Stretch* (FN)
9. Alice Faye, Patsy Kelly and Gregory Ratoff in *Sing, Baby Sing* (Fox)
10. Leif Erickson and Virginia Weidler in *Girl of the Ozarks* (Par)
11. Adolph Menjou, Alice Faye and Michael Whalen in *Sing, Baby Sing* (Fox)
12. Binnie Barnes, Victor McLaglen and William Hall in *The Magnificent Brute* (Univ)

1. Elsie Randolf in *This'll Make you Whistle* (HW)
2. Joan Marsh and Eddie Nugent in *Dancing Feet* (Rep)
3. Stuart Erwin, Margaret Irving, Franchot Tone, Louise Henry and Madge Evans in *Exclusive Story* (MGM)
4. Ted Healy, Patricia Wilder and James Stewart in *Speed* (MGM)
5. Freddie Bartholomew, Mickey Rooney and Jackie Cooper in *The Devil is a Sissy* (MGM)
6. Greta Garbo and Robert Taylor in *Camille* (MGM)
7. June Lang and Michael Whalen in *The Country Doctor* (Fox)
8. Basil Rathbone, Marlene Dietrich and Charles Boyer in *Garden of Allah* (DS)
9. Ann Rutherford, Ben Lyon and Russell Hardy in *Down to the Sea* (Rep)
10. Betty Compson and John Halliday in *Hollywood Boulevard* (Par)
11. Russell Hardy and Ann Rutherford in *Down to the Sea* (Rep)

7 △ ▽ 10

9 △ ▽ 11

1

2 3

4 5

6

7 8

1. Jack Oakie and Sally Eilers in *Florida Special* (Par)
2. Robert Cummings and Eleanore Whitney in *Three Cheers for Love* (Par)
3. Frances Langford, Sir Guy Standing and Ernest Cossart in *Palm Springs* (GB *Palm Springs Affair*) (Par)
4. Spencer Tracy, Jean Harlow and William Powell in *Libeled Lady* (MGM)
5. Wheeler Oakman, Tim McCoy and Walter Miller in *Ghost Patrol* (Pur)
6. Frances Farmer and Grant Withers in *Border Flight* (Par)
7. Douglas Dumbrille, Donald Cook and Charlotte Wynters in *The Calling of Dan Matthews* (Col)
8. Mae West and Randolph Scott in *Go West Young Man* (Par)
9. Bill Cody
10. Ethel Jackson
11. Cecilia Parker
12. Rose Hobart
13. Lila Lee
14. Pauline Brooks

11 △ ▽ 13

12 △ ▽ 14

9 10

1 2

3

4 5

6 △ ▽ 9

7 △ ▽ 10

8

1. Gracie Allen, Jack Benny, Ray Milland and George Burns in *The Big Broadcast of 1937* (Par)
2. Frank McHugh, Glenda Farrell, John Eldredge, Genevieve Tobin, Patricia Ellis and George Brent in *Snowed Under* (FN)
3. Lane Chandler and John Wayne in *Winds of the Wasteland* (Rep)
4. Reginald Gardiner
5. Frank Rice, John Wayne and Harry Harvey in *The Oregon Trail* (Rep)
6. Syd Saylor, Tex Ritter and Snub Pollard in *Headin' for the Rio Grande* (GN)
7. Humphrey Bogart, Margaret Lindsay and Donald Woods in *Isle of Fury* (WB)
8. Irving Bacon, Harry Richman, Jack Pennick and Rochelle Hudson in *The Music Goes Round* (Col)
9. John Wayne, George Humbert and John 'Fuzzy' Knight in *The Sea Spoilers* (Univ)
10. Esther Ralston

2

4

6

1

5 △ ▽ 9

8 △ ▽ 11

7 △ ▽ 10

12

13

14

The Charge of the Light Brigade (WB) was, as one would expect, a film epic in the true sense of the word. The action of the movie was split between the first part devoted to adventures on the North West Frontier of India and the second to the war in the Crimea. It is still a great success whenever and wherever it is shown.

1. Errol Flynn leads the charge
2. Dismounted action for the 27th Lancers
3. Olivia de Havilland and Patric Knowles
4. Olivia de Havilland and Errol Flynn
5. The tribesmen attack the fort
6. Spring Byington, Patric Knowles, Olivia de Havilland and Nigel Bruce
7. Olivia de Havilland, Errol Flynn and David Niven
8. Manning the ramparts
9. Errol Flynn
10. Helen Sanborn
11. Errol Flynn and Scotty Beckett
12. Errol Flynn
13. Cannon to right of them, cannon to left of them
14. Olivia de Havilland and Errol Flynn
15. Patric Knowles
16. David Niven, Errol Flynn and Donald Crisp
17. The tribesmen massacre the lancers and their womenfolk

continued on the next page

15 △ ▽ 16

17

1

2 3

4 5

7 8 △ ▽ 10

6 △ ▽ 9

11

12 **13**

14 **15**

The Charge of the Light Brigade continued

1 **11 & 12.** Olivia de Havilland and Patric Knowles
2 3 **13 & 16.** Olivia de Havilland and Errol Flynn
4. Patric Knowles, Olivia de Havilland and Errol Flynn
5. Errol Flynn
6. Henry Stephenson
7. Donald Crisp, Olivia de Havilland and Errol Flynn
8. Patric Knowles, Nigel Bruce and Spring Byington
9. Errol Flynn
10. (Centre Group) Patric Knowles, Olivia de Havilland, Donald Crisp, Spring Byington and Errol Flynn
14. Errol Flynn, David Niven, Walter Holbrook, E E Clive, Charles Sedgwick and Charles David
15. Patric Knowles, Olivia de Havilland and Errol Flynn
17. Olivia de Havilland, Spring Byington and Patric Knowles
18. Patric Knowles and Olivia de Havilland
19. Spring Byington, Nigel Bruce and Donald Crisp
20. Olivia de Havilland

16 △ ▽ 18

▽ 19

17 △ ▽ 20

1

2 3

Romeo and Juliet (MGM) was treated with true Hollywood reverence. It was another of the studio's star-studded movies.

1. Leslie Howard
2. Leslie Howard and Norma Shearer
3. Norma Shearer
4. Edna May Oliver, C Aubrey Smith, Violet Kemble Cooper and Norma Shearer
5. Norma Shearer
6. Leslie Howard, Basil Rathbone and John Barrymore
7. John Barrymore
8. Basil Rathbone
9. Katherine DeMille
10. Ralph Forbes
11. Violet Kemble Cooper
12. C Aubrey Smith
13. John Barrymore
14. Reginald Denny and John Barrymore
15. Reginald Denny, Basil Rathbone and John Barrymore
16. Leslie Howard and Edna May Oliver
17. Violet Kemble Cooper, Edna May Oliver, Norma Shearer and C Aubrey Smith
18. Reginald Denny and Basil Rathbone
19. Reginald Denny, John Barrymore, Leslie Howard and Basil Rathbone

4 5

6 7

8

9 10

11   12   13

14

15   16

17   18   19

1

2 3

4

5 6

7 8

9 △ ▽ 12

10 △ ▽ 13   11 △ ▽ 14

15 16 17

18 19

20 21

22 △ ▽ 24   23 △ ▽ 25

1. Marjorie Gateson, Cary Grant and Joan Bennett in *Big Brown Eyes* (Par)
2. Marian Nixon in *Tango* (Inv)
3. Johnny Mack Brown in *Undercover Man* (Rep)
4. James Burke (c) and Gertrude Michael in *Forgotten Faces* (Par)
5. Billy Gilbert (r) in *Three of a Kind* (Inv)
6. Kermit Maynard and Roger Williams in *Wildcat Trooper* (Amb)
7. Ray Milland
8. James Dunn, Mae Clarke and Fritz Lieber in *Hearts in Bondage* (Rep)
9. Joan Blondell and Joe E Brown in *Sons O' Guns* (WB)
10. Roland Young
11. Donald Cook in *Ring Around the Moon* (Che)
12. Jean Parker and Robert Donat in *The Ghost Goes West* (LF)
13. Leonora Corbett and Otto Kruger in *Living Dangerously* (BIP)
14. Sara Haden, Jane Withers and Slim Summerville in *Can This Be Dixie?* (SW/Fox)
15. Gene Raymond and Helen Broderick in *The Bride Walks Out* (RKO)
16. Catherine Cotter, Bill Cody and Bill Cody Jr in *Outlaws of the Range* (Spe)
17. Tom Keene, Rita Cansino (Hayworth) and Duncan Renaldo in *Rebellion* (Cre)
18. Hoot Gibson, Harry Carey and Henry B Walthall in *The Last Outlaw* (RKO)
19. Lois Wild, Francis X Bushman Jr and Rin Tin Tin Jr in *Caryl of the Mountains* (Rel/WS)
20. Brian Donlevy and Frances Dee in *Half Angel* (Fox)
21. Whitney Bourne and Jimmy Savo in *Once in a Blue Moon* (Par)
22. Bob Livingston and Heather Angel in *The Bold Caballero* (Rep)
23. Phillips Holmes, Mae Clarke and Irving Pichel in *The House of a Thousand Candles* (Rep)
24. Henry Wilcoxon and Betty Furness in *The President's Mystery* (Rep)
25. Mae Clarke and James Cagney in *Great Guy* (GN)

331

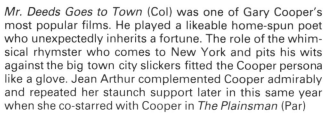

Mr. Deeds Goes to Town (Col) was one of Gary Cooper's most popular films. He played a likeable home-spun poet who unexpectedly inherits a fortune. The role of the whimsical rhymster who comes to New York and pits his wits against the big town city slickers fitted the Cooper persona like a glove. Jean Arthur complemented Cooper admirably and repeated her staunch support later in this same year when she co-starred with Cooper in *The Plainsman* (Par)

1. Gary Cooper and Jean Arthur
2. Gary Cooper and Lionel Stander
3. Jean Arthur and Gary Cooper
4. Jean Arthur
5. Lionel Stander, Muriel Evans and Gary Cooper
6. Raymond Walburn and Gary Cooper
7. Lionel Stander, Gary Cooper and H B Warner (foreground)
8. Gary Cooper, H B Warner, Gustav Von Seyffertitz and Douglas Dumbrille

5△ ▽7

6△ ▽8

1. Bruce Seton and Ann Harding in *Love from a Stranger* (Tra)
2. Helen Vinson
3. Ned Sparks and Gordon Harker in *Two's Company* (B&D)
4. Eddie Cantor (l) in *Strike me Pink* (SG)
5. Cicely Courtneidge and Ernest Truex in *Everybody Dance* (G'boro)
6. Charles Chaplin
7. Melvyn Douglas
8. Lucie Mannheim and George Arliss in *East Meets West* (Gau)
9. Etta McDaniel and Ann Rutherford in *The Lonely Trail* (Rep)
10. Walter C Kelly and Phil Regan in *Laughing Irish Eyes* (Rep)
11. Hazel Forbes and Nils Asther in *The Marriage of Corbal* (US *The Prisoner of Corbal* (Cap)

7△ ▽ 9

8 △ ▽10

1   2

3   4   5

6   7   8

9 △   10 △ ▽ 12   11 △ ▽ 13

14 15

16

1. Arthur Lake and Theodore Von Eltz in *I Cover Chinatown* (Stn)
2. Guy Kibbee, Sybil Jason, Jane Bryan and Dick Purcell in *The Captain's Kid* (FN)
3. Fred Kohler, Georgie Bellings, Ralph Bellamy and Gloria Shea in *Dangerous Intrigue* (Col)
4. Ann Sothern in *Don't Gamble with Love* (Col)
5. Ken Maynard in *The Cattle Thief* (Col)
6. Margaret Morris(s) and Conway Tearle(s) in *Desert Guns* (Bet)
7. Tim McCoy and Joan Woodbury in *The Lions Den* (Pur)
8. Alan Hale, Walter Abel, Margot Grahame and Wallace Ford in *Two in the Dark* (RKO)
9. Paul Guilfoyle, June Clayworth and James Dunn in *Two-Fisted Gentlemen* (Col)
10. Paul Stanton , Sara Haden, Robert Kent, Gloria Stuart, in *The Crime of Dr Forbes* (Fox)
11. William Boyd, Sidney Blackmer and James Ellison in *Heart Of The West* (Par)
12. Douglas Walton and Steffi Duna in *I Conquer the Sea* (AP)
13. Rod La Rocque and Ian Keith in *The Preview Murder Mystery* (Par)
14. Evelyn Venable, J Edward Bromberg and Jane Darwell in *Star for a Night* (Fox)
15. Margaret Sullavan, Henry Fonda and Charles Butterworth in *The Moon's Our Home* (Par)
16. Victor Varconi, Steffi Duna and Frank Morgan in *Dancing Pirate* (RKO)
17. Kay Francis, Roland Young, Helen Flint, Patric Knowles, Frieda Ivescourt and George Brent in *Give Me Your Heart* (GB *Sweet Aloes*) (WB)
18. Katherine Hepburn, David Manners and Herbert Marshall in *A Woman Rebels* (RKO)
19. Montagu Love, Arthur Hohl and Reginald Barlow in *Lloyds of London* (Fox)

▽18   17 △ ▽19

1

2

3

4

5

6

7

8

9

12 △ ▽ 14

10

11 △ ▽ 13

1. Mae West
2. Will Hay
3. Jane Withers
4. Polly Moran
5. Charles Trowbridge
6. Danielle Darrieux
7. Jean Gabin
8. Wayne Morris
9. Robert Young
10. Jerome Cowan
11. Sally Gray
12. Gail Patrick
13. Frances Farmer
14. Greta Garbo

1

2 3

4

5 6

7

8 △ ▽ 11

9 10

12 △ ▽ 14

13

1. Selmer Jackson
2. Gale Sondergaard
3. Fay Holden
4. Frances Day
5. Eddie Quillan
6. Erich von Stroheim
7. John Boles
8. J Carrol Naish
9. Michael Whalen
10. John Carradine
11. Nancy Carroll
12. Grant Withers
13. Virginia Gilmore
14. Lily Pons

337

1

2

3

4

5

6

7 △ ▽ 10

8 △ ▽ 9

11   12   13

14   15   16

The Plainsman (Par/CdeM) in which Gary Cooper played Wild Bill Hickok, was one of the star's most popular Westerns. It was another Cecil B DeMille epic.

1. Chief Thundercloud, Paul Harvey and Jean Arthur
2. Victor Varconi and Gary Cooper
3. Charles Judels and Gary Cooper
4. Charles Bickford and Porter Hall
5. Jean Arthur and Gary Cooper
6, 7, 8, 12 and 17 Gary Cooper and Jean Arthur
9. Purnell Pratt, James Ellison and Gary Cooper
10. Gary Cooper and Victor Varconi
11. Helen Burgess, Jean Arthur and James Ellison
13. Jean Arthur
14. Gary Cooper, Anthony Quinn and James Ellison
15. Jean Arthur and Gary Cooper
16. Fred Kohler Sr and Gary Cooper
18. James Ellison and Helen Burgess
19. Victor Varconi, Gary Cooper and Jean Arthur
20. Bud Osborne, Harry Woods, Robert Wilbur and Charles Bickford

17 △ ▽ 19   18 △ ▽ 20

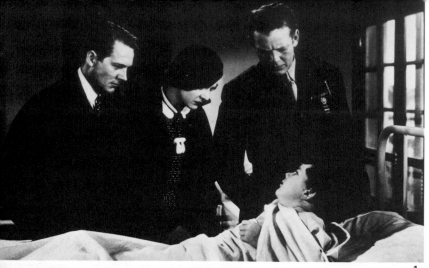

6 △ ▽ 8

7 △ ▽ 9

1. Charles Bickford (r) in *Pride of the Marines* (Col)

2. Buck Jones in *For the Service* (Univ)

3. Sheila Mannors and Johnny Mack Brown in *Desert Phantom* (Sup/WS)

4. Bela Lugosi, Patricia Ellis and Michael Loring in *Postal Inspector* (Univ)

5. Paul Lukas, Ruth Chatterton, Mary Astor and Walter Huston in *Dodsworth* (SG)

6. Ann Rutherford and John Wayne in *The Lawless Nineties* (Rep)

7. Rex Bell and Joan Barclay in *Men of the Plains* (Coy)

8. Clifford Heatherley and Buster Keaton in *An Old Spanish Custom* (Hof)

9. John Howard and Marsha Hunt in *Easy to Take* (Par)

340

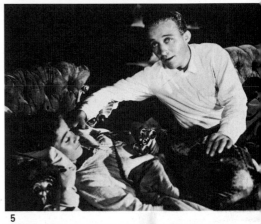

1. William Janney, Bill Boyd, Irving Bacon, George 'Gabby' Hayes and Gail Sheridan in *Hopalong Cassidy Returns* (Par)

2. Bob Allen (c/r) in *The Unknown Ranger* (Col)

3. Bob Custer (r) in *Ambush Valley* (Rel/WS)

4. John Miljan (s) in *Murder at Glen Athol* (Inv)

5. Edith Fellows and Bing Crosby in *Pennies From Heaven* (Col)

6. Bryant Washburn, Betty Compson and Creighton Hale in *The Millionaire Kid* (Rel)

7. Paul Draper, Dick Powell and Ruby Keeler in *Colleen* (WB)

8. Kay Linaker, Onslow Stevens, Noel Madison and Robert E Homans in *Easy Money* (Inv)

9. 'Pinky' Tomlin, Sally Eilers and James Dunn in *Don't Get Personal* (Univ)

10. Elizabeth Patterson, Edward Everett Horton and Peggy Conklin in *Her Master's Voice* 'WaW/ Par)

11. Victor Jory (l) and George Bancroft (r) in *Hell Ship Morgan* (Col)

12. Sonja Henie and Adolphe Menjou in *One in a Million* (Fox)

341

1 2

3 4 5

6 △ ▽9 7 8 △ ▽10

11   12

13

The Great Ziegfeld (MGM) was one of the most spectacular of all the musicals turned out by MGM during the Thirties. It was not only a movie dedicated to Hollywood showmanship-it also paid homage to the much-lauded beauty of The American Girl. As the ever-popular song went: 'A pretty girl is like a melody'.

1. Herman Bing, William Powell and Reginald Owen
2. Reginald Owen, William Powell and Raymond Walburn
3. Frank Morgan
4. Myrna Loy and William Powell
5. Luise Rainer and William Powell
6. William Powell and the Ziegfeld Girls
7. William Powell and Raymond Walburn
8. Marcelle Corday and Luise Rainer
9. Nat Pendleton
10. Susan Kaaren, William Powell and Jean Chatburn
11. Virginia Bruce and Luise Rainer
12. Dennis Morgan and the Ziegfeld Girls
13. Ralph Morgan
14. The 'A Pretty Girl is Like a Melody' number
15. Jean Chatburn and William Powell
16. Joseph Cawthorn, Ann Gillis and William Powell
17. Ray Bolger and the Ziegfeld Girls

14 △ ▽ 16   15 △ ▽ 17

Snow White and her wicked stepmother
© The Walt Disney Company

Above: Walt Disney © The Walt Disney Company
Below: Fred Astaire

The year 1937 saw something unique in film entertainment – the first animated feature (in those days content to be called a full-length cartoon). *Snow White and the Seven Dwarfs* was an enormous gamble on the part of Walt Disney' studios in terms of both cost ($1.5 million, a colossal sum in its day) and reputation.

The film had been three years in the making, and Hollywood film folk couldn't believe their ears when they heard what Walt was up to. Audiences were accustomed to cartoons lasting no more than seven or eight minutes and it seemed incredible that people would want to sit through one lasting nearly an hour and a half.

But Disney was vindicated. *Snow White* was from the start an enormous hit and made $8.5 million on its initial release.

It was a tremendous technical achievement, employing over 700 artists to create the two million drawings the film needed, using many techniques new to cartoon production and three-strip Technicolor throughout (not an innovation for Disney, however, who had made his first Technicolor cartoon as early as 1932). In addition it had a string of catchy tunes to boost its popularity, among them 'Some Day My Prince Will Come' and 'Whistle While You Work'.

It was not until 1953 that Disney formed its own distribution company, Buena Vista, and *Snow White* was released by RKO. This was the busiest year in RKO's history. The Astaire-Rogers team was still one of its top attractions as they tripped the light fantastic in *Shall We Dance?*

After making seven films in a row with Ginger Rogers *Damsel in Distress* found Astaire with a new leading lady. She was Joan Fontaine, not a singer or dancer by any means but decidedly more suited than Ginger Rogers would have been to playing the aristocratic English girl who is pursued by an American dancing star. As she didn't contribute to the musical side of the film, the comedy team of George Burns and Gracie Allen were included in the cast and joined Astaire in a couple of the numbers.

Joan Fontaine had just appeared for RKO in *Quality Street*, based on J.M. Barrie's period play. It stars Katharine Hepburn, and Kate next found herself teamed with Ginger Rogers who was beginning to break away from musicals in a bid to show that she was as good an actress as dancer. The film that teamed her with Hepburn is *Stage Door*, a comedy about life in a boarding house for actresses.

This was Hepburn's thirteenth film (she made her first in 1932) but one of her luckiest to date. It needed to be – she desperately wanted a hit to boost her sagging career. With this film she revealed an unexpected flair for comedy that was to help her maintain her popularity for many years to come.

Paul Muni

In *Stage Door* she plays a society girl determined to get on the stage. Ginger Rogers plays a brash creature more interested in landing a wealthy husband. The two stars make the most of the scintillating dialogue. A more tragic creature, a girl who commits suicide on failing to secure a coveted role, is portrayed by Andrea Leeds whose performance in the film won her an Oscar nomination. Other ladies in the female-dominated cast are Gail Patrick, Constance Collier and Lucille Ball. The last-named was still only getting minor roles in films with no indication that in 1953 she would become the head of a TV company, Desilu Productions, and go on to buy out the RKO studios in 1957.

Leslie Howard

Stage Door was nominated for a Best Picture Oscar, but the film that actually picked up that accolade was *The Life of Emile Zola* presenting Paul Muni as the famous novelist campaigning for the release of a Jewish officer, Captain Dreyfus, from wrongful imprisonment on Devil's Island after he has been falsely condemned of a treason charge by anti-semitic members of the French army. This is one of the big-scale biographical films that Muni made for Warners, to whom he was under contract.

Above: The Dead End Kids
Below: Humphrey Bogart in *Dead End* (SG)

Another Warner star was Bette Davis but in 1937 she claimed the studio was treating her badly by not giving her roles worthy of her talent. Of the four films she made this year, the best is *It's Love I'm After* which is a rare thing for her – a romantic comedy. It co-stars that perfect English gentleman, Leslie Howard, and they play actors always bickering off stage. In one sequence they do a scene from *Romeo and Juliet*; the previous year Howard had played Shakespeare's immortal lover in MGM's version of the play.

In 1937 Warners loaned out Humphrey Bogart to producer Sam Goldwyn for *Dead End*. In it he plays a gangster – 'Baby Face' Martin – who returns to the New York slum where he was raised, renewing acquaintance with such people as his old girl-friend (Claire Trevor) who by now has sunk to prostitution. His notoriety as a gangster has made him a hero with some local boys, an unruly lot who appealed so much to audiences that they became known as the Dead End Kids and were given their own series of B movies. The film provides an uncharacteristically dramatic part for

John Boles

Anne Shirley

Above: Nelson Eddy and Jeanette MacDonald in
Maytime (MGM)
Below: Allan Jones

Marjorie Main as Bogart's mother; later she was to become a popular screen comedienne.

She appears in another 1937 Goldwyn production, *Stella Dallas*, This was a remake of a famous 1925 weepie and stars Barbara Stanwyck as an uncouth girl who traps a well-bred man (John Boles) into marrying her. Anne Shirley plays the daughter for whom Stella makes sacrifices so that she, the daughter, can have all the advantages in life that her mother never managed to achieve for herself. The final sequence, with the estranged mother gazing tearfully through a window at the marriage of her daughter, is one of the cinema's great melodramatic moments. This is Stanwyck's own favourite performance of the Thirties. The director was King Vidor who, like so many others, was full of admiration for the dedication and professionalism Stanwyck always brings to her portrayals.

High on MGM's incredible array of popular stars was the team of Jeanette MacDonald and Nelson Eddy who sang their way through lavish screen versions of well-known operettas.

Of the seven films they made together over six years, their most successful was *Maytime* in 1937. Based loosely on the Sigmund Romberg stage show, it was set in Paris in the nineteenth century and cast MacDonald as an opera singer who, despite being married to her impresario (John Barrymore), falls madly in love with a penniless baritone (Eddy). Barrymore eventually kills Eddy, but he doesn't kill his wife's love for the singer. She goes on loving him until her own death (a natural one) when they are reunited in ghostly fashion and walk transparently hand-in-hand while singing one of the many reprises of 'Will You Remember?'

The film was intended as MGM's first feature in Technicolor but the studio finally had to be content with monochrome photography and an occasional sequence in sepia. This was as a result of cutbacks on the death of studio head Irving Thalberg. There was, however, belated consolation for MacDonald and Eddy in that the film finally chosen to be Metro's first in colour (in 1938) was one of theirs, *Sweethearts*.

In 1937 MacDonald had another box office success with *The Firefly* in which she played a Spanish spy during the Napoleonic war. But her partner this time was Allan Jones who had a big hit singing 'The Donkey Serenade'.

Jones, a popular tenor of the day (and father of Jack Jones, a singer of the seventies), found himself once again in the crazy world of the Marx Brothers when they had *A Day at the Races* (he had already survived *A Night at the Opera* with them in 1935). This time he played a racehorse owner romancing Maureen O'Sullivan, but their affair, as one would expect, was completely overshadowed by the antics of Groucho, Harpo and Chico. Groucho played a horse doctor labouring under the name of Hugo Z. Hackenbush who poses as a neurologist at a sanatorium owned by the wealthy Mrs Upjohn. This long-suffering lady was portrayed by Margaret Dumont, the magnificent butt of Groucho's put-down humour in seven of their films. She stood up splendidly to his insults.

The gags the Brothers performed in the film – both the one-liners and the complete routines – had been tried out in advance before live audiences to merit inclusion in the film. It was one of the best of the five the Brothers made for MGM.

In complete contrast, MGM was at the same time surrounding Garbo with opulence in *Conquest* (known in Britain as *Marie Walewska*) in which she plays the Polish mistress of Napoleon. The Emperor is portrayed by Charles Boyer, newly established as a great romantic figure of the cinema. Garbo possibly never had a better leading man but this film doesn't give her enough chances to shine – in fact, it's the one film of her American career in which her leading man has the more dramatic role.

The top money-making star of 1937 (indeed from 1935-1938) was a nine-year-old at Twentieth Century-Fox, Miss Shirley Temple.

They gave her two title roles in 1937: *Heidi*, a Swiss orphan who goes to live with her grumpy grandfather and wins him over; and *Wee Willie Winkie*, a girl adopted by a British regiment in India. Here again she has a crusty grandfather to win over (C. Aubrey Smith) as well as a notorious enemy chieftain (Cesar Romero).

Over at Universal, the big name was Deanna Durbin. Having saved them from bankruptcy the year before with her debut film *Three Smart Girls*, they now rushed her into *One Hundred Men and a Girl*. The men are unemployed musicians whom the girl manages to form into a symphonic orchestra conducted by the great Leopold Stokowski (in real life his name was romantically linked with that of Garbo). The film provides a mixture of popular songs and popular classical music, something Hollywood studios were partial to in those days. Among Durbin's songs is 'It's Raining Sunbeams.'

Frank Capra, the director renowned for his films (usually packed with heart warming comedy) about everyday folk chasing their 'American Dream', had a shot at drama in 1937 when he made *Lost Horizon*, based on James Hilton's celebrated novel. It stars Ronald Colman as one of five survivors of a plane crash who come across an idyllic Tibetan community called Shangri La (the film introduced the word into our vocabulary) where life seems to be eternal. Budgeted at $2 million, it was an unusually costly production for Columbia, not the most generous of studios, and its boss Harry Cohn regretted it when a preview audience responded unfavourably to the film's opening sequence showing a revolution somewhere in Asia. The solution was to edit most of the sequence, shortening the film by some 20 minutes, but it was a wise decision that helped the film to considerable popularity.

Charles Boyer in *Conquest* (GB *Marie Walewska*) (MGM)

Greta Garbo in *Conquest* (GB *Marie Walewska*) (MGM)

Above: Shirley Temple
Below: Ronald Colman

Janet Gaynor

Carole Lombard

Above: Laurence Olivier and Morton Selten in
Fire Over England (Pen)
Below: Raimu

There were two successes this year for producer David O. Selznick – *A Star Is Born* (presenting Janet Gaynor as a film actress whose star waxes as her actor-husband's wanes) and *Nothing Sacred*. Both starred Fredric March, and in the latter he played a reporter on a small-town newspaper that exploits a young woman who claims she is dying of radium poisoning. Hardly a fit subject for a comedy you might think (and many people were dubious at the time), but it was nicely carried off by the cast, especially Carole Lombard as the girl. She was one of the best light comediennes of her day but, tragically, she died in a plane crash in 1942.

Both these Selznick films were shot in the comparatively new process of three-strip Technicolor that had first been used on a feature *(Becky Sharp)* two years earlier. 1937 saw the first such feature film made in England. It was *Wings of the Morning* for which Twentieth Century-Fox brought Henry Fonda from America and Annabella from France. She plays two parts – a gypsy of 1889 who marries an Irish count but loses her position when he dies, and her granddaughter of 1937 who gets a job at the same place, working in the stabes disguised as a boy! The film's title was the name of a horse – Fonda played a horse trainer, and there were climactic scenes at the Epsom Derby.

Someone who was at his very best in 1937 was the irascible British comedian Will Hay. The classic *Oh, Mr Porter!* presents him as an incompetent stationmaster in the wilds of Ireland who becomes embroiled with gun-runners. Hay and his regular stooges – chubby, cheeky Graham Moffatt and single-toothed, scruffy old Moore Marriott – never had better material. For many cinema lovers this is one of the best British comedy films of all time.

Laurence Olivier was just beginning to find his feet as a film actor and had a starring role as an emissary of Elizabeth I in *Fire Over England*. Flora Robson was an ideal choice to play the queen facing threats from the Spanish Armada, and Raymond Massey plays Philip of Spain. Olivier's love interest in the film is provided by Vivien Leigh – and it provided him with love interest *off* the set, too. The romance of these actors drew a lot of attention. After divorces from their respective spouses, they became husband and wife in 1940.

Among the French films of 1937, one that enjoyed a tremendous success overseas was *Un Carnet de Bal*. The title translates as *A Dance Programme*. In the old days a girl would carry one at a dance, and men would sign it to reserve dances with her. In the film a lonely widow (Marie Bell) comes across one dating from her youth and seeks out the men who signed it. She discovers that all have been failures in life. The film has an impressive array of French talent including Françoise Rosay (who was to do some filming in Britain in the Forties), Louis Jouvet, Harry Baur, Pierre Blanchar, Raimu and Fernandel. Its theme, 'Valse Grise' became very popular. The film was directed by Julien

Duvivier. It brought him much acclaim and led to his going to Hollywood where his work included a remake of *Un Carnet de Bal* in 1941; it was called *Lydia* and starred Merle Oberon.

Françoise Rosay and Louis Jouvet were also in Marcel Carné's *Drôle de Drame*, a crazy comedy set in an uproariously funny Gallic version of Edwardian London. Making digs at English detective fiction, it presents Jouvet as a bishop trying to pin a murder on his cousin, played by the great Michel Simon, who poses as a botanist while really being a thriller-writer! However, there is also at work in the neighbourhood a romantic but clearly demented murderer (Jean-Louis Barrault) known as 'the slaughter-house killer.'

French film-makers were no better at depicting Dublin. This was the setting for *Le Puritain*, based on a crime story by Liam O'Flaherty. Jean-Louis Barrault plays a religious fanatic who stalks and stabs streetwalkers. The delightfully-named Vivian Romance played a woman at risk and Pierre Fresnay was a police inspector.

Russia was another foreign setting for a French film, *La Citadelle du Silence (The Citadel of Silence)*, and it was well conveyed. The film concerned the daughter of a revolutionary who marries a prison governor, simply to free the man she really does love. She is played by Annabella (who came to Britain to star in *Wings of the Morning* and then went to America where in 1939 she became the wife of Tyrone Power).

The most important film to come out of France at this time was *La Grande Illusion*. Made when the Nazis were causing a lot of trouble in Europe, it was regarded as a pacifist film. Based by director Jean Renoir on his own experiences, it was set in a PoW camp in the First World War and explored the relationship between prisoners and their captors. Erich von Stroheim masqueraded magnificently as the German prison commander, and Pierre Fresnay played a French officer, an internee. Both were aristocrats who begin to realize that the war has put an end to their class of society. Two other officers who clash with the commandant were played by Jean Gabin, a mechanic in civilian life, and Marcel Dalio, a Jew.

In Russia Stalin commissioned *Lenin in October* from Mikhail Romm and Dimitri Vasiliev to celebrate the twentieth anniversary of the Revolution. Though there have been many films on Lenin this is one of the best, thanks in large part, to a splendid central performance by Boris Shchukin. The film opens with Lenin's arrival at the Finland Station and traces his rise to power, culminating in a splendidly-staged storming of the Winter Palace.

Another, though lesser, hero of the Revolution, scientist Timiriazev, is portrayed in *Baltic Deputy* by leading Russian actor Nikolai Cherkassov. His role as a lonely old professor befriended by sailors of the Baltic Fleet – whom he eventually helps in turn – brought him world fame.

Louis Jouvet

Jean Gabin

Above: Jean Gabin and Pierre Fresnay in *La Grand Illusion* (FrF)
Below: Erich von Stroheim in *La Grand Illusion* (FrF)

Film Favourites 1937

Movies that have now become classics in their own right were legion in 1937. *Lost Horizon* was probably tops.

Douglas Fairbanks Jr as Rupert of Hentzau in *The Prisoner of Zenda* (DS)

Dorothea Kent and Wendy Barrie in *A Girl with Ideas* (Univ)

PICTUREGOER'S *Famous Films* SUPPLEMENT

Captains Courageous

With
SPENCER TRACY
Freddie BARTHOLOMEW
Lionel BARRYMORE

Cover of Picturegoer 'give-away'

Cary Grant, Roland Young and Constance Bennett in *Topper* (HR)

Wallace Ford and John Mills in *OHMS* (US *You're in the Army Now*) (Gau)

Herman Bing, Nelson Eddy, Jeanette MacDonald and John Barrymore in *Maytime* (MGM)

Flora Robson and Laurence Robson in *Fire Over England* (Pen)

Walter Abel

Left: Miriam Hopkins and Joel McCrea in *Woman Chases Man* (SG)

Shirley Temple in *Heidi* (Fox)

Sabu and Walter Hudd in *Elephant Boy* (AK)

Wendy Barrie

Claire Trevor in *Dead End* (SG)

Maureen O'Sullivan, Virginia Bruce and Franchot Tone in *Between Two Women* (MGM)

Deanna Durbin and Leopold Stokowski in *One Hundred Men and a Girl* (Univ)

Edward Everett Horton and Eve Arden in *Oh Doctor* (Univ)

Larry 'Buster' Crabbe, June Martel and Harvey Stephens in *Forlorn River* (Par)

Barbara Stanwyck and Robert Taylor in *This is My Affair* (GB *His Affair*) (Fox)

Jon Hall and John Carradine in *The Hurricane* (SG)

Gene Autry and Smiley Burnette in *Round-Up Time in Texas* (Rep)

Stepin Fetchit

Right: Margo and Ronald Colman in *Lost Horizon* (Col)

Felix Aylmer and Anna Neagle in *Victoria the Great* (Imp)

Frieda Inescort, Bonita Granville, Walter Woolf King and Olivia de Havilland in *Call It a Day* (WB)

Peter Lorre and Sidney Blackmer in *Thank You, Mr Moto* (Fox)

Joan Bennett and Warner Baxter in *Walter Wanger's Vogues of 1938* (WaW)

Ann Sothern and Burgess Meredith in *There Goes the Groom* (RKO)

Cesar Romero and Phyllis Brooks in *Dangerously Yours* (Fox)

Roland Young, Cary Grant and Joan Bennett in *Topper* (HR)

Jean Harlow and Robert Taylor in *Personal Property* (GB *The Man in Possession*) (MGM)

Leslie Howard and Bette Davis in *It's Love I'm After*

Spencer Tracy and Gladys George in *They Gave Him a Gun* (MGM)

Mischa Auer, Adolphe Menjou and Deanna Durbin in *One Hundred Men and a Girl* (Univ)

Fred Astaire, Gracie Allen and George Burns in *Damsel in Distress* (RKO)

Wendy Barrie and Joel McCrea in *Dead End* (SG)

Michael Whalen, June Lang and Shirley Temple in *Wee Willie Winkie* (Fox)

Andrea Leeds and Katharine Hepburn in *Stage Door* (RKO)

Fred Astaire, Harriet Hoctor and Edward Everett Horton in *Shall We Dance?* (RKO)

Joan Bennett and Jack Benny in *Artists and Models Abroad* (GB *Stranded in Paris*) (Par)

Right: Dame May Whitty and Robert Montgomery in *Night Must Fall* (MGM)

1

2

3

4

5

6

7 △ ▽ 10

8

9 △ ▽ 11

1. Glenda Farrell, Rosemary Lane (c), Curt Bois (r) and Louella Parsons (r) in *Hollywood Hotel* (WB)
2. Humphrey Bogart in *San Quentin* (FN)
3. Walter Woolf King and Olivia de Havilland in *Call It a Day* (WB)
4. Roland Young (l) and Franklin Pangborn (r) in *Topper* (HR)
5. Allan Jones and Jeanette MacDonald in *The Firefly* (MGM)
6. Warren Hull and Jean Rogers in *Night Key* (Univ)
7. C Aubrey Smith and Shirley Temple in *Wee Willie Winkie* (Fox)
8. Peter Lorre in *Thank you, Mr Moto* (Fox)
9. Lloyd Nolan and Mae West in *Every Day's a Holiday* (Par)
10. Nan Grey, Deanna Durbin and Barbara Read in *Three Smart Girls* (Univ)
11. Ann Dvorak in *Merry-go-round* (Rep)

1   2

3

4   5

6△▽9   7

8

1. Laurence Olivier in *Fire Over England* (LF/Pen)
2. Raymond Massey and Laurence Olivier in *Fire Over England* (LF/Pen)
3. Loretta Young and Virginia Bruce in *Wife, Doctor and Nurse* (Fox)
4. Ben Weldon, Charles Starrett and Edward Deane in *Westbound Mail* (Col)
5. Spencer Tracy, Gladys George and Franchot Tone in *They Gave Him a Gun* (MGM)
6. Virginia Bruce and Kent Taylor in *When Love is Young* (RP/Univ)
7. Charles Boyer and Claudette Colbert in *Tovarich* (HW)
8. John Beal and Florence Rice in *Beg, Borrow or Steal* (MGM)
9. Barbara Stanwyck, Brian Donlevy and Victor McLaglen in *This is my Affair* (GB *His Affair*) (Fox)

355

1

2

3

4

5

6

7

8

1. George Brent and Josephine Hutchinson in *Mountain Justice* (FN)

2. William Powell and Luise Rainer in *The Emperor's Candlesticks* (MGM)

3. Errol Flynn and Phyllis Barry in *The Prince and the Pauper* (FN)

4. George Sanders and Dolores Del Rio in *Lancer Spy* (Fox)

5. Michael Whalen, Claire Trevor and Andrew Tombes in *Time Out for Romance* (Fox)

6. Billy and Bobby Mauch in *The Prince and the Pauper* (FN)

7. Simone Simon and James Stewart in *Seventh Heaven* (Fox)

8. Bette Davis and Humphrey Bogart in *Marked Woman* (FN)

9. Claude Rains, Errol Flynn and Bobby Mauch in *The Prince and the Pauper* (FN)

10. Ann Sothern and Mary Boland in *There Goes the Groom* (RKO)

11. John Beal (r) in *The Man Who Found Himself* (RKO)

12. Dick Powell and Madeleine Carroll in *On the Avenue* (Fox)

9 △ ▽ 11

10 △ ▽ 12

1. Ginger Rogers and Gail Patrick in *Stage Door* (RKO)
2. Ginger Rogers and Fred Astaire in *Shall We Dance* (RKO)
3. Arthur Hohl, George Sanders, Wallace Beery and Mickey Rooney in *Slave Ship* (Fox)
4. J M Kerrigan and Clark Gable in *Parnell* (MGM)
5. Dorothy Lamour in *High, Wide and Handsome* (Par)
6. Margaret Lindsay, Pat O'Brien and Henry Fonda in *Slim* (WB)
7. Noah Beery Jr and Dorothea Kent in *Some Blondes are Dangerous* (Univ)
8. Shirley Temple and Helen Westley in *Heidi* (Fox)
9. C Aubrey Smith, Ronald Colman, David Niven and Raymond Massey in *The Prisoner of Zenda* (DS)
10. Lewis Stone and Jameson Thomas in *The Man Who Cried Wolf* (Univ)
11. C Aubrey Smith, David Niven, Ronald Colman and Madeleine Carroll in *The Prisoner of Zenda* (DS)
12. James Stewart and Robert Young in *Navy Blue and Gold* (SZ/MGM)
13. Ronald Colman and Douglas Fairbanks Jr in *The Prisoner of Zenda* (DS)

11 △ ▽ 13

10 △ ▽ 12

1. Rose Stradner and Edward G Robinson in *The Last Gangster* (MGM)

2. Allen Jenkins and Humphrey Bogart in *Dead End* (SG)

3. Melvyn Douglas and Grace Moore in *I'll Take Romance* (Col)

4. Molly Lamont and John Trent in *A Doctor's Diary* (Par)

5. Edward Everett Horton, Jack Oakie and Lily Pons in *Hitting a New High* (RKO)

6. Loretta Young, George Sanders and Tyrone Power in *Love is News* (Fox)

7. Edward Everett Horton and Porter Hall in *Let's Make a Million* (Par)

8. Jean Harlow and Robert Taylor in *Personal Property* (GB *The Man in Possession*) (MGM)

9. Ray Milland and Wendy Barrie in *Wings Over Honolulu* (Univ)

10. Fredric March and Janet Gaynor in *A Star is Born* (DS)

11. Buddy Ebsen, Eleanor Powell and George Murphy in *Broadway Melody of 1938* (MGM)

12. Robert Wilcox, Judith Barrett and Harry Davenport in *Armored Car* (Univ)

1   2

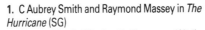

4

5

1. C Aubrey Smith and Raymond Massey in *The Hurricane* (SG)
2. Chester Morris (I) in *Devil's Playground* (Col)
3. Donald Woods, Ann Dvorak and Selmer Jackson in *The Case of the Stuttering Bishop* (FN)
4. Luise Rainer in *The Good Earth* (MGM)
5. Rex Harrison and Vivien Leigh in *Storm in a Teacup* (VSP/LF)
6. George Cheseboro and Fred Scott in *Roaming Cowboy* (Spe)
7. Lionel Barrymore, Clark Gable and Cliff Edwards in *Saratoga* (MGM)
8. Onslow Stevens and Hedda Hopper in *You Can't Buy Luck* (RKO)
9. Kent Taylor and Wendy Barrie in *Prescription for Romance* (Univ)
10. Frank Shields, Anne Nagel and Mickey Rooney in *The Hoosier Schoolboy* (KG/MoP)
11. James Ellison and Jean Parker in *The Barrier* (HS/Par)
12. Errol Flynn, Walter Abel, Margaret Lindsay, Anita Louise and Henry O'Neill in *Green Light* (Cos/FN)

7

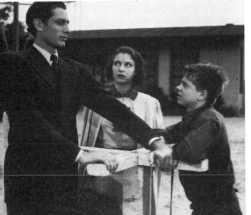

8 △ ▽ 10   9 △ ▽ 12

11

1. Clifford Evans
2. Bette Davis and Wayne Morris in *Kid Galahad* (FN)
3. Jerry Uhlick
4. Helen Mack and Robert Cummings in *Last Train from Madrid* (Par)
5. Berton Churchill
6. Eleanor Powell in *Rosalie* (MGM)
7. Joan Crawford and William Powell in *The Last of Mrs Cheyney* (MGM)
8. Gordon Elliott and Ann Dvorak in *Midnight Court* (WB)
9. Marlene Dietrich and Robert Donat in *Knight without Armour* (LF)
10. Dick Foran in *Guns of the Pecos* (FN)
11. Deanna Durbin in *One Hundred Men and a Girl* (Univ)
12. Alan Hale, Grant Mitchell and Joan Fontaine in *Music for Madame* (RKO)
13. Joel McCrea and Barbara Stanwyck in *Internes Can't Take Money* (GB *You Can't Take Money*) (Par)
14. Leslie Howard, Olivia de Havilland and Patric Knowles in *It's Love I'm After* (FN)
15. Fred MacMurray and Charlie Ruggles in *Exclusive* (Par)

1. Mary Carlisle and Bing Crosby in *Double or Nothing* (Par)
2. Florence Rice and Robert Young in *Married Before Breakfast* (MGM)
3. John Beal, William Powell, Myrna Loy and Florence Rice in *Double Wedding* (MGM)
4. Anna May Wong
5. Joan Crawford in *Mannequin* (MGM)
6. Mickey Rooney and Robert Montgomery in *Live, Love and Learn* (MGM)
7. Helen Twelvetrees, Dickie Jones and Buck Jones in *Hollywood Round-Up* (Col)
8. Donald O'Connor
9. Loretta Young, Harold Huber and Frances Drake in *Love under Fire* (Fox)
10. Leo Gorcey
11. Don Ameche and Loretta Young in *Love under Fire* (Fox)

8 △ ▽ 10   9 △ ▽ 11

1

2

3

4

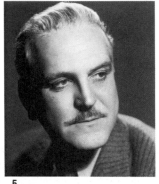

5

6

7

8

9

10

1. Tom Tyler and Harlene Wood in *The Feud of the Trail* (Vic)

2. Mary Livingstone

3. Claire Trevor

4. Luise Rainer and Spencer Tracy in *The Big City* (MGM)

5. Frank Morgan

6. James Gleason

7. Jon Hall

8. Fred Astaire and Joan Fontaine in *Damsel in Distress* (RKO)

9. Jack Randall and Charles King in *Danger Valley* (MoP)

10. Pat O'Brien and Sybil Jason in *The Great O'Malley* (WB)

11. Robert Taylor

12. Robert McWade, Robert Taylor and Marjorie Weaver in *This Is My Affair* (GB *His Affair*) (Fox)

13. Robert Newton

14. Harry Tyler, Rosalind Keith, William Humphries and John Tyrell in *Find the Witness* (Col)

11 △ ▽ 13

12 △ ▽ 14

362

1

2 3

4 △ ▽ 8

5

7

6

9 △ ▽ 10

1. Jane Withers and Walter Brennan in *Wild and Woolly* (Fox)
2. Miriam Hopkins
3. Ann Sothern and Robert Young in *Dangerous Number* (MGM)
4. Edward Ellis, Francis Dee and John Wayne in *A Man Betrayed* (Rep)
5. Don Terry
6. Cora Witherspoon, Guy Kibbee and Dorothy Moore in *The Big Shot* (RKO)
7. Nancy Kelly
8. Marie Wilson
9. Lionel Barrymore
10. Bryant Washburn

1. Don Ameche and Ann Sothern in *Fifty Roads to Town* (Fox)
2. Mickey Rooney, Lionel Barrymore and Cecilia Parker in *A Family Affair* (MGM)
3. Kent Taylor and Nan Grey in *Love in a Bungalow* (Univ)
4. Jean Muir, Joe Crehan, Henry O'Neill and Helen MacKellar in *Draegerman Courage* (FN)
5. June Lang, Eddie Cantor and Gypsy Rose Lee in *Ali Baba Goes To Town* (Fox)
6. William Gargan and Jean Rogers in *Reported Missing* (Univ)
7. Douglas Montgomery, Otto Kruger and Jacqueline Wells in *Counsel For Crime* (Col)
8. Walter Pidgeon and Gloria Stuart in *Girl Overboard* (Univ)
9. Melvyn Douglas and Marlene Dietrich in *Angel* (Par)

1. Warner Baxter and Joan Bennett in *Vogues of 1938* (WW)
2. Kay Francis and Errol Flynn in *Another Dawn* (WB)
3. Charles Bickford
4. Ann Sothern and Gene Raymond in *There Goes My Girl* (RKO)
5. Franchot Tone, Lynne Carver, Robert Young and Joan Crawford in *The Bride Wore Red* (MGM)
6. Elizabeth Patterson
7. Joel McCrea and Miriam Hopkins in *Woman Chases Man* (SG)
8. John Payne, Billy Burrud, Betty Furness and J Edward Bromberg in *Fair Warning* (Fox)
9. Patric Knowles
10. ZaSu Pitts
11. Ida Lupino and John Boles in *Fight For Your Lady* (RKO)
12. Frank McHugh

1. Greta Garbo and Charles Boyer in *Conquest* (GB *Marie Walewska*) (MGM)
2. Charles Boyer, Maria Ouspenskaya and Greta Garbo in *Conquest* (GB *Marie Walewska*) (MGM)
3. Paul Kelly and Leona Maricle in *The Frame-Up* (Col)
4. Greta Garbo and Charles Boyer in *Conquest* (GB *Marie Walewska*) (MGM)
5. Claude Gillingwater, Greta Garbo and George Houston in *Conquest* (GB *Marie Walewska*) (MGM)
6. Mady Correll, Warren William and Ward Bond in *Midnight Madonna* (Par)
7. Lew Ayres and Mary Carlisle in *Hold 'Em Navy* (Par)

8. Joseph Calleia
9. Walter Catlett and Charles Williams in *Four Days Wonder* (Univ)
10. Vivienne Osborne and Jack Oakie in *Champagne Waltz* (Par)
11. Miriam Hopkins and Ivan Lebedeff in *Wise Girl* (RKO)

10 △ ▽ 11

8 △ ▽ 11

1. The Ritz Brothers in *Life Begins In College* (Fox)
2. Charles Boyer and Jean Arthur in *History Is Made at Night* (WaW)
3. Evelyn Daw and James Cagney in *Something to Sing About* (GN)
4. Guy Kibbee, Lucie Kaye and Tom Brown in *Jim Hanvey – Detective* (Rep)
5. Marian Marsh, John Trent, William Demarest and Ed Brophy in *The Great Gambini* (Par)
6. John Barrymore, John Sutton and John Howard in *Bulldog Drummond's Revenge* (Par)
7. George Raft and Gary Cooper in *Souls at Sea* (Par)
8. Basil Rathbone and Jane Bryan in *Confession* (WB)
9. Ken Murray, George Murphy, Alice Faye and Frank Jenks in *You're A Sweetheart* (Univ)
10. Ronald Sinclair, Mickey Rooney and Judy Garland in *Thoroughbreds Don't Cry* (MGM)
11. Tala Birell and Cesar Romero in *She's Dangerous* (Univ)

367

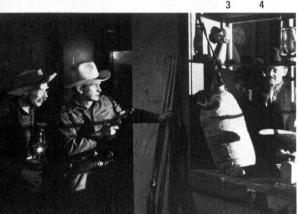

1. James Craig, Gilbert Roland and J Carrol Naish in *Thunder Trail* (Par)

2. Ray Corrigan, Rita Hayworth, Max Terhune and Bob Livingston in *Hit the Saddle* (Rep)

3. Johnny Mack Brown and Tom London in *Bar Z Bad Men* (Rep)

4. Johnny Mack Brown and Dick Curtis in *Guns in the Dark* (Rep)

5. Johnny Mack Brown and Dick Curtis in *Boothill Brigade* (Rep)

6. Bob Steele in *The Gun Ranger* (Rep)

7. Glenn Strange (l) and Dick Foran in *Blazing Sixes* (WB)

8. Louise Stanley and Tex Ritter in *Sing Cowboy Sing* (GN)

9. Stanley Fields and Smith Ballew (r) in *Roll Along, Cowboy* (Pri/Fox)

10. Tex Ritter and William Faversham in *Arizona Days* (GN)

11. Dick Foran (r) in *Prairie Thunder* (WB)

12. Bob Steele and Claire Rochelle in *Ridin' the Lone Trail* (Rep)

1

2

3

4

5

6

7

8

9

10

11

12

13 △ ▽15

14 △ ▽ 16

1. Smiley Burnette, Gene Autry and William Farnum in *Public Cowboy No.1* (Rep)

2. Gene Autry and Hope Manning in *The Old Corral* (Rep)

3. Iris Meredith, Joe Girard, Horace Murphy and Tex Ritter in *The Mystery of the Hooded Horsemen* (GN)

4. Max Terhune, Julia Thayer, Ray Corrigan, Sammy McKim and Bob Livingston in *Gunsmoke Ranch* (Rep)

5. Buck Jones and Kay Linaker in *Black Aces* (Univ)

6. Judith Allen and Gene Autry in *Boots and Saddles* (Rep)

7. Bill Boyd and Judith Allen in *Texas Trail* (Par)

8. Dickie Howard and Buck Jones in *Boss of Lonely Valley* (Univ)

9. Smiley Burnette and Gene Autry in *Git Along Little Dogies* (Rep)

10. Bill Boyd in *North of the Rio Grande* (Par)

11. Max Terhune, Bob Livingston, Sammy McKim and Ray Corrigan in *Roarin' Lead* (Rep)

12. Gene Autry and Smiley Burnette in *Rootin' Tootin' Rhythm* (Rep)

13. Russell Hayden, Bill Boyd and Lee J Cobb in *Rustler's Valley* (Par)

14. Lita Chevret and Buck Jones in *Sandflow* (Univ)

15. Morris Ankrum and Bill Boyd in *Hills of Old Wyoming* (Par)

16. Horace Murphy, Snub Pollard and Tex Ritter in *Riders of the Rockies* (GN)

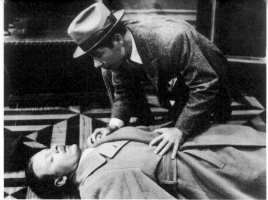

1. Mary Carlisle and Lynne Overman in *Hotel Haywire* (Par)

2. Joe E Brown in *Fit for a King* (RKO)

3. Alan Hale and Barbara Stanwyck in *Stella Dallas* (SG)

4. Kay Franics, Verree Teasdale and Victor Jory in *First Lady* (WB)

5. Anita Louise and George Brent in *The Go-Getter* (WB)

6. Warren Hull and Beverly Roberts in *Her Husband's Secretary* (FN)

7. Walter Winchell, Bert Lahr and Ben Bernie in *Love and Hisses* (Fox)

8. Annabella, Stewart Rome, Edward Underdown and Henry Fonda in *Wings of the Morning* (Fox)

9. Movita and Warren Hull in *Paradise Isle* (MoP)

10. Franklin Pangborn, Rochelle Hudson and Jack Haley in *She Had to Eat* (Fox)

11. Henry Fonda and Bette Davis in *That Certain Woman* (WB)

12. Ray Walker and Jack Holt in *Outlaws of the Orient* (Col)

13. Ben Blue and Judy Canova in *Artists and Models* (Par)

11 △ ▽ 13

10 △ ▽ 12

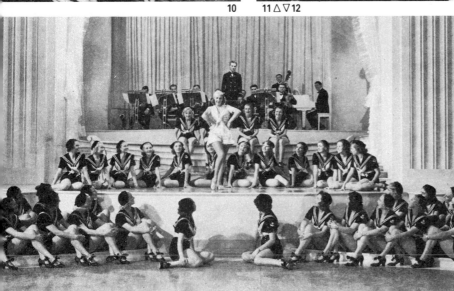

1. Joe E Brown and Florence Rice in *Riding on Air* (RKO)
2. Beulah Bondi and Victor Moore in *Make Way for Tomorrow* (Par)
3. Alice Faye and Tony Martin in *You Can't Have Everything* (Fox)
4. Delma Byron and Allan Lane in *Laughing at Trouble* (Fox)
5. Warren Hull and Patricia Ellis in *Rhythm in the Clouds* (Rep)
6. Gracie Fields, Owen Nares and Cyril Ritchard in *The Show Goes On* (ATP)
7. John Eldredge, Sally Blane and Claire Trevor in *One Mile From Heaven* (Fox)
8. Lynne Overman, Ruth Coleman and Edward Everett Horton in *Wild Money* (Par)
9. Ben Bernie, Patsy Kelly and Walter Catlett in *Wake Up and Live* (Fox)
10. Glenda Farrell and Barton MacLane in *Fly Away Baby* (WB)
11. Miriam Hopkins and Louis Hayward in *The Woman I Love* (GB *The Woman Between*) (RKO)
12. Ruby Keeler in *Ready, Willing and Able* (WB)

371

4

6

7 △ ▽ 11

8

10

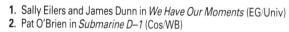

1. Sally Eilers and James Dunn in *We Have Our Moments* (EG/Univ)
2. Pat O'Brien in *Submarine D–1* (Cos/WB)
3. Martha Raye, Bing Crosby and Bob Burns in *Waikiki Wedding* (Par)
4. Heather Angel, Ray Milland and Porter Hall in *Bulldog Drummond Escapes* (Par)
5. Bob Burns and Martha Raye in *Mountain Music* (Par)
6. Walter Catlett, Dick Powell, Ted Healy, Fred Waring in *Varsity Show* (WB)
7. Raymond Massey and Elisabeth Bergner in *Dreaming Lips* (Tra)
8. Joan Gardener and Beniamino Gigli in *Forever Yours* (GN)
9. Robert Woolsey, Lupe Velez, Bert Wheeler and Marjorie Lord in *High Flyers* (RKO)
10. Warner Oland, Keye Luke and Harold Huber in *Charlie Chan at Monte Carlo* (Fox)
11. Harold Huber, Donald Woods, Keye Luke and Warner Oland in *Charlie Chan on Broadway* (Fox)

1 2

3

1. Ann Dvorak and Harry Carey in *Racing Lady* (RKO)
2. Arthur Loft, Bud Wiser, Harry Strang, Rita Hayworth and Charles Quigley in *The Game That Kills* (Col)
3. Tex Ritter and Rita Hayworth in *Trouble in Texas* (GN)
4. Rochelle Hudson and Robert Kent in *That I May Live* (F)
5. Virginia Grey, Bruce Cabot and Jean Chatburn in *Bad Guy* (MGM)
6. Jim Corey, Dick Foran and Harry Woods in *Land Beyond the Law* (WB)
7. Bob Livingston, Ray Corrigan and Max Terhune in *Ghost Town Gold* (Rep)
8. Cicely Courtneidge, Frank Cellier and Jack Hulbert in *Take My Tip* (Gau)
9. Ray Corrigan, Max Terhune and Bob Livingston in *Ghost Town Gold* (Rep)
10. Bob Steele and Warner Richmond in *Doomed at Sundown* (Rep)
11. Jack Randall (r) in *Stars Over Arizona* (MoP)
12. George Chesebro and Dick Foran in *Empty Holsters* (WB)

8 △ ▽ 11   9   10 △ ▽ 12

1

2

3

4

5

6

7

8

9

1. Guy Kibbee and Betty Furness in *Mama Steps Out* (MGM)

2. Ricardo Cortez and Marjorie Weaver in *The Californians* (Fox)

3. Spring Byington and Jed Prouty in *Borrowing Trouble* (Fox)

4. Gladys George (l) and John Beal (r) in *Madame X* (MGM)

5. Ann Southern and Jack Oakie in *Super Sleuth* (RKO)

6. John Loder, Roland Young and Cedric Hardwicke in *King Solomon's Mines* (G'boro)

7. Shirley Temple

8. Don Ameche

9. Carole Lombard and John Barrymore in *True Confession* (Par)

10. Hugh Herbert, Marcia Ralston and Allen Jenkins in *Sh! The Octopus* (FN)

11. Cecil Parker and Viven Leigh in *Dark Journey* (LF/VSP)

12. Beverly Roberts and Boris Karloff in *West of Shanghai* (FN)

13. Gilbert Roland and Brian Donlevy in *Midnight Taxi* (Fox)

10 △ ▽ 12

11 △ ▽ 13

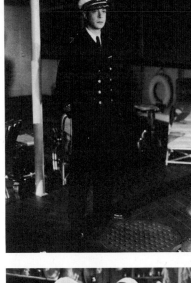

1

2

3

4

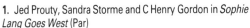

5

6

7

9

8

1. Jed Prouty, Sandra Storme and C Henry Gordon in *Sophie Lang Goes West* (Par)
2. Fernand Gravet in *The King and the Chorus Girl* (GB *Romance is Sacred*) (WB)
3. John Boles and Doris Nolan in *As Good As Married* (Univ)
4. Virginia Brissac, Barton MacLane and Glenda Farrell in *The Adventurous Blonde* (FN)
5. Louise Dresser, Claudette Colbert and Benny Bartlett in *Maid of Salem* (Par)
6. Thomas E Jackson, Carol Hughes and George Meeker in *The Westland Case* (Univ)
7. Leslie Howard and Joan Blondell in *Stand-In* (WaW)
8. Fay Bainter, Franchot Tone and Katharine Hepburn in *Quality Street* (RKO)
9. Ann Dvorak and Gavin Williams in *She's No Lady* (Par)
10. Howard Hickman, Smith Ballew, Leroy Mason and Heather Angel in *Western Gold* (Fox)
11. Arthur Housman, Arthur Treacher and Patricia Ellis in *Step Lively, Jeeves!* (Fox)
12. Henry O'Neil and Dick Powell in *The Singing Marine* (FN)
13. Jessie Matthews and Nat Pendleton in *Gangway* (Gau)

10 △ ▽ 12

11 △ ▽ 13

1. James Dunn, William Bakewell and June Travis in *Exiled to Shanghai (Rep)*
2. John Wayne and Gwen Gaze in *I Cover the War* (Univ)
3. Matty Kemp, Rosalind Keith and Charles Quigley in *Criminals of the Air* (Col)
4. Jane Darwell, Phyllis Brooks and Cesar Romero in *Dangerously Yours* (Fox)
5. Loretta Young and Claire Trevor in *Second Honeymoon* (Fox)
6. Peggy Bates and Barton MacLane in *Wine, Women and Horses* (WB)
7. Sonja Henie
8. Wallace Beery, Ted Healy and Una Merkel in *Good Old Soak* (MGM)
9. Margaret Lindsay and Joan Blondell in *Back in Circulation* (WB)

376

1

2   3

4   5

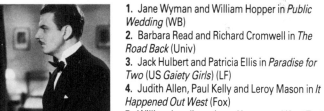

1. Jane Wyman and William Hopper in *Public Wedding* (WB)
2. Barbara Read and Richard Cromwell in *The Road Back* (Univ)
3. Jack Hulbert and Patricia Ellis in *Paradise for Two* (US *Gaiety Girls*) (LF)
4. Judith Allen, Paul Kelly and Leroy Mason in *It Happened Out West* (Fox)
5. William Lundigan, Irene Hervey and Kent Taylor in *The Lady Fights Back* (Univ)
6. Maureen O'Sullivan, Walter Pidgeon and Edna May Oliver in *My Dear Miss Aldrich* (MGM)
7. Constance Worth and Vinton Hayworth in *China Passage* (RKO)
8. J Carrol Naish, Bradley Page, Marjorie Lord and Emma Dunn in *Hideaway* (RKO)
9. Ken Maynard, Claudia Dell and Vince Barnett in *Boots of Destiny* (GN)
10. Johnny Downs, Eleanore Whitney, Charlie Ruggles and Grady Sutton in *Turn off the Moon* (FR/Par)
11. Jane Withers Robert Kent and Harold Huber in *Angel's Holiday* (JSt/Fox)
12. Barry Fitzgerald, Ray Milland, Oscar Homolka and Lloyd Nolan in *Ebb Tide* (Par)

8 △ ▽ 10   9 △ ▽ 11

12

377

1

2

3

4

3

5

5

6

7

8

9 △ ▽ 11

10 △ ▽ 12

Wells Fargo (Par) related the foundation and development of the world-famous express service. With an array of star names and a first class promotion, the producers anticipated a sure-fire paybox attraction. They were not disappointed.

1. Joel McCrea, Robert Cummings and Bob Burns
2. Scotty Beckett and Ralph Morgan
3. Frances Dee and Mary Nash
4. Lloyd Nolan, Porter Hall and Joel McCrea
5. Joel McCrea and Frances Dee
6. Joel McCrea and Peggy Stewart
7. Johnny Mack Brown and Frances Dee
8. Joel McCrea and Frances Dee
9. Lloyd Nolan and Porter Hall
10. Frances Dee and Joel McCrea
11. Joel McCrea, Henry O'Neill, Ralph Morgan and Mary Nash
12. Peggy Stewart (c)
13. Joel McCrea and Peggy Stewart
14. Joel McCrea, Frances Dee and Ralph Morgan
15. Frances Dee and Mary Nash
16. Joel McCrea and Frances Dee
17. Frances Dee and Joel McCrea
18. Joel McCrea and Bob Burns
19. Joel McCrea, Clarence Kolb, Frances Dee and Henry O'Neill
20. Frances Dee and Joel McCrea
21. Henry O'Neill, Joel McCrea and Bob Burns
22. Johnny Mack Brown, Frances Dee, Ralph Morgan and Mary Nash.
23. Mary Nash and Frances Dee

13

14 15

16

17 18

19

20 △ ▽ 23

21 △ ▽ 22

1

2

3

4

5

6

7

8

9

10 △ ▽ 15

11

13 △ ▽ 17

14 △ ▽ 16

12

18   19

20

21   22

23   24   25

26   27   28

29 △ ▽ 31   30 △ ▽ 32

1. Hal Taliaferro. Bob Allen, Bud Osborne and Tom London in *Law of the Ranger* (Col)

2. Douglas Walter (l), Arletta Duncan and Esther Dale in *Damaged Goods* (GN)

3. Orin Heyward and William Gargan in *She Asked For It* (Par)

4. Toby Wing in *Sing While You're Able* (Mel)

5. Jeanne Martel, Edward Nugent and Grady Sutton in *Two Minutes to Play* (Vic)

6. Charles Starrett (l) and Lew Meehan (r) in *Trapped* (Col)

7. Tom Keene and David Sharpe in *Where Trails Divide* (MoP)

8. Chico, Harpo and Groucho Marx and Frank Albertson in *A Day at the Races* (MGM)

9. Rex Lease, Slim Whitaker and Ed Cassidy in *The Silver Trail* (Rel/WS)

10. Carl 'Cherokee' Matthews and Fred Scott in *Melody of the Plains* (Spe)

11. Fred Allen

12. Allan 'Rocky' Lane

13. James Stephenson and Betty Lynne in *Dangerous Fingers* (Ria)

14. Smith Ballew

15. Rosalind Keith and Don Terry in *A Fight to the Finish* (Col)

16. Roscoe Karns, Ruth Coleman and Grant Richards in *A Night of Mystery* (Par)

17. Bob Livingston and Grace Bradley in *Larceny on the Air* (Rep)

18. Joe Sawyer and William Benedict in *A Dangerous Adventure* (Col)

19. William Hopper, Frank Orth (c) and Ann Sheridan in *The Footloose Heiress* (WB)

20. Charles Starrett and Frankie Darro in *Anything for a Thrill* (CoP)

21. Jeanette MacDonald and Nelson Eddy in *Maytime* (MGM)

22. Harvey Clark, Russell Hayden, Gwen Gaze, John Warburton and Bill Boyd in *Partners of the Plains* (Par)

23. Wallace Ford and Isabel Jewell in *Swing It, Sailor* (GN)

24. Frank Ball and Bob Steele in *The Red Rope* (Rep)

25. Roscoe Karns and Judith Allen in *Navy Spy* (GN)

26. Edna Mae Harris and Joe Louis in *Spirit of Youth* (GN)

27. Ralph Bellamy and Joan Perry in *Counterfeit Lady* (Col)

28. Henry Wilcoxon and Anna Sten in *A Woman Alone* (US *Two Who Dared*) (GK)

29. Buck Jones and John Elliott in *Smoke Tree Range* (Univ)

30. Frank Coghlan Jr in *Blazing Barriers* (MoP)

31. Bob Terry, Tom Tyler and Roger Williams in *Brothers of the West* (Vic)

32. John Beach, Bill Boyd and James Ellison in *Borderland* (Par)

381

1

2

3

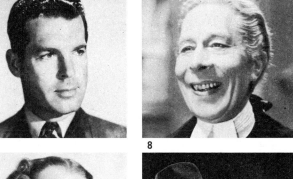

4

5

6 △

7

8

10 △ ▽ 12

11 △ ▽ 13

9 △

14   15   16

17   18

19   20

21 △ ▽23   22 △ ▽24

1. Cecilia Parker in *Sweetheart of the Navy* (GN)

2. Douglas Walton, Van Heflin and Rita La Roy in *Flight from Glory* (RoS/RKO)

3. Ruth Coleman, Colin Tapley and Lew Ayres in *The Crime Nobody Saw* (Par)

4. George Ernest, Spring Byington, Jed Prouty, Florence Roberts and Frank Conroy in *Big Business* (Fox)

5. Sylvia Sidney and Henry Fonda in *You Only Live Once* (WaW)

6. Donald Cook and Thomas E Jackson in *Beware of Ladies* (Rep)

7. Fred MacMurray

8. George Arliss in *Dr Syn* (Gau)

9. Brian Donlevy and Rochelle Hudson in *Born Reckless* (Fox)

10. Betty Furness

11. Gordon Oliver and Marian Marsh in *Youth On Parole* (Rep)

12. Dame May Whitty, Eily Malyon, Rosalind Russell and Merle Tottenham in *Night must Fall* (MGM)

13. Brandon Evans (l) and George O'Brien (c) in *Windjammer* (RKO)

14. Helen Broderick, Edward Gargan, James Carlyle and Colleen Clare in *We're on the Jury* (RKO)

15. Jack La Rue and Jack Holt in *Trapped by G-Men* (Col)

16. David Carlyle and Carol Hughes in *Meet the Boy Friend* (Rep)

17. Bert Wheeler, Robert Woolsey and Esther Muir in *On Again, Off Again* (RKO)

18. Marvin Stephens, Stuart Erwin and Jane Withers in *Checkers* (Fox)

19. Elsie Randolph and Jack Buchanan in *Smash and Grab* (JB)

20. Arthur Margetson, Margaretta Scott and Clive Brook in *Action for Slander* (VS/LF)

21. Terry Walker and Benny Baker in *Blonde Trouble* (Par)

22. Roscoe Karns and Lynne Overman in *Partners in Crime* (Par)

23. David Niven and Annabella in *Dinner at the Ritz* (NW)

24. Jane Withers and Thomas Beck in *Forty-five Fathers* (JSt/Fox)

13 14

16

15

17 18

1. John Morley and Barbara Pepper in *Too Many Wives* (RKO)
2. Terry Walker and James Ellison in *23½ Hours Leave* (GN)
3. Frank McHugh and Carol Hughes in *Marry the Girl* (WB)
4. George Regas, Nena Quartero and Buck Jones in *Left Handed Law* (Univ)
5. Edmund Lowe and Madge Evans in *Espionage* (MGM)
6. George O'Brien and Maude Eburne in *Hollywood Cowboy* (RKO)
7. Marion Claire and Bobby Breen (r) in *Make a Wish* (SL)
8. Jessie Matthews and Robert Flemyng in *Head Over Heels* (Gau)
9. Bruce Seton and Sally Gray in *Cafe Colette* (GF)
10. Bill Boyd and Russell Hayden in *Hopalong Rides Again* (Par)
11. June Travis and William Hopper in *Over the Goal* (FN)
12. Edward Everett Horton and Genevieve Tobin in *The Man in the Mirror* (JHP/War)
13. Edward Arnold, Jean Arthur and Ray Milland in *Easy Living* (Par)
14. Lynn Roberts and William Henry in *Mama Runs Wild* (Rep)
15. Samuel S Hinds, Barbara Reed and Noah Beery Jr in *The Mighty Treve* (Univ)
16. Eddie Acuff and Lyle Talbot in *What Price Vengeance* (Ria)
17. Jean Rogers and Scott Colton in *The Wildcatter* (Univ)
18. Lola Lane and Ramon Novarro in *The Sheik Steps Out* (Rep)
19. George Murphy and Josephine Hutchinson in *The Women Men Marry* (MGM)
20. Bruce Cabot and Beatrice Roberts in *Love Takes Flight* (GN)
21. Joe Cook and Marjorie Gateson in *Arizona Mahoney* (Par)

19 20

21

1

2

3

1. Lona Andre and Ken Maynard in *Trailing Trouble* (GN)
2. Gene Autry in *Oh Susanna* (Rep)
3. Jack Holt and Grace Bradley in *Roaring Timber* (Col)
4. Dick Purcell and Ben Welden in *Missing Witnesses* (WB)
5. Nan Grey and Richard Carle in *The Man in Blue* (Univ)
6. Jean Muir and Gordon Oliver in *White Bondage* (WB)
7. Lee Brown and Betty Grable in *This Way Please* (Par)
8. Dick Purcell, Patricia Ellis and James Melton in *Melody for Two* (WB)
9. Hedy Lamarr in *Ecstase* (Jew)
10. Richard Arlen (c) in *Silent Barriers* (Gau)
11. James Millican, Richard Dix and Joan Perry in *The Devil is Driving* (Col)
12. Lyda Roberti and Pert Kelton in *Nobody's Baby* (HR/MGM)

4

5

6

7 △ ▽10

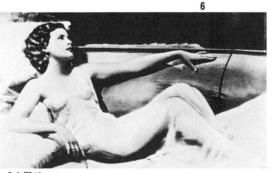

8 △ ▽11

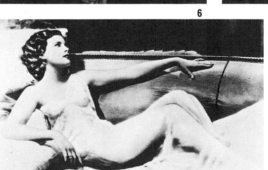

9 △ ▽12

3

1. Marion Weldon and Charles Starrett in *Dodge City Trail* (Col)
2. Virginia Field and George Murphy in *London by Night* (MGM)
3. Robert Armstrong and Irene Hervey in *The Girl Said No* (GN)
4. Suzanne Karen, Maude Eburne and Joe E Brown in *When's Your Birthday?* (RKO)
5. Eleanor Whitney, Johnny Downs and Roscoe Karns in *Clarence* (Par)
6. Jimmy Savo, Billy House, Bert Lahr and Mischa Auer in *Merry Go Round of 1938* (Univ)
7. Lyle Talbot and Polly Rowles in *Westbound Limited* (Univ)
8. Pauline Moore and Allan Lane in *Charlie Chan at the Olympics* (Fox)
9. Franklin Pangborn in *The Mandarin Mystery* (Rep)
10. Ann Harding, Donald Calthrop and Basil Rathbone in *Love from a Stranger* (Tra)
11. Karen Morley, Roscoe Karns and Eduardo Ciannelli in *On Such a Night* (EC/Par)

6

8 △ ▽ 11

9 △ ▽ 10

1

2 3

4

5

6 7

8

9 10

11 12

13 14

15

1. Eleanor Hunt and Conrad Nagel in *The Gold Racket* (GN)
2. Van Heflin and Marian Marsh in *Saturday's Heroes* (RKO)
3. Jane Wyman and Kenny Baker in *Mr Dodd takes the Air* (WB)
4. Armida, John Beal and Harry Carey in *Border Cafe* (RKO)
5. Dick Purcell, Alan Baxter and Margaret Irving in *Men in Exile* (FN)
6. Florence Roberts, George Ernest, Jed Prouty and Spring Byington in *Hot Water* (Fox)
7. Lee Tracy and Margot Grahame in *Criminal Lawyer* (RKO)
8. Gordon Jones and Betty Furness in *They Wanted to Marry* (RKO)
9. Gordon Jones, Victor McLaglen and Preston Foster in *Sea Devils* (RKO)
10. Shemp Howard and Buck Jones in *Headin' East* (Col)
11. John Barrymore, John Howard and Reginald Denny in *Bulldog Drummond Comes Back* (Par)
12. Jeanne Madden (I) and Donald Woods in *Talent Scout* (GB *Studio Romance*) (FN)
13. Will Hay and Lilli Palmer in *Where There's a Will* (G'boro)
14. Robertson Hare and Jack Hulbert in *The Two of Us* (G'boro)
15. Franchot Tone and Maureen O'Sullivan in *Between Two Women* (MGM)
16. Joyce Compton and Stuart Erwin in *Small Town Boy* (GN)
17. Hugh Sinclair and Constance Cummings in *Strangers on a Honeymoon* (Gau)
18. Victor Moore, Anne Shirley and Alan Bruce in *Meet the Missus* (AL/RKO)
19. Eleanor Hunt and Conrad Nagel in *Bank Alarm* (GN)

16 17

18 19

12 13

14 15

1. Joan Fontaine and Preston Foster in *You Can't Beat Love* (RKO)
2. Diana Gibson and Lee Tracy in *Behind the Headlines* (RKO)
3. Tom Tyler in *Orphan of the Pecos* (Vic)
4. William Gargan (l) and Don Wilson (r) in *Behind the Mike* (Univ)
5. Etienne Girardot, Jack Haley, Ann Sothern, Walter Catlett, Bennie Bartlett, John Carradine and Mary Boland in *Danger - Love at Work* (Fox)
6. Beverly Roberts and Patric Knowles in *Expensive Husbands* (WB)
7. Horace Murphy and Johnny Mack Brown in *The Gambling Terror* (Rep)
8. Jimmie Lucas, John Wayne and Diana Gibson in *Adventure's End* (Univ)
9. Ronald Reagan and June Travis in *Love is on the Air* (GB *The Radio Murder Mystery*) (FN)
10. Conrad Veidt and Annabella in *Under the Red Robe* (Fox)
11. Karen Morley, Robert Baldwin and Katherine Alexander in *The Girl from Scotland Yard* (Par)
12. Cecilia Parker and Eric Linden in *Girl Loves Boy* (GN)
13. Kent Taylor, Wendy Barrie and Walter Pidgeon in *A Girl with Ideas* (Univ)
14. Gene Raymond and Harriet Hilliard in *Life of the Party* (RKO)
15. Douglas Fairbanks Jr and Valerie Hobson in *When Thief Meets Thief* (GB *Jump for Glory*) (Cri)
16. Leah Ray, Tony Martin and Dixie Dunbar in *Sing and Be Happy* (MF/Fox)
17. Robert Wilcox and Dorothea Kent in *Carnival Queen* (Univ)
18. Richard Dix and Fay Wray in *It Happened in Hollywood* (Col)
19. Jack Haley and Rosina Lawrence in *Pick A Star* (HR/MGM)
20. Barbara Stanwyck and Herbert Marshall in *Breakfast for Two* (RKO)

16 17

18 19 20

1

2

3

Captains Courageous (MGM) was a milestone in Spencer Tracy's brilliant career. For his performance in this film he received the accolade of the Academy Award for Best Actor of the year.

1. Spencer Tracy, Freddie Bartholomew and Lionel Barrymore
2. Jack La Rue and Freddie Bartholomew
3. Freddie Bartholomew, Melvyn Douglas and Charles Trowbridge
4. John Carradine and Lionel Barrymore
5. Lionel Barrymore and Mickey Rooney
6. Lionel Barrymore, John Carradine and Spencer Tracy
7. Mickey Rooney, John Carradine, Charles Grapewin, Lionel Barrymore, Spencer Tracy and Freddie Bartholomew
8. Spencer Tracy, Freddie Bartholomew and Lionel Barrymore
9. Freddie Bartholomew (l)
10. Melvyn Douglas, Lionel Barrymore and Mickey Rooney
11. Freddie Bartholomew
12. Melvyn Douglas (l)
13. Melvyn Douglas and Freddie Bartholomew

4

5

6

7

8 △ ▽ 11

9 △ ▽ 12

10 △ ▽ 13

1

4

5   6

7   8

9 △ ▽ 11   10 △ ▽ 12   ▽ 13

14

The Life of Emile Zola (WB) won the Academy Award for the Best Film of the year for Warner Brothers, an honour largely due to Paul Muni's magnificent performance as Zola. Joseph Schildkraut won the Award for best Supporting Actor.

1. Paul Muni and Gloria Holden
2. & 3. Paul Muni
4. Vladimir Sokoloff, Paul Muni and Erin O'Brien Moore
5. Paul Muni and Gloria Holden
6. Paul Muni and Erin O'Brien Moore
7. Paul Muni and Louis Hayward
8. John Litel and Paul Muni
9. Paul Muni and Vladimir Sokoloff
10. Donald Crisp and Paul Muni
11. Paul Muni (I)
12. Paul Muni
13. Paul Muni and Gloria Holden
14. Donald Crisp and Paul Muni

393

1

2

3

4

5

6

7

8

9

10 △ ▽ 13

11

12 △ ▽ 14

1. Raymond Walburn
2. Katherine DeMille
3. Susan Hayward
4. Harriet Hilliard
5. Dorothy Kent
6. Dick Foran
7. Grace Bradley
8. Victor Varconi
9. Jack Carson
10. Broderick Crawford
11. Tim Holt
12. Sally Eilers
13. Bonita Granville
14. John Howard

394

1

2

3

4

5

6

7

8

9 △ ▽ 13

10

11 △ ▽ 14

12

1. Grace Moore
2. Rita Hayworth
3. Tallulah Bankhead
4. Dame May Whitty
5. Laraine Day
6. Hedy Lamarr
7. Jack La Rue
8. Eric Blore
9. Richard Denning
10. Maxie Rosenbloom
11. Barry K Barnes
12. Grant Mitchell
13. Jane Carr
14. Max Terhune

395

Walt Disney was taking a huge financial risk when the brilliant artists in his studio set to work on the first feature-length animated cartoon film ever made, namely *Snow White and the Seven Dwarfs* (Walt Disney). It was a work of sheer genius and even today this wonderful movie still enchants the hearts of millions of children all over the world and continues to reap massive profits for the Disney organisation. Every song was a musical gem. Age has not diminished its splendour. All stills reproduced © The Walt Disney Company.

17   18   19   20

21   22

23   24

25

1. Robert Emmett O'Connor
2. Donald Crisp
3. Gwili Andre
4. Robert Greig
5. Dick Foran (c) and Anne Nagel in *The Devil's Saddle Legion* (WB)
6. Judith Barrett and Robert Wilcox in *Let Them Live* (Univ)
7. Margaret Lockwood, Desmond Tester and Maurice Chevalier in *The Beloved Vagabond* (T)
8. Johnny Mack Brown and Iris Meredith in *Trail of Vengeance* (Rep)
9. Walter Connolly and Carole Lombard in *Nothing Sacred* (DS)
10. Bobs Watson, Marjorie Mein, Phyllis Brooks and George Lynn in *City Girl* (Fox)
11. Henry Fonda and Dorothy Stickney in *I Met my Love Again* (WaW)
12. Tom Tyler, Lon Chaney Jr and Lucile Browne in *Cheyenne Rides Again* (Vic)
13. Edward Kennedy
14. William Gargan, J P McGowan and James McGrath in *Fury and the Woman* (Ria)
15. Roscoe Ates
16. Lafe McKee
17. John Wray
18. J Farrell MacDonald
19. Olympe Bradna
20. James Newill and Carol Hughes in *Renfrew of the Royal Mounted* (GN)
21. Frank Craven, Shirley Ross and Edward Arnold in *Blossoms on Broadway* (BPS/Par)
22. Fred Scott and Lois January in *Moonlight on the Range* (Spe)
23. Sammy McKimm, Ray Corrigan, Max Terhune and Lynn Roberts in *Heart of the Rockies* (Rep)
24. Marjorie Lord, Barbara Pepper George Shelley in *Forty Naughty Girls* (WSm/RKO)
25. Gene Autry, Polly Rowles and Smiley Burnette in *Springtime in the Rockies* (Rep)

Bette Davis in *Jezebel* (WB)

Claude Rains in *The Adventures of Robin Hood* (FN)

Errol Flynn in *The Adventures of Robin Hood* (FN)

CHAPTER NINE

1938

BETTE AND BETTER STILL

The year 1938 was when Bette Davis vindicated herself. Under contract to Warner Brothers for the past six years, she became dissatisfied with the films they were selecting for her. She began to refuse parts and went to Europe where she was offered a couple of pictures, but an injunction was issued by Warners. She sued them in an English court but lost. Obliged to return to Hollywood to honour the contract she had with Warners, she was surprised to find her legal expenses met by them and an excellent film awaiting her. *Jezebel* was just what she wanted – and what her fans wanted. It won her the Best Actress Oscar and was nominated best film of the year.

She plays a headstrong Southern girl. In one memorable scene she scandalizes the town by attending a society ball in a red gown – unmarried women were supposed to wear white. It says much for William Wyler's direction that fans of the film always remember that red dress vividly – even though the film was black-and-white. As a result she loses her fiance (Henry Fonda) but atones for her sins when yellow fever strikes and she accompanies the afflicted Fonda to an island for plague victims from which they have no hope of returning. This is one of cinema's great climactic scenes.

The Sisters, Bette Davis's other film this year, was not in the same league but still a good example of the 'woman's picture' of the period.

Flynn, one of the most handsome and virile actors of the day, was the perfect choice for the title role in *The Adventures of Robin Hood*, directed by Michael Curtiz, one of his best films ever and a leading action film of the decade. Errol Flynn tackled his part with gusto and good humour. Olivia de Havilland was an appealing and spirited Maid Marian, while Basil Rathbone and Claude Rains were at their evil best as the dastardly villains Sir Guy of Gisbourne and Prince John respectively, and Eugene Pallette was prominent (in more ways than one) as Friar Tuck.

The whole affair was a splendid romp in ravishing Technicolor. Although this film was nominated for the

Best Picture Oscar, that award went to *You Can't Take It With You* which also won an Oscar for its director, Frank Capra. Based on a Moss Hart-George Kaufman play, it was a madcap affair about an eccentric family. The mother (played by the delightful Spring Byington) is writing a novel simply because a typewriter was once wrongly delivered to the house. The father (Samuel S. Hinds) makes fireworks in the basement. A Russian ballet master (Mischa Auer) has somehow taken up residence, giving rise to much pirouetting by the younger daughter (Ann Miller). Pandemonium reigns.

The sanest member of the family is the older daughter (Jean Arthur) who falls for the son (James Stewart) of a millionaire determined to acquire the land the house stands on. Eviction looms.

Perhaps the craziest of the crazy 'screwball' comedies of the Thirties is *Bringing Up Baby*. The baby of the title is a pet leopard for which the eccentric Susan Vance (Katharine Hepburn) is 'babysitting' until her brother returns from the Amazon.

Into the maelstrom of Susan's life falls David Huxley (Cary Grant), a stuffy, absent-minded palaeontologist whose purpose in life is to find the missing intercostal clavicle that will complete his precious brontosaurus skeleton. Instead he finds himself on a mad cross-country chase with Miss Vance in the pursuit of the cuddly Baby.

James Stewart and Jean Arthur in *You Can't Take it With You* (Col)

Walter Catlett and Katharine Hepburn in *Bringing Up Baby* (RKO)

Howard Hawkes' direction gleefully combines action with insanity and secures achingly funny performances from both his stars.

In 1938 Laurel and Hardy made their last two features for MGM, with whom they had been associated throughout the Thirties.

Swiss Miss presents them as mousetrap salesmen who come to a Tyrolean hotel. The film has leanings towards operetta – the love interest was provided by a couple of opera singers – and thus the comedians' contributions are somewhat spasmodic. One of their best scenes shows them trying to get a piano across a rope bridge, impeded by a gorilla intent on getting across from the other direction.

But there were no singing interruptions in their film, *Blockheads*. This begins with Ollie finding his old buddy Stan still guarding First World War trenches 20 years after the end of hostilities (nobody had told him the war was over) and goes on to show the rumpus that erupts when Ollie takes him home to meet the new wife.

Spencer Tracy, one of the big stars at MGM, won the 1938 Best Actor Oscar (for the second year running) for his portrayal of Father Flanagan in *Boys' Town*. There really was such a person – and such a place. Boys' Town was a home for delinquent youths founded by a Nebraskan priest. The most troublesome resident in the film is played with typical verve by Mickey Rooney. He eventually reforms, of course – in an unabashedly sentimental manner that delighted audiences of the day.

Above: Oliver Hardy
Below: Spencer Tracy in *Boys' Town* (MGM)

Ann Rutherford and Mickey Rooney in *Judge Hardy's Children* (MGM)

Norma Shearer in *Marie Antoinette* (MGM)

Tyrone Power in *Marie Antoinette* (MGM)

Lionel Atwill and Fernand Gravet in *The Great Waltz* (MGM)

The indefatigable Rooney made eight films in 1938, among them three in the enormously popular Andy Hardy series – *Judge Hardy's Children*, *Out West With the Hardys* and *Love Finds Andy Hardy*. The last is notable for having in its cast the fledgling talents of Lana Turner and Judy Garland. Turner had played small parts in five films for other studios, and MGM, sensing great potential, decided to try her out as the object of Andy Hardy's schoolboy affections. She stayed with the studio for 16 years and became one of their biggest assets, a leading sex symbol of the Forties. Garland, too, became one of their greatest attractions.

Mickey Rooney won an Oscar this year. Together with Deanna Durbin he was awarded a Special Oscar for bringing to the screen the spirit and personification of youth, and as a juvenile player setting a high standard of ability and achievement. By 1938, at the age of 18, he had already made 67 shorts and 35 features!

In 1938 a prestige film for MGM was *Marie Antoinette* starring Norma Shearer who had been away from the screen for two years following the death of her husband, Irving Thalberg, the young genius who was the head of production. MGM's renowned art and wardrobe departments excelled themselves in making the court of Louis XVI a very opulent place – very much France a la Hollywood.

Louis XVI is portrayed as feeble-minded and petulant by Robert Morley, 'imported' from England to make his film debut. Louis XV is played to the hilt by the legendary John Barrymore, and Gladys George makes the most of a brief role as Madame du Barry. The grand sets seemed to inspire grand performances as events led inexorably to the climactic guillotine scenes. Norma Shearer, in the title role, did well enough to be given her sixth Oscar nomination. To portray Antoinette's Swedish lover, Count Axel de Fersen, MGM borrowed handsome Tyrone Power from Twentieth Century-Fox.

At his home studio Power made two big films. One of them, *In Old Chicago,* was a lively piece of fiction culminating in an actual event, the great Chicago fire of 1871. The conflagration provided one of the year's great screen spectacles. It was Fox's reply to MGM's highly-praised earthquake in *San Francisco* two years earlier. Alice Brady won the Supporting Actress Oscar for her portrayal of Mrs O'Leary whose cow starts the fire by kicking over a lantern in its stable. Power plays one of her two sons, a gambler. The other is a more respectable citizen, a lawyer who rises to become mayor, played by Don Ameche. Alice Faye plays the saloon singer who comes between them.

Power, Ameche and Faye were also teamed in *Alexander's Ragtime Band*, one of the year's best musicals.

A big-scale musical at MGM was *The Great Waltz*, the first American film directed by France's Julien Duvivier. Purporting to tell the love life of Johann Strauss II, it is as gooey as Viennese confectionery but filmed with considerable flair (its photography won an Oscar). The famous waltz king is played by Fernand Gravet, a Frenchman, his wife by Luise Rainer, an Austrian, and the opera singer who comes between them by Miliza Korjus from Hungary. 'Pronounce her name 'Gorgeous',' said the adverts.

Despite an Oscar nomination for her performance, Korjus never made another film; in fact, this was her only one. But someone just beginning a prominent career at the time was Hedy Lamarr. *Ecstase* which she had made in her native Sweden in 1933, had caused a sensation with its glimpses of her running naked through woodland. Consequently she was lured to America and in 1938 made an impressive English-speaking debut in *Algiers*. In it she played a Parisienne visiting the Casbah who attracts a French crook (Charles Boyer). Smitten by her, he longs to return home but cannot leave Algiers without being arrested. The film is a remake (by John Cromwell) of Julian Duvivier's 1936 French classic, *Pépé le Moko*. Lamarr was perhaps no great actress but she was breathtakingly beautiful. It's said she never cared to smile for fear it caused lines on her beautiful face!

Another thespian on the brink of a big career was Bob Hope. After some years in vaudeville he graduated to comedy roles in Broadway musicals and made a number of comedy shorts. However, it wasn't until he decided to concentrate on radio that his career really took off. He became such a national favourite that he found the film world beckoning him back to his first feature – *The Big Broadcast of 1938*. In it he sings what was to become his signature tune, 'Thanks for the Memory', which won the year's Oscar for best song. Presented as a duet with Shirley Ross, it was such a hit that the two were quickly signed up for another film which was given the title *Thanks for the Memory*. In it they had another successful song, 'Two Sleepy People'.

One of the top British films of 1938 was *Pygmalion*. This was the first major attempt to film a work by George Bernard Shaw, whose writing had hitherto been considered too 'wordy' for the cinema. And Shaw himself had never been too keen. It was producer Gabriel Pascal who persuaded the great man of letters to change his mind.

Leslie Howard is ideal as the arrogant Professor of Phonetics, Henry Higgins. He shared the direction with Anthony Asquith.

Wendy Hiller makes an impressive movie debut as Eliza Doolittle, the Cockney guttersnipe whom Higgins turns into a lady. Another memorable performance is given by Wilfrid Lawson as Eliza's dustman father. Others in a cast of top British talent are Marie Lohr as Mrs Higgins, David Tree as Freddy, and Scott Sunderland as Colonel Pickering.

In 1938 Hitchcock made *The Lady Vanishes* now regarded as the best of his British films. Margaret Lockwood, one of the most popular British stars of the day, has the leading role as a girl aboard a trans-European train who takes it on herself to investigate the disappearance of a little old

Miliza Korjus in *The Great Waltz* (MGM)

Top: Hedy Lamarr
Above: A scene from *Ecstase* (Jew)

Wendy Hiller in *Pygmalion* (PFP)

Naunton Wayne and Basil Radford in *The Lady Vanishes* (Gau/G'boro)

Charles Laughton in *Vessel of Wrath* (US *The Beachcomber*) (Mfl)

Above: Rosalind Russell and Robert Donat in *The Citadel* (MGM)
Below: Nikolai Cherkassov in *Alexander Nevsky* (Mosfilm)

lady (Dame May Whitty). Co-starring as the young man who helps her unravel the mystery is Michael Redgrave in his film debut. Outstanding support is given by Basil Radford and Naunton Wayne as Charters and Caldicott, a couple of cricket-obsessed passengers whose main concern on the eventful train journey is getting home to England in time for a test match. British audiences liked these characters so much that they appeared in other films.

British actor Charles Laughton, after some triumphs in Hollywood, returned home in 1938 to make a couple of films for producer Erich Pommer, with whom he formed Mayflower Pictures. Laughton was at his boisterous best in both of them. In *St Martin's Lane* (US: *Sidewalks of London*) he plays a street musician who is attracted to a young dancer who becomes a star. She was played by Vivien Leigh.

In the other Mayflower production, *Vessel of Wrath* (US: *The Beachcomber*), Laughton plays a tippling, ribald beachcomber. Based on a Somerset Maugham story and set in the Dutch East Indies, it also stars Elsa Lanchester (Laughton's wife) a missionary's spinster sister who at first despises the beachcomber but whose attitude towards him changes – she even fancies him – when they find themselves stranded together on an island. In the supporting cast is Robert Newton who also appeared in the inferior 1954 version when he played the Laughton part.

Another quality British production was *The Citadel* based on a novel by A.J. Cronin. Robert Donat has the lead as an idealistic doctor in a Welsh mining community who temporarily succumbs to the get-rich-quick world of Harley Street. It was the second film to be made in England by MGM; the first had been *A Yank at Oxford*, also released in 1938 but started the previous year. They sent over King Vidor to direct – and, as leading lady, Rosalind Russell who was somewhat miscast as Donat's long-suffering wife. But as compensation there are many excellent British actors in the supporting cast, among them Ralph Richardson, Rex Harrison and Emlyn Williams.

In 1938 Russian's legendary director, Sergei Eisenstein, presented one of his infrequent films, his first to be completed in nine years and his first sound film. It was *Alexander Nevsky*, named after the prince who defeated German invaders, the Teutonic Knights, in 1242. Starring Nikolai Cherkassov, it was a rousing historical pageant culminating in the famous battle on the frozen Lake Peipus. In keeping with all Eisenstein's films, it was beautifully photographed, with the excitement heightened by a score especially composed by Prokofiev. The soundtrack for the final battle scene was pure music without any natural sounds.

Mark Donskoi, a director who had studied with Eisenstein, did the master proud when he made *The Gorky Trilogy*, three films which he adapted from Maxim Gorky's autobiography. *The Childhood of Maxim Gorky* (1938) is the first. It is a lyrical account of the author's early years in a small town near the Volga with his warm, life-giving grandmother (played by the great Russian actress Massalikinowa) and his tyrannical grandfather.

In *My Apprenticeship* (1939) our hero has grown to adolescence and tried a series of jobs. *My Universities* (1940) are not imposing buildings with gowned professors but the universities of human experience – of relationships, of revolutions, of the whole quest for knowledge of life.

All three films are full of beautiful imagery and convey, with warmth and verve, an impressively realistic account of life in Tsarist Russia.

Germany's well-known *Olympische Spiele/Olympia (Berlin Olympiad)* is one of the best and most beautiful records of the Games there has ever been. However, it was at the same time a completely overt piece of Nazi propaganda. All the glory of the Games, all the triumphs of victors, all the beauty of the participants is shown to be but a reflection of the Party's ideals and achievements. The film was premiered on Hitler's birthday.

It is a two-part documentary made by Leni Riefenstahl, the woman director who had already pleased Hitler immensely four years earlier with her documentary about the 1934 Nuremberg Rally – *Triumph des Willens (Triumph of the Will)*.

Meanwhile, in France, Jean Gabin continued to be one of the great stars of the Gallic cinema. His two main films of 1938 were a little sombre. In *Quai des Brumes (Port of Shadows)*, directed by Marcel Carne from a screenplay by Jacques Prevert, he plays an army deserter on the run. In a seedy little café in fog-bound and menacing Le Havre he meets Nellie (Michele Morgan) an attractive but unhappy girl. He persuades her to run away in the hope of finding a better life with him – but, alas, they are doomed.

La Bete Humaine (Judas Was a Woman) has Gabin as an engine driver. He falls in love with a conductor's wife (Simone Simon) and she inviegles him into agreeing to kill her husband, but he winds up killing the woman (who has proved equally unfaithful to him) instead.

The drab side of life, something the French could portray so convincingly and artistically, was also shown in *Hotel du Nord*. The title referred to a rundown hostelry on the side of a canal that has attracted all manner of weird and strange people.

Our final film in this survey of 1938 is *La Femme du Boulanger (The Baker's Wife)*, a delicious comedy from Marcel Pagnol set in a delightful Provençal village. The great character actor Raimu plays the baker who threw the village into turmoil by refusing to work when his young, delectable wife (Ginette Leclerc) runs off with a shepherd (Charles Moulin). The villagers have to band together to effect a reconciliation so that normal life – i.e., life with bread – can be resumed. This is a charming film – quintessential French comedy; indeed for French cinema, this was a vintage year.

Three scenes from *Olympische Spiele / Olympia* (LR)

Jean Gabin and Michel Simon in *Quai des Brumes (Port of Shadows)* (Rbv)

Above: Jean Gabin in *La Bete Humaine (Judas was a Woman)* (XX)
Below: Raimu in *La Femme du Boulanger (The Baker's Wife)* (XX)

Bing Crosby was in full spate, crooning his love songs unceasingly. Harold Lloyd was still in tip-top form, rocking them in the aisles with his helter-skelter comedy routines. George O'Brien had never hesitated in his hot pursuit of baddies across the boundless prairies. Little did the film world know that the holocaust was only a few months ahead.

Donald O'Connor, Fred MacMurray and Bing Crosby in *Sing You Sinners* (Par)

Milton Berle, Bob Burns and Jack Oakie in *Radio City Revels* (RKO)

Earle Hodgins, Walter Miller, George O'Brien in *Lawless Valley* (RKO)

Phyllis Welch and Harold Lloyd in *Professor Beware* (Par)

Glenda Farrell and Barton MacLane in *Blondes at Work* (WB)

Dick Foran, Helen Mack and Edmund Lowe in *Secrets of a Nurse* (Univ)

Minna Gombell, Dick Powell, Walter Catlett and Thurston Hall in *Going Places* (FN)

Claire Trevor and Michael Whalen in *Walking Down Broadway* (Fox)

Dolores Del Rio and George Sanders in *International Settlement* (Fox)

Vicki Lester, Allan Lane and Victor Moore in *This Marriage Business* (RKO)

Claire Trevor, Inez Courtney and Cesar Romero in *Five of a Kind* (Fox)

George O'Brien and Stanley Fields in *The Painted Desert* (RKO)

Anne Shirley and Frank Albertson in *Mother Carey's Chickens* (RKO)

Reginald Gardiner, Nelson Eddy and Jeanette MacDonald in *Sweethearts* (MGM)

Margaret Tallichet, Martha O'Driscoll, Kenneth Howell, Jean Lucius, Marjorie Deane and Peggy Moran in *Girl's School* (Col)

Picture Gallery for 1938

8 △▽ 10   ▽11

1. Eddie 'Rochester' Anderson
2. Franchot Tone, Robert Young and Robert Taylor in *Three Comrades* (MGM)
3. Dick Powell, Penny Singleton, Olivia de Havilland and Charles Winninger in *Hard to Get* (WB)
4. Barbara Stanwyck and Herbert Marshall in *Always Goodbye* (Fox)
5. Jane Withers, Jean Rogers and Eddie Collins in *Always in Trouble* (Fox)
6. Tim Holt and Harry Carey in *The Law, West of Tombstone* (RKO)
7. Jacqueline Wells, Allen Brook, Scott Colton and Patricia Farr in *All American Sweetheart* (Col)
8. Donald Crisp, Sam McDaniel and Ronald Reagan in *Sergeant Murphy* (WB)
9. Humphrey Bogart, Bobby Jordan and Huntz Hall in *Crime School* (WB)
10. Dorothy Lamour, Martha Raye, Shirley Ross and W C Fields in *The Big Broadcast of 1938* (Par)
11. Deanna Durbin in *Mad About Music* (Univ)

1. Mary Maguire, Addison Richards and Ann Sheridan in *Alcatraz Island* (FN)

2. Ruth Terry, George Murphy and Donald Meek in *Hold that Co-ed* (GB *Hold that Girl*) (Fox)

3. Melvyn Douglas, Walter Kingsford and Thurston Hall in *There's Always a Woman* (Col)

4. Tyrone Power and Annabella in *Suez* (Fox)

5. Dick Curtis, Paul Kelly and C Henry Gordon in *Adventure in Sahara* (Col)

6. Barbara Stanwyck and Henry Fonda in *The Mad Miss Manton* (RKO)

7. Dick Purcell and Ann Sheridan in *Mystery House* (FN)

8. Maureen O'Sullivan, John Beal and Wallace Beery in *Port of Seven Seas* (MGM)

9. Fred Stone and Hattie McDaniel in *Quick Money* (RKO)

10. Robert Montgomery and Janet Gaynor in *Three Loves Has Nancy* (MGM)

11. Thurston Hall, Ralph Forbes and Kay Francis in *Women Are Like That* (FN)

12. Margaret Lindsay, George Brent, Bette Davis and Henry Fonda in *Jezebel* (Col)

9 △ ▽ 11

10 △ ▽ 12

1

2

3

4

5

6 △ ▽8

7 △ ▽9

1. Ann Sheridan
2. Wendy Hiller
3. Maureen O'Hara
4. June Clyde
5. Marjorie Reynolds
6. Florence Desmond
7. Gloria Swanson
8. Evelyn Keyes
9. Anna Sten

1 2

3 4

5 △ ▽ 7 6 △ ▽ 8

9

1. Fernand Gravet
2. Errol Flynn
3. James Ellison
4. Ray Bolger
5. Alan Baxter
6. Dennis O'Keefe
7. Richard Greene
8. Ray Walker
9. Johnny Weissmuller

411

1 2

3

4

5

6 △ ▽ 9

7

8 △ ▽ 10

1. Andrea Leeds and Joel McCrea in *Youth Takes a Fling* (JP/Univ)
2. Cecilia Parker, Lewis Stone and Mickey Rooney in *Love Finds Andy Hardy* (MGM)
3. Mary Astor, Herbert Marshall and Virginia Bruce in *Woman Against Woman* (MGM)
4. Robert Montgomery and Virginia Bruce in *Yellow Jack* (MGM)
5. Donald Crisp and Kay Francis in *Comet Over Broadway* (WB)
6. Robert Barrat, Dennis O'Keefe and Wallace Beery in *Bad Man of Brimstone* (MGM)
7. Neil Hamilton, Madge Evans and Preston Foster in *Army Girl* (Rep)
8. Clark Gable and Leo Carrillo in *Too Hot to Handle* (MGM)
9. Pola Negri
10. Barbara Stanwyck and William Holden in *Golden Boy* (Col)

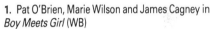

1. Pat O'Brien, Marie Wilson and James Cagney in *Boy Meets Girl* (WB)

2. Alice Faye and Tony Martin in *Sally, Irene and Mary* (Fox)

3. Spencer Tracy, Myrna Loy and Clark Gable in *Test Pilot* (MGM)

4. Richard Arlen, Beverly Roberts and Lyle Talbot in *Call of the Yukon* (Rep)

5. Andrew Tombes, June Lang, Dick Baldwin and Sidney Toler in *One Wild Night* (Fox)

6. Claude Gillingwater, Virginia Bruce, Etienne Girardot, Irving Pichel, Fredric March and Arthur Lake in *There Goes My Heart* (HR)

7. Fay Bainter, Bob Burns, Jean Parker and John Beal in *Arkansas Traveler* (Par)

8. Maureen O'Sullivan and Robert Taylor in *The Crowd Roars* (MGM)

9. Rita Hayworth and Charles Quigley in *Convicted* (Col)

10. Ann Miller and Spring Byington in *You Can't Take It With You* (Col)

11. James Stewart, Jean Arthur, Lionel Barrymore, Spring Byington, Edward Arnold, Ann Miller, Mischa Auer, Donald Meek, Samuel S Hinds and Halliwell Hobbes in *You Can't Take It With You* (Col)

1

2 3

4

5 6

7

8 9

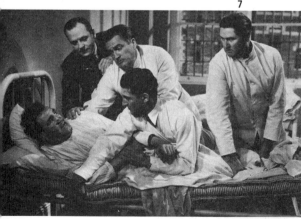

10 △ ▽13

11 △ ▽14

12 △ ▽15

16　17

18

19

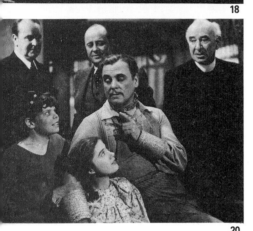

20

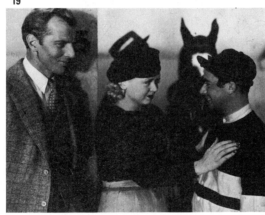

21

1. Gary Cooper, Claudette Colbert and Tyler Brooke in *Bluebeard's Eighth Wife* (Par)
2. Felix Aylmer, John Lodge and Margaret Lockwood in *Bank Holiday* (US *Three On a Weekend*) (G'boro)
3. Will Fyffe
4. Frances Drake and John Boles in *She Married an Artist* (Col)
5. Louise Hovick (Gypsy Rose Lee), Brian Donlevy and Victor McLaglen in *Battle of Broadway* (Fox)
6. Leon Ames, Peter Lorre and Billy Bevan in *Mysterious Mr Moto* (Fox)
7. Lee Bowman and Anne Shirley in *A Man to Remember* (RKO)
8. Phil Harris
9. Arthur Lake, June Johnson and Preston Foster in *Double Danger* (RKO)
10. Tom Kennedy (I) in *Crime Ring* (RKO)
11. Allan Lane and Frances Mercer in *Crime Ring* (RKO)
12. Sheila Bromley and Ronald Reagan in *Accidents Will Happen* (WB)
13. Vera Zorina in *The Goldwyn Follies* (SG)
14. Evelyn Venable and Grant Richards in *My Old Kentucky Home* (MoP)
15. Tex Ritter and Carmen La Roux in *Starlight over Texas* (MoP)
16. Harry Carey, Judith Allen and Milburn Stone in *Port of Missing Girls* (MoP)
17. Melvyn Douglas and Virginia Bruce in *Arsene Lupin Returns* (MGM)
18. Louis Hayward (I) in *Midnight Intruder* (Univ)
19. Richard Cromwell and Marsha Hunt in *Come On, Leathernecks* (Rep)
20. Joseph King, Arthur Loft, Frank Sheridan (t), Tommy Bond, Edith Fellows and Leo Carrillo (b) in *City Streets* (Col)
21. Herman Brix and Toby Wing in *Silks and Saddles* (Tre)
22. Lucille Ball and James Ellison in *Next Time I Marry* (RKO)
23. Ward Bond and Ralph Byrd in *Born to be Wild* (Rep)
24. Helen Chandler and Stuart Erwin in *Mister Boggs Steps Out* (GN)
25. Eddie Collins, Phyllis Brooks, Sidney Toler and Sen Yung in *Charlie Chan in Honolulu* (Fox)
26. Jackie Cooper, Louise Lorimer and Robert Warwick in *Gangster's Boy* (MoP)

22 △　▽ 24

23 △　▽ 25

26

1 2

3

4

5 △ ▽ 7

6 △ ▽ 8

Rebecca of Sunnybrook Farm (Fox) was yet another example of Hollywood taking the title of a well-known book to entice filmgoers into the cinemas. The previous year Shirley Temple had dealt capably with the vague adaptation of *Wee Willie Winkie* (Fox) from Rudyard Kipling's story. As if to add insult to injury, Twentieth Century Fox went to the length of changing Wee Willie Winkie into a girl. *Rebecca of Sunnybrook Farm* had little to do with Kate Douglas Wiggin's famous novel. The movie was just a vehicle for Shirley Temple's talents and popular songs which she had sung in previous films.

1. Clarence Wilson, Shirley Temple, Phyllis Brooks, Helen Westley, Gloria Stuart and William Demarest.
2. Gloria Stuart and Shirley Temple
3. Shirley Temple and Gloria Stuart
4. Shirley Temple and Helen Westley
5. Shirley Temple
6. Slim Summerville and Shirley Temple
7. Shirley Temple and Bill Robinson
8. Bill Robinson, Shirley Temple, Phyllis Brooks, Gloria Stuart, William Demarest and Helen Westley.

1. Margaret Sullavan and James Stewart in *The Shopworn Angel* (MGM)

2. Joyce Compton, (l) and Jacqueline Wells (r) *Spring Madness* (MGM)

3. William Bakewell in *Crime Afloat* (Tre)

4. Stan Laurel, Walter Woolf King and Oliver Hardy in *Swiss Miss* (MGM)

5. Jane Wyman, Cora Witherspoon, Frank McHugh and Burton Churchill in *He Couldn't Say No* (WB)

6. Eleanor Lynne and Mickey Rooney in *You're Only Young Once* (MGM)

7. Jane Bryan, Eddie Albert, Ronald Reagan and Wayne Morris in *Brother Rat* (FN)

8. Louis Hayward (l) in *The Saint in New York* (RKO)

9. Sonja Henie and Louise Hovick in *My Lucky Star* (Fox)

10. Mickey Rooney and Wallace Beery in *Stablemates* (MGM)

11. Freddie Bartholomew and Judy Garland in *Listen Darling* (MGM)

12. Marjorie Weaver, Warner Baxter and Fritz Feld in *I'll Give a Million* (Fox)

8 △ ▽ 10

▽ 11

9 △ ▽ 12

1
2
3

4
5

1. Roy Rogers, Mary Hart and Stanley Andrews in *Shine on Harvest Moon* (Rep)
2. Merle Oberon and Gary Cooper in *The Cowboy and the Lady* (UA)
3. Bob McKenzie, William Boyd and Russell Hayden in *Heart of Arizona* (Par)
4. William B Davidson, Ronald Reagan, Pat O'Brien, Priscilla Lane and Dick Powell in *The Cowboy from Brooklyn* (WB)
5. Smiley Burnette, Pert Kelton, Peggy Moran and Gene Autry in *Rhythm of the Saddle* (Rep)
6. Lynne Roberts and Roy Rogers in *Billy the Kid Returns* (Rep)
7. Gene Autry in *Gold Mine in the Sky* (Rep)
8. Nelson Eddy and Jeanette MacDonald in *The Girl of the Golden West* (MGM)
9. Tim McCoy and Kathleen Eliot in *West of Rainbow's End* (Con/MoP)
10. Evalyn Knapp and Smith Ballew in *Rawhide* (Pri)

6
7

8
9
10

418

1

2

3   4   5

6 △ ▽ 8   7

1. Charles Starrett and Frank Ellis in *Outlaws of the Prairie* (Col)
2. Bob Baker and Joan Barclay in *The Singing Outlaw* (Univ)
3. Steve Clark and Bob Steele in *Paroled to Die* (Rep)
4. Tom Tyler
5. Smiley Burnette, Gene Autry and Helen Valkis in *The Old Barn Dance* (Rep)
6. Karl Hackett and Tim McCoy in *Phantom Ranger* (MoP)
7. Buck Jones and Hank Worden in *The Stranger from Arizona* (Col)
8. George Houston (r) in *Frontier Scout* (GN) 1937
9. Gene Autry in *Western Jamboree* (Rep)
10. Harry Woods and Roy Rogers in *Come On, Rangers!* (Rep)

9   10

419

1. Charles D Brown, Joan Fontaine and Alan Curtis in *The Duke of West Point* (ES)

2. Freddie Bartholomew and Mickey Rooney in *Lord Jeff* (GB *The Boy from Barnardo's*) (MGM)

3. Ginger Rogers, Fred Astaire, Ralph Bellamy and Luella Gear in *Carefree* (RKO)

4. Willard Parker, Edward G Robinson and Jane Bryan in *A Slight Case of Murder* (FN)

5. Anton Walbrook

6. Wilfrid Lawson, Arthur Wontner and Linden Travers in *The Terror* (ABPC)

7. James Craig

8. Akim Tamiroff

9. Ellen Drew, Ronald Colman, Francis J McDonald and Stanley Ridges in *If I Were King* (Par)

10. Dame May Whitty, Margaret Lockwood, Naunton Wayne and Michael Redgrave in *The Lady Vanishes* (Gau/G'boro)

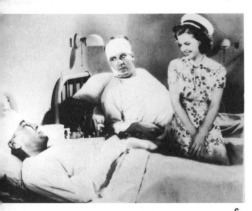

1. Frank Craven, Spring Byington and Billy Mauch in *Penrod and His Twin Brother* (WB)
2. Bobby Breen in *Hawaii Calls* (SL/RKO)
3. Beverly Roberts and Dick Purcell in *The Daredevil Drivers* (FN)
4. Rosalind Russell, Rex Harrison and Robert Donat in *The Citadel* (MGM)
5. Jack Oakie, Chester Clute and Jean Ronverol in *Annabel Takes A Tour* (RKO)
6. Robert Armstrong, Dick Foran and Ann Sheridan in *She Loved A Fireman* (FN)
7. Mary Astor, Frank Morgan and Reginald Owen in *Paradise For Three (GB Romance for Three)* (MGM)
8. George O'Brien and Laraine Johnson in *Border G Man* (RKO)
9. Fredric March (cr) and Margot Grahame (r) in *The Buccaneer* (Par)

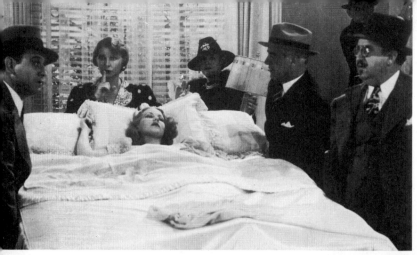

6 △ ▽ 9

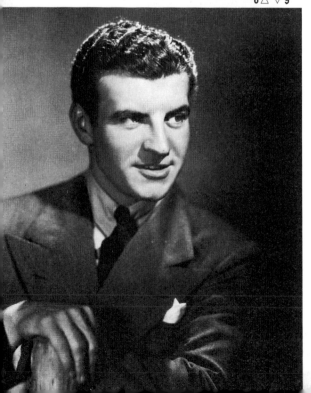

1. Helen Broderick, Ann Sothern and Billy Gilbert (r) in *She's Got Everything* (RKO)

2. Reginald Owen, Terry Kilburn, Barry Mackay and Lynne Carver in *A Christmas Carol* (MGM)

3. James Cagney and Humphrey Bogart in *Angels with Dirty Faces* (FN)

4. James Cagney in *Angels with Dirty Faces* (FN)

5. Walter Huston and James Stewart in *Of Human Hearts* (MGM)

6. James Cagney, George Bancroft and Humphrey Bogart in *Angels with Dirty Faces* (FN)

7. Tom Keene and Leroy Mason in *The Painted Trail* (MoP)

8. Fanny Brice, Henry Armetta, Judy Garland and Allan Jones in *Everybody Sing* (MGM)

9. Robert Preston

10. Craig Reynolds and Evelyn Venable in *Female Fugitive* (MoP)

11. Merle Oberon and Laurence Olivier in *Divorce of Lady X* (LF)

10 △ ▽ 11

1. Helen Broderick and Constance Bennett in *Service De Luxe* (Univ)

2. John Boles, Gladys Swarthout and John Barrymore in *Romance in the Dark* (Par)

3. Deanna Durbin in *That Certain Age* (Univ)

4. Cary Grant and Katharine Hepburn in *Bringing Up Baby* (RKO)

5. John Payne

6. Henry Fonda and Madeleine Carroll in *Blockade* (WaW)

7. Tyrone Power and Alice Faye in *In Old Chicago* (Fox)

8. Edmund Lowe in *Every Day's a Holiday* (Par)

9. Martha Raye in *Give me a Sailor* (Par)

10. Fay Bainter

11. Jack Oakie and Lucille Ball in *The Affairs of Annabel* (RKO)

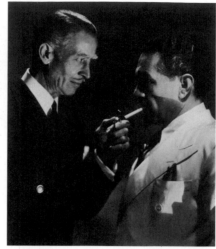

1

3

4

6

5

8

9

10

11

2

7

1. John Howard, Louise Campbell and John Barrymore in *Bulldog Drummond's Peril* (Par)
2. H B Warner and J Carrol Naish in *Bulldog Drummond in Africa* (Par)
3. Max Terhune, John Wayne and Ray Corrigan in *Santa Fe Stampede* (Rep)
4. Jane Wyman, Robert Warwick and William Hall in *The Spy Ring* (Univ)
5. Virginia Weidler and Fred MacMurray in *Men with Wings* (Par)
6. Shirley Temple and Jimmy 'Schnozzle' Durante in *Little Miss Broadway* (Fox)
7. James Stewart and Charles Coburn in *Of Human Hearts* (MGM)
8. Madge Evans and John Boles in *Sinners in Paradise* (KG/Univ)
9. Loretta Young, David Niven, Pauline Moore and Marjorie Weaver in *Three Blind Mice* (Fox)
10. Walter Brennan, Loretta Young and Richard Greene in *Kentucky* (Fox)
11. William Lundigan and Doris Lloyd in *The Black Doll* (Univ)

1. Donald Grayson and Charles Starrett in *Cattle Raiders* (Col)
2. James Mason in *The Return of the Scarlet Pimpernel* (LF)
3. Griffith Jones and Alan Napier in *Wife of General Ling* (JoSt/Pre)
4. Ray Milland and Dorothy Lamour in *Her Jungle Love* (Par)
5. Bette Davis in *The Sisters* (WB)
6. Lucille Gleason and James Gleason in *The Higgins Family* (Rep)
7. Bette Davis and Errol Flynn in *The Sisters* (WB)
8. Borrah Minnevitch, Robert Wilcox, Jane Withers, Rochelle Hudson and Howard Hickman in *Rascals* (Fox)
9. Harriet Hilliard and Fred MacMurray in *Cocoanut Grove* (Par)
10. Robert Wilcox, Rochelle Hudson, Jane Withers and Borrah Minnevitch in *Rascals* (Fox)
11. John Garfield and Priscilla Lane in *Four Daughters* (WB)

425

1   2

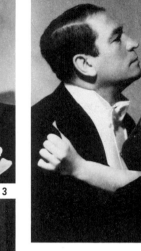

3

5

6

1. Renee Saint-Cyr and Tom Walls in *Strange Boarders* (G'boro)
2. Bing Crosby and Mary Carlisle in *Doctor Rhythm* (Par)
3. Maurice Chevalier and Jack Buchanan in *Break the News* (JB)
4. Victor McLaglen and Beatrice Roberts in *The Devil's Party* (Univ)
5. Richard Cromwell, Rochelle Hudson and Patric Knowles in *Storm Over Bengal* (Rep)
6. Elsa Lanchester and Charles Laughton in *Vessel of Wrath* (US *The Beachcomber*) (Mfl)
7. Claire Trevor, Edward G Robinson and Maxie Rosenbloom in *The Amazing Dr Clitterhouse* (FN)
8. Lew Ayres, Lionel Barrymore and Lynne Carver in *Young Dr Kildare* (MGM)
9. Jackie Cooper, Bonita Granville and Fay Bainter in *White Banners* (WB)
10. Joe Sawyer, Helen Mack and Robert Wilcox in *Gambling Ship* (Univ)
11. Dick Baldwin and Peter Lorre in *Mr Moto's Gamble* (Fox)
12. James Dunn, Ralph Morgan and Linda Gray in *Shadows Over Shanghai* (GN)

7

8 △ ▽ 10   11   9 △ ▽ 12

1. Robert Douglas in *The Challenge* (AK)
2. Dolores Costello and Bonita Granville in *Beloved Brat* (GB *A Dangerous Age*) (FN)
3. Priscilla Lane and Wayne Morris in *Love, Honor and Behave* (WB)
4. David Niven, Basil Rathbone and Errol Flynn in *Dawn Patrol* (WB)
5. Vera Zorina
6. Harpo, Lucille Ball, Chico and Groucho Marx in *Room Service* (RKO)
7. Roscoe Karns, Lloyd Nolan, Anna May Wong, Akim Tamiroff, Anthony Quinn and Harvey Stephens in *Dangerous to Know* (Par)
8. Ralph Bellamy, Ann Sothern and Robert Elliott in *Trade Winds* (WaW)
9. Lloyd Nolan and J Carrol Naish in *King of Alcatraz* (Par)
10. Robert Preston and J Carrol Naish in *Illegal Traffic* (Par)
11. Weldon Heyburn and Anne Nagel in *Saleslady* (MoP)
12. Pierre Watkin, Lloyd Nolan and J Carrol Naish in *Tip-Off Girls* (Par)
13. Lewis Stone, Mickey Rooney, Cecilia Parker and Fay Holden in *Judge Hardy's Children* (MGM)

1

2

3

4

5

6

7

8

9 △ ▽ 11

12

10 △ ▽ 13

1

2

3

4

5

6

7

8

9

11 △ ▽ 13

1. The Ritz Brothers in *Kentucky Moonshine* (Fox)
2. Stanley Lupino and Fred Emney in *Hold My Hand* (ABPC)
3. Raymond Parker, Preston Foster and Kay Linaker in *The Last Warning* (Univ)
4. Walter Pidgeon, Myrna Loy, Franchot Tone and Rosalind Russell in *Man Proof* (MGM)
5. Victor Moore
6. Margaret Lockwood in *Owd Bob* (G'boro)
7. Corbet Morris, Marjorie Gateson, Tom Kennedy, Jack Holt and Beverly Roberts in *Making the Headlines* (Col)
8. Arthur Loft, Jacqueline Wells, Robert Paige, and Oscar O'Shea in *Main Event* (Col)
9. Freddie Bartholomew, Warner Baxter, Arleen Whelan and H B Warner in *Kidnapped* (Fox)
10. Diana Churchill and Jean Muir in *Jane Steps Out* (ABPC)
11. Irene Dunne and Douglas Fairbanks Jr in *Joy of Living* (RKO)
12. John Payne and Stella Ardler in *Love on Toast* (Par)
13. Christine McIntyre and Fred Scott in *Songs and Bullets* (Spe)

10 △ ▽ 12

428

1

2 3

4

5 6

7

10 △ ▽ 12

11 △ ▽ 13

8 9

1. William Lundigan (I) in *Freshman Year* (Univ)

2. Frank Albertson, Phillip Terry, Fay Holden, Maureen O'Sullivan and Mickey Rooney in *Hold That Kiss* (MGM)

3. Anthony Bushell and Jane Baxter in *Hideout in the Alps* (GN)

4. Mary Boland, Mischa Auer and Edward Everett Horton in *Little Tough Guys in Society* (Univ)

5. Don Ameche and Robert Young in *Josette* (Fox)

6. Gordon Jones and Robert Cummings in *I Stand Accused* (Rep)

7. Henry Fonda and Joan Bennett in *I Met My Love Again* (WaW)

8. Carole Lombard and Ralph Bellamy in *Fools for Scandal* (WB)

9. Bobs Watson and Lloyd Nolan in *Hunted Men* (Par)

10. Ed Cobb (s) and Charles Starrett in *Law of the Plains* (Col)

11. Binnie Barnes and Arleen Whelan in *Gateway* (Fox)

12. Sonja Henie and Don Ameche in *Happy Landing* (Fox)

13. Margaret Lockwood

429

1. Anne Shirley
2. Florence Desmond, Edward Rigby, Julian Vedey and George Carney in *Kicking the Moon Around* (US *The Playboy*; *Millionaire Merry Go Round*) (Vog)
3. Adele Pearce and Tex Ritter in *Utah Trail* (GN)
4. Preston Foster, Nan Grey and Charles Bickford in *The Storm* (KG/Univ)
5. Paul Guilfoyle, Sally Eilers and Ann Miller in *Tarnished Angel* (RKO)
6. Colin Tapley and Jayne Regan in *Booloo* (Par)
7. Philip Reed
8. Lyle Talbot
9. Jack Randall and Charles King in *Gun Packer* (MoP)
10. Ann Miller
11. Charles Halton, Otto Kanger (seated) and Edward G Robinson in *I am the Law* (Col)
12. George O'Brien

9△ ▽ 12

▽11

1. Annabella
2. Junior Durkin and Junior Coghlan in *Juvenile Court* (Col)
3. Fred Scott and Marion Weldon in *Knight of the Plains* (Spe)
4. Tommy Kelly and David Holt in *The Adventures of Tom Sawyer* (UA)
5. John Garfield
6. Ken Maynard, Joan Barclay and Joe Girard in *Whirlwind Horseman* (GN)
7. Christine McIntyre, Fred Scott and Al St John in *The Rangers Roundup* (Spe)
8. Constance Moore and William Lundigan in *State Police* (Univ)
9. Gloria Dickson, Dick Foran and Gale Page in *Heart of the North* (FN)
10. Dave O'Brien and Dorothy Page in *Water Rustlers* (Cor/GN)

6 △ ▽ 9

7

8 △ ▽ 10

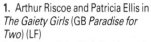

1. Arthur Riscoe and Patricia Ellis in *The Gaiety Girls* (GB *Paradise for Two*) (LF)

2. Dorothea Kent, Tom Brown and Frank Jenks in *Goodbye Broadway* (Univ)

3. Allen Jenkins, Hugh Herbert, Gloria Dickson, Rosemary Lane and Rudy Vallee in *Golddiggers in Paris* (GB *The Gay Imposters*) (WB)

4. Oliver Hardy and Minna Gombell in *Blockheads* (HR/StL)

5. Sigrid Gurie in *Algiers* (WaW)

6. Alan Hale and Charles Boyer in *Algiers* (WaW)

7. Brian Aherne and Constance Bennett in *Merrily We Live* (HR)

8. Charles Boyer in *Algiers* (WaW)

9. Joe E Brown, Lucien Littlefield and Ethel Wales in *The Gladiator* (Col)

10. Ken Howell, Russell Gleason, June Carlson, George Ernest, Florence Roberts, Spring Byington and Jed Prouty in *Down on the Farm* (Fox)

11. Carmen Bailey and Buck Jones in *California Frontier* (Col)

12. Anne Nagel, Charles Trowbridge and Robert Kent in *Gang Bullets* (MoP)

13. Joe Penner, June Travis and Bradley Page in *Go Chase Yourself* (RKO)

14. Frank Jenks

15. Olivia de Havilland, George Brent and Tim Holt in *Gold Is Where You Find It* (WB)

16. Jimmy Durante (I) in *Forbidden Music* (Wo)

17. Francoise Rosay (I) in *Maternité* (GB *Mother Love*) (FMP)

18. Max Terhune, Jean Joyce, Bob Livingston, Stelita Peluffe and Ray Corrigan in *Outlaws of Sonora* (Rep)

19. Lewis Stone, Dennis O'Keefe and Ann Morriss in *The Chaser* (MGM)

433

1. Ray Corrigan, Max Terhune and John Wayne in *Pals of the Saddle* (Rep)
2. Nils Asther
3. Tim McCoy, Betty Compson, John Merton and Joan Barclay in *Two Gun Justice* (Con/MoP)
4. Rita Oehmen, Robert Glecker and George O'Brien in *Gun Law* (RKO)
5. Bob Livingston (l) and Ray Corrigan (c) in *The Purple Vigilantes* (Rep)
6. Lucille Ball
7. Danielle Darrieux and Douglas Fairbanks Jr in *The Rage of Paris* (Univ)
8. Frances Robinson, Samuel S Hinds and Noah Beery Jr in *Forbidden Valley* (Univ)
9. William B Davidson
10. John Beal

3

4

5 △ ▽8

7△ ▽9   ▽ 10

1. Ralph Bellamy, Josephine Hutchinson and William Gargan in *The Crime of Dr Hallet* (Univ)
2. Jack Luden, 'Tuffy' and Eleanor Stewart in *Stagecoach Days* (Col)
3. Robert Montgomery and Virginia Bruce in *The First Hundred Years* (MGM)
4. Marjorie Reynolds and Bob Baker in *Western Trails* (Univ)
5. Al St John, Jack Randall and Ted Adams in *Gunsmoke Trail* (MoP)
6. Glenda Farrell
7. Robert Taylor and Maureen O'Sullivan in *A Yank at Oxford* (MGM)
8. Hal Taliaferro, Beth Marion, Jimmy Robinson, Marin Sais and Jack Luden in *Phantom Gold* (Col)
9. The Dead End Kids
10. Frank Craven

5 △ ▽ 8

6

7 △ ▽ 9

▽ 10

435

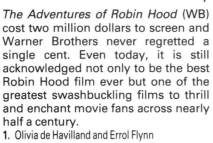

1

2

3

The Adventures of Robin Hood (WB) cost two million dollars to screen and Warner Brothers never regretted a single cent. Even today, it is still acknowledged not only to be the best Robin Hood film ever but one of the greatest swashbuckling films to thrill and enchant movie fans across nearly half a century.

1. Olivia de Havilland and Errol Flynn
2. Errol Flynn
3. Errol Flynn and Eugene Pallette
4. Errol Flynn and Basil Rathbone
5. Melville Cooper, Basil Rathbone, Olivia de Havilland and Errol Flynn
6. Ian Hunter, Alan Hale, Olivia de Havilland and Errol Flynn
7. Claude Rains, Basil Rathbone and Melville Cooper
8. Errol Flynn
9. Olivia de Havilland and Errol Flynn
10. Errol Flynn
11. Olivia de Havilland and Errol Flynn
12, 13, 14 and 15. Errol Flynn
16. Basil Rathbone and Errol Flynn
17. Herbert Mundin and Errol Flynn

4

5

6   7

8

9

10

11

12 13

14 15

16 17

1

2

3

4△▽7

5△▽8

6△▽9

10 11 12 13

14 15 16 17

18

Marie Antoinette (MGM) was Norma Shearer's first film for two years. Since her husband Irving Thalberg, MGM's wonderman, had died, she had been living quietly in retirement. Her re-entry into the film world as the ill-fated Queen of France was a triumph

1. Robert Morley
2. Gladys George, John Barrymore, Reginald Gardiner, Barnett Parker and Albert van Dekker
3. Norma Shearer
4. Tyrone Power and Norma Shearer
5. Cecil Cunningham and Norma Shearer
6. Norma Shearer
7. Barnett Parker, Robert Morley and Norma Shearer
8. Robert Morley and Norma Shearer
9. Tyrone Power and Norma Shearer
10. Norma Shearer and Joseph Schildkraut
11. Norma Shearer
12. Norma Shearer
13. Scotty Beckett, Norma Shearer and Marilyn Knowlden
14. Norma Shearer
15. Norma Shearer
16. Joseph Schildkraut, Barnett Parker, Norma Shearer and Reginald Gardiner
17. Norma Shearer and Tyrone Power
18. Gladys George and Norma Shearer
19. Tyrone Power and Norma Shearer
20. Norma Shearer
21. Tyrone Power and Norma Shearer
22. Norma Shearer and Robert Morley
23. Tyrone Power and Norma Shearer
24. Robert Morley, Marilyn Knowlden, Scotty Beckett and Norma Shearer

19 △ ▽ 21   22   23   20 △ ▽ 24

1

2

4

5

6

7

8

9

440

10

11

13

12

14

15   **16**

The Great Waltz was produced by MGM because Louis B Mayer had always been fond of the music of Johann Strauss. The movie was a lush production with beautiful songs and melodies and entrancing dancing. Mayer must have been happy with the success of the film.

1. Fernand Gravet and Miliza Korjus
2. Fernand Gravet, Miliza Korjus and Luise Rainer
3. Albertina Rasch ballet dancers
4. Fernand Gravet and Luise Rainer
5. Louis Hightower and Nita James
6. Luise Rainer
7. Fernand Gravet
8. Minna Gombell and Hugh Herbert
9. Miliza Korjus and the Albertina Rasch ballet dancers
10. Fernand Gravet and Luise Rainer
11. Miliza Korjus and Albertina Rasch ballet dancers
12. Fernand Gravet and Luise Rainer
13. Albertina Rasch ballet dancers
14. Lionel Atwill and Luise Rainer
15. Fernand Gravet and Miliza Korjus
16. Fernand Gravet and Sig Rumann

1

2

3

4

5

6

7

8

9 △ ▽ 12

10 △ ▽ 11

1. J Farrell MacDonald, Mary Russell, Arthur Loft, Gene Morgan, Edward Keane, Frank Wilson, Ann Doran and Roland Got in *Extortion* (Col)

2. Rosalind Russell, Errol Flynn, Olivia de Havilland and Walter Connolly in *Four's a Crowd* (WB)

3. Anna Neagle and Anton Walbrook in *Sixty Glorious Years* (Imp)

4. Sabu and Desmond Tester in *The Drum* (LF)

5. Kay Francis and Dickie Moore in *My Bill* (FN)

6. Richard Greene and Loretta Young in *Four Men and a Prayer* (Fox)

7. Edward Greene, Phyllis Brooks and the Ritz Brothers in *Straight, Place and Show* (GB *They're Off*)(Fox)

8. Jimmy Durante (c) in *Start Cheering* (Col)

9. William Powell and Annabella in *The Baroness and the Butler* (Fox)

10. John Luden, Lafe McKee and Eleanor Stewart in *Rolling Caravans* (Col)

11. Paul Guilfoyle, Lee Patrick and Lee Tracy in *Crashing Hollywood* (RKO)

12. Vivien Leigh and Charles Laughton in *St Martin's Lane* (Mfl)

13. Joan Fontaine, Derrick de Marney and Lillian Bond in *Blonde Cheat* (RKO)

14. Sigrid Gurie and Gary Cooper in *The Adventures and Marco Polo* (SG)

15. Max Terhune, John Wayne, Ray Corrigan and Sammy McKim in *Red River Range* (Rep)

16. Alan Hale, Gary Cooper and Ernest Truex in *The Adventures of Marco Polo* (SG)

17. Randolph Scott and Hope Hampton in *The Road to Reno* (Univ)

18. Hope Hampton in *The Road to Reno* (Univ)

19. Glynis Johns, Ralph Richardson and Edna Best in *South Riding* (LF VSP)

20. Penny Singleton, Arthur Lake, Kathleen Lockhart, Gordon Oliver and Dorothy Moore in *Blondie* (Col)

13   14

15   16

17 △ ▽ 19   18 △ ▽ 20

Vivien Leigh in *Gone with the Wind* (MGM/DS)

Leslie Howard in *Gone with the Wind* (MGM/DS)

Barbara O'Neil in *Gone with the Wind* (MGM/DS)

Ona Munson in *Gone with the Wind* (MGM/DS)

CHAPTER TEN
1939
GONE WITH THE WIND

The Thirties were brought to a magnificent close with the unveiling of *Gone With the Wind* which has proved to be one of the best-loved films of all time. This saga of the American Civil War and its aftermath had created exceptional interest since it first appeared in the mid-Thirties as a book that sold a million copies in its first six months, and even greater interest was generated by the making of the film.

Never in the history of movies had there been such a widely-publicised search for actors. Readers of the book insisted that Clark Gable was the only person suitable to play the soldier of fortune, Rhett Butler.

The choice of Vivien Leigh to play the tempestuous girl who loves him was a last-minute one. In fact, the film had already begun shooting when she joined the cast. Many people were surprised that a British actress should be chosen to play a scheming Southern girl but, of course, she justified producer Selznick's faith in her.

British-born Leslie Howard was cast as Ashley Wilkes, whom Scarlett wants for herself, and Olivia de Havilland as Melanie – the woman Ashley chooses to marry instead.

Vivien Leigh received one of the nine Oscars bestowed on the film. Others were for the Best Film of the year and Best Direction. The Supporting Actress Award went to Hattie McDaniel who played Scarlett's 'Mammy' – she was the first black actor ever to receive an Oscar. At the time no other film had ever won that many Academy Awards.

Producer David O. Selznick was determined to make *Gone With the Wind* the monumental film of his illustrious career. He slaved away at it for three years, during which time the production suffered setbacks that would have made a lesser man abandon the project. It underwent several revisions by various writers and, although Victor Fleming is credited as director, George Cukor and King Vidor also held the reins at various times.

What finally emerged is a magnificent example of old Hollywood at its entertaining best – a stirring spectacle with outstanding contributions from every department.

Ray Bolger, Jack Haley, Judy Garland and Bert Lahr in the *Wizard of Oz* (MGM)

Until it was sold to TV in the Seventies, few films in history were reissued as regularly as *Gone With the Wind*. But another which has been a perennial favourite is MGM's *The Wizard of Oz*, which is one of the great fantasy films of all time and made a world-famous star of Judy Garland.

Dorothy (Judy Garland) is a Kansas farm girl who is planted by a tornado in the land of Oz where she meets a scarecrow (Ray Bolger), a Tin Man (Jack Haley) and a Cowardly Lion (Bert Lahr) who help her find the Wizard of Oz (Frank Morgan) – the one they believe can send her back home.

Frank Baum's classic story was embellished with some memorable songs. 'Over the Rainbow' the most popular, was nearly cut from the final print because it was thought to slow up the action. Garland eventually adopted it as her signature tune.

Shirley Temple, now 11 years old, was still one of America's most popular stars. This year she appeared in *Susannah of the Mounties* and *The Little Princess*, her first film in Technicolor.

J Farrell MacDonald and Shirley Temple in *Suzannah of the Mounties* (Fox)

Over at MGM, Garbo was still queen. Having made a series of dramas for them throughout the decade, this year she agreed to tackle comedy and the one chosen was *Ninotchka*. 'Garbo laughs,' said the advertisements. Ernst Lubitsch, a master of sophisticated comedy, was signed as director, and Garbo gives a delightful performance as a Russian emissary who, on being sent to Paris to sell some jewels, succumbs to the city, capitalism and a suave playboy (Melvyn Douglas).

If MGM had been considered daring to let Garbo laugh, it was even more daring to produce a film full of females. There is not one man on view in *The Women*. Based on the celebrated play by Clare Boothe, it concerns the marital ups-and-downs of several well-heeled New York ladies. Norma Shearer heads them as a respectable woman whose husband is stolen from her by a social-climbing shop assistant (Joan Crawford). Rosalind Russell, one of the best wisecrackers in the business, is in her element as the bitchy gossip gleefully stirring things up. Paulette Goddard and Joan Fontaine also grace the cast, and that ample comedienne Mary Boland sparkles as a much-married matron whose motto in life is 'L'amour, l'amour, toujours l'amour'.

Above: Norma Shearer
Below: Rosalind Russell and Joan Crawford in *The Woman* (MGM)

There were said to be 140 women in the film, and all were deftly deployed by George Cukor, here clearly confirming his reputation of being the 'woman's director' who elevated his female characters from the slot of being mere 'love interest.'

James Stewart had two fine films to his credit this year – *Destry Rides Again* and *Mr Smith Goes to Washington*. The latter is one of the outstanding comedies Frank Capra made throughout the decade. It is a typical Capra tale about an idealistic individual taking on heartless big business and crooks in positions of trust.

There is plenty of humour, although of a more earthy

Marlene Dietrich in *Destry Rides Again* (Univ)

Claire Trevor and John Wayne in *Stagecoach* (WaW)

Claudette Colbert and Henry Fonda in *Drums Along the Mohawk* (Fox)

kind than in Stewart's other big film, *Destry Rides Again*. His co-star is the incomparable Marlene Dietrich – who obviously relished her part as a saloon girl and made it one of her most memorable roles. She has a couple of numbers to sing and is remembered to this day for her rendition of 'See What the Boys in the Back Room Will Have'. Stewart plays a mild-mannered sheriff's deputy who dislikes guns but still manages to restore law and order to Bottleneck.

The really big Western of the year is *Stagecoach*. Although its lasting claim to fame is the fact that it made a star of John Wayne after struggling in lesser films for a decade, it is also a solid and highly professional piece of filmcraft, one of the many directed by John Ford.

Although it tells a simple story, Ford makes it a very exciting experience. It is a variation on the theme of strangers brought together by fate to share a common experience. In this case they are passengers crowded together on a perilous stagecoach journey across Arizona. Wayne plays an outlaw – the Ringo Kid – being escorted to jail by a marshal (George Bancroft).

Other passengers are a reformed prostitute (Claire Trevor) who takes a shine to the Kid, a gambler (John Carradine), a pregnant woman (Louise Platt) and an alcoholic doctor (Thomas Mitchell) called upon to deliver the baby that unexpectedly arrives in the midst of all the excitement. Filmed largely on location, *Stagecoach* gave cinema audiences their first sight of Monument Valley, used in many later Westerns.

John Ford made two more remarkable films in 1939, both starring Henry Fonda. *Drums Along the Mohawk* (co-starring Claudette Colbert) weaves a tale of action, humour and drama around settlers in New York State facing attacks by Indians as well as the turmoils of the War of Independence.

Young Mr Lincoln shows Abe Lincoln as a young lawyer defending two youngsters accused of murder. The future President is already exhibiting his idealism through his efforts to merge and abide by the laws of both man and God.

After years of struggling in B pictures, Rita Hayworth at last got her first starring role – from Columbia – and she makes quite an impact as a philandering wife in *Only Angels Have Wings*. Starring Cary Grant, this was a typical tale of male camaraderie from director Howard Hawks, this time concerned with a tightly knit group of pilots flying cargo planes in remote regions of the Andes.

Another actress beginning to make her presence felt was Ingrid Bergman. Her first Hollywood film was *Intermezzo* (GB *Escape to Happiness*). It is a remake of a film she had made in her native Sweden in 1936. In the new version she is joined by Leslie Howard as a violinist – a married one – with whom she has an affair.

Prominent among the crop of upcoming stars was Bob Hope. In 1939 Paramount gave him his best role to date in *The Cat and the Canary*. Co-starring Paulette Goddard, it

is a spoof on the haunted-house thriller, complete with the reading of a Will and disappearing beneficiaries.

In 1939 Universal were still leading the chillers field, the best of which was *Son of Frankenstein*, the third in their celebrated series. Boris Karloff still shambles around as the easily-resuscitated monster, and Basil Rathbone has the title role as the Baron's offspring unable to resist dabbling in the frightful family business. It is all well-executed among some stylish sets.

Happier notes were struck at Universal by singing star Deanna Durbin, appearing in *Three Smart Girls Grow Up*, a sequel to the 1936 film in which she made her debut. And in *First Love* she received her first screen kiss – from Robert Stack.

Paramount's biggest film this year was *Union Pacific*, created by Cecil B. DeMille. It tells of the building of the railroad that opens up the West in the nineteenth century. Joel McCrea stars as a trouble-shooter employed by the railroad. He has plenty of trouble to face, some of it from businessmen bent on delaying the building of the railroad.

Brian Donlevy, who plays one of the villains, also turns up in another big western, *Jesse James* (directed by Henry King) – again as a railroad man. The part of the legendary outlaw went to Tyrone Power, with Henry Fonda as his brother Frank.

There was no shortage of Westerns in 1939. Another big one was Michael Curtiz's *Dodge City*, the first 'horse opera' for Errol Flynn. He plays an Irish-born adventurer faced with cleaning up the trouble-torn town of the title. He has two leading ladies – Ann Sheridan and Olivia de Havilland.

The latter had appeared with him the previous year in the rousing *Adventures of Robin Hood*, and in 1939 she was also with him in *The Private Lives of Elizabeth and Essex* – again directed by Michael Curtiz. But this time she wasn't the leading lady. The role of Elizabeth I of England went to Bette Davis. She had originally wanted Laurence Olivier to play Essex, with whom the queen has a love affair, and she was not happy when she got Flynn, whom she considered to be a superficial actor. In *Elizabeth and Essex*, Flynn certainly does not appear to make much effort to rise above her flamboyant style of acting.

Davis was at long last getting the type of roles at Warners that she wanted. However, she had excellent roles in two films directed by Edmund Goulding. In *The Old Maid* she plays a puritanical woman who allows her illegitimate daughter to be raised by her cousin (Miriam Hopkins), and in *Dark Victory*, which she has described as her own favourite film, she is a good-time society girl who discovers she is dying of a brain tumour.

Warners, who were famous for their social dramas, this year released *Confessions of a Nazi Spy*, directed by Anatole Litvak, the first American feature film to warn of the threat of Nazism. Telling how G-Men uncover a ring of German spies in the United States, it is based on actual events and

Boris Karloff and Basil Rathbone in *Son of Frankenstein* (Univ)

Brian Donlevy in *Union Pacific* (Par/CdeM)

Above: Tyrone Power in *Jesse James* (Fox)
Below: George Brent and Bette Davis in *Dark Victory* (WB)

Paul Lucas in *Confessions of a Nazi Spy* (WB)

Humphrey Bogart and James Cagney in *The Roaring Twenties* (WB)

Laurence Olivier and Merle Oberon in *Wuthering Heights* (SG)

Maureen O'Hara in *The Hunchback of Notre Dame* (RKO)

stars Paul Lukas and Edward G. Robinson at his most forceful as the FBI prosecutor.

Two of Warners' top stars, James Cagney and Humphrey Bogart, are together in *The Roaring Twenties* (directed by Raoul Walsh and Anatole Litvak), one of the last in the gangster cycle for which the studio was renowned. However, this is a gangster film with a very different flavour.

Eddie Bartlett (Cagney) returns from the First World War to find he cannot get a job. Even so, he only turns to bootlegging through doing a good deed for another, and even when he becomes a 'big shot' he continues to look after those who need him. Indeed, it is because he will not agree to the demands of ruthless gang boss George Melly (Bogart) to 'silence' their war buddy Lloyd Hart (Jeffrey Lynn) – the only one who went 'straight' – that Eddie meets his end.

Fox provided one of the big spectacles of the year with *The Rains Came* (directed by Clarence Brown). The story is set in India, and Tyrone Power plays an Indian surgeon at a hospital that becomes a place of refuge when floods bring devastation and plague. A spoilt rich English girl with whom he has an affair is played by Myrna Loy, and her elderly husband, a bore, by Nigel Bruce.

Bruce hit lucky this year when chosen to play Dr Watson opposite Basil Rathbone's Sherlock Holmes in *The Hound of the Baskervilles*. This is the best of many versions of the famous story. Rathbone and Bruce were a perfect choice to portray Conan Doyle's famous sleuths and repeated their roles 14 times over the next seven years.

While this was the beginning of a popular partnership, one was about to end in 1939. Fred Astaire and Ginger Rogers made the last in their series of musicals for RKO (although they were to be reunited by MGM in 1948). Their 1939 film was *The Story of Vernon and Irene Castle*, a famous dancing partnership at the beginning of the century.

Ginger Rogers proves herself to be a very capable straight actress in *Bachelor Mother*, directed by Garson Kanin, a comedy about an unmarried shopgirl who is mistaken for the mother of an abandoned baby. Her co-star, David Niven, was chosen to play the spineless Edgar Linton in Sam Goldwyn's beautifully conceived production of *Wuthering Heights* which stars Merle Oberon as Linton's wife, Cathy, and Laurence Olivier as Heathcliffe – her impassioned lover. The brooding nature of the story is perfectly captured by Gregg Toland's atmospheric camerawork and Alfred Newman's music, and a splendid cast – including Flora Robson and Hugh Williams – respond well to the masterly direction of William Wyler.

One of the big RKO films of 1939 is *The Hunchback of Notre Dame* – a superb recreation, by director William Dieterle and art director Van Nest Polglase, of Victor Hugo's story of French medieval life. Charles Laughton gives an inspired performance as Quasimodo, the grossly deformed bellringer of Notre Dame who falls in love with gypsy girl Esmeralda (Maureen O'Hara).

The Best Actor Oscar for 1939 went to Britain's Robert Donat for his touching performance in *Goodbye, Mr Chips* (directed by Sam Wood), which covers 60 years in the life of a master at an English public school. There is delightful support from Greer Garson as his wife whose charming nature turns him from a shy teacher into a self-confident one. This was made in Britain by MGM who were so taken with Greer Garson that they put her under contract and transplanted her to Hollywood.

Margaret Lockwood, still one of Britain's most popular stars, made two films this year for director Carol Reed. *A Girl Must Live* is a comedy not unlike the gold-digger type associated with America. Lockwood plays a schoolgirl (she was then 23!) who becomes involved with chorus girls (Lilli Palmer and Renee Houston) and winds up marrying the young peer (Hugh Sinclair) that they are all chasing.

Robert Donat in *Goodbye Mr Chips* (MGM)

Her other film, *The Stars Look Down*, is a very different drama based on a novel by A.J. Cronin (whose *The Citadel* became an important British film in 1938). It stars Michael Redgrave; he and Lockwood had appeared together in Hitchcock's *The Lady Vanishes* the previous year. He plays a miner struggling to become an MP, with Lockwood as the vulgar girl he ill-advisedly marries. The film enjoyed the distinction of being the first feature film shown on British television.

Terry Kilburn and Robert Donat in *Goodbye Mr Chips* (MGM)

In Britain Alexander Korda continued turning out big action films in colour, this year producing the best of many versions of A.E.W. Mason's famous novel *The Four Feathers* (directed by Zoltan Korda). Its central character is a young man (John Clements) who, when accused of being a coward because he won't go to fight in the Sudan, proves his courage by going out there in disguise and performing some extremely heroic feats. The film co-starred Ralph Richardson and C. Aubrey Smith.

Britain's declaration of war with Germany came too late in the year to have much impact on British film production of 1939 or to be reflected in its stories. One exception was *The Lion Has Wings*, a semi-documentary rushed out by Alexander Korda (with the help of several British directors) to show events leading up to the outbreak of war. There were some fictional linking sequences enacted by Ralph Richardson as an RAF officer and Merle Oberon as his wife. Although naive by today's standards, it was undeniably a morale-booster in its day and heralded a new era in British film production.

Above: Renée Houston
Below: Margaret Lockwood

In 1939 Russia presented *My Apprenticeship* – the second film in *The Gorky Trilogy* (covered in Chapter 9) and *The Vyborg Side* – the third film in *The Maxim Trilogy* (covered in Chapter 6). Another 'follow on' was *Lenin in 1918*, inspired by the success of *Lenin in October* the previous year, and in which Shchukin again plays the great leader.

A remarkable period in film-making was coming to a close in France. One of the last big films of the Thirties is *Le Jour se Leve (Daybreak)* starring the ubiquitous Jean

Jean Renoir

Gabin. He plays a factory worker who commits murder and holes up in his drab little room when besieged by the police.

Waiting for them to take him, he passes the night reflecting on events that have led to his being trapped, in particular his relationship with his mistress (Arletty) and with the girl friend (Jacqueline Laurent) of the man (Jules Berry) he was goaded into killing. With its poetic realism, this stands out as an archetypal French film of the period.

As well as producing this film about daybreak, France produced one named after the end of the day. Called *La Fin de Jour*, and starring Michel Simon and Louis Jouvet, it shows life in a home for retired actors and was directed by Julien Duvivier.

But perhaps the very best French film of the Thirties was Jean Renoir's *La Regle de Jeu (Rules of the Games)*. Although on the surface it told of the interaction between guests and domestic staff at a weekend house party, it was an allegory about life and living and the current sorry state of the world. Renoir, who had written the screenplay, also appeared in the film as an onlooker commenting on events and their implication.

Blatantly anti-Fascist, it was shortened by its distributors after public protests on its initial release. When war broke out, the censor banned it. Later the Germans destroyed all prints they could lay their hands on, including the original negative. After the war, a new copy was assembled from odds and ends, and in 1962 many international critics proclaimed it the third greatest film ever made.

Japanese cinema was also having an exciting year in 1939. There was Hiroshi Shimizu's lyrical *Four Seasons of Children* which looks at country children's reactions to their world of the earth and living things and to the squabbling world of the adults in their lives. Mikio Naruse's decidedly different *The Whole Family Works* shows the cluttered, chaotic life of a printer's family, all 11 of whom have to work so that the family can eat.

But the best-remembered Japanese film of the year is almost certainly Kenji Mizoguchi's *Story of the Late Chrysanthemums*. This is a richly romantic love story that gives a fictionalized account of a famous *kabuki* actor's fall from grace as a result of the love affair he is having with a young girl. However, the girl gives up her life for him, and there is the most dazzling series of shots that cut between the crescending climax of his theatre performance and scenes of her deathbed. As the actor takes his applause, his bows become more and more frozen as he 'realizes' what is happening to his beloved.

Some countries that had not produced much of note in the Thirties were by 1939 well-geared for prodigious output in the Forties. Italian film-making, though, had been severely affected by the restraints of Fascism.

That said, there certainly were an extraordinary number of classic films that came out of the Thirties – which for quality and quantity will possibly never be matched.

Film Favourites 1939

This was the War year. For Hollywood, it was the American Civil War with MGM's triumphant *Gone with the Wind*. For Europe, it was the commencement of World War II – and the glamour of the Thirties was over. During the next decade the world was to change as did the style of the movies.

Irene Dunne and Fred MacMurray in *Invitation to Happiness* (Par)

Robert Cummings and Nan Grey in *Three Smart Girls Grow Up* (Univ)

Claude Rains

Eddie Dean, Stanley Price, William Boyd, Pedro de Cordoba, Betty Moran and Russell Hayden in *Range War* (Par)

Basil Rathbone and Nigel Bruce in *The Adventures of Sherlock Holmes* (GB *Sherlock Holmes*) (Fox)

Victor McLaglen in *Captain Fury* (HR)

Graham Moffatt in *Where's That Fire* (Fox)

Above: Victor McLaglen, Joseph Calleia and Sally Eilers in *Full Confession* (RKO)

Left: Tyrone Power and Nancy Kelly in *Jesse James* (Fox)

Charles Starrett, Iris Meredith and Dick Curtis in *Western Caravans* (Col)

Bette Davis and Errol Flynn in *The Private Lives of Elizabeth and Essex* (WB)

Ann Sothern and Robert Young in *Maisie* (MGM)

Huntz Hall, Leo Gorcey, John Garfield, Billy Halop and Bobby Jordan in *They Made me a Criminal* (WB)

Frankie Thomas, Gabriel Dell, Bonita Granville, Leo Gorcey and Huntz Hall in *Angels Wash Their Faces* (FN)

Throughout the Thirties, Humphrey Bogart and James Cagney excelled in gangster films. Here they are in *The Roaring Twenties* (WB) produced in 1939 and definitely another roaring success. Alan Baxter is next to Cagney.

Douglas Fairbanks Jr and Joan Fontaine in *Gunga Din* (RKO)

John Carroll

Constance Moore and Robert Cummings in *Charlie McCarthy, Detective* (Univ)

Charles Boyer and Irene Dunne in *When Tomorrow Comes* (Univ)

John Barrymore, Don Ameche and Claudette Colbert in *Midnight* (Par)

Rosemary Lane, Frank McHugh, Lola Lane, Gail Page, Claude Rains, May Robson, Dick Foran, Priscilla Lane and Jeffrey Lynn in *Four Wives* (FN)

Johnny Weissmuller and Maureen O'Sullivan in *Tarzan Finds a Son* (MGM)

Guinn (Big Boy) Williams, Errol Flynn and Alan Hale in *Dodge City* (WB)

Richard Greene and Richard Dix in *Here I am a Stranger* (HJB/Fox)

Jackie Cooper in *What A Life* (Par)

John Hubbard

Ward Bond, Chill Wills and George O'Brien in *Trouble in Sundown* (RKO)

Paulette Goddard

Broderick Crawford, Gary Cooper and David Niven in *The Real Glory* (SG)

Wallace Beery, Chester Morris and Virginia Grey in *Thunder Afloat* (MGM)

7 △ ▽ 10

9 △ ▽ 11

Picture Gallery for 1939

1. Dorothy Lamour
2. Donald Barry and Helen Mack in *Calling All Marines* (Rep)
3. Alice Eden, John Archer and Anne Shirley in *Career* (RKO)
4. Ginny Simms, Hobart Cavanaugh, Edward Everett Horton and Kay Kyser in *That's Right-You're Wrong* (RKO)
5. Judy Garland
6. Charles Boyer and Irene Dunne in *When Tomorrow Comes* (Univ)
7. Victor McLaglen, William Frawley, Tom Brown, Nan Grey, Donald Briggs and Constance Moore in *Ex-Champ* (GB *Golden Gloves*) (Univ)
8. John Hamilton, Walter Abel and Beverly Roberts in *First Offenders* (Col)
9. David Niven and Ginger Rogers in *Bachelor Mother* (RKO)
10. Jackie Cooper and Betty Field in *What a Life* (Par)
11. George Raft and Stanley Ridges in *I Stole a Million* (Univ)

6

1. Francis Ford, Guinn Williams and Noah Beery Jr in *Bad Lands* (RKO)

2. Loretta Young and David Niven in *Eternally Yours* (WaW)

3. William Gargan and Rosella Towne in *The Adventures of Jane Arden* (WB)

4. Bob Baker and Glenn Strange in *Honor of the West* (Univ)

5. Mary Astor

6. Laraine Day and Lew Ayres in *The Secret of Dr Kildare* (MGM)

7. Ronald Sinclair, Edith Fellows, Clarence Kolb, Dorothy Seece, Tommy Bond, Charles Peck and Jimmy Leake in *Five Little Peppers and How They Grew* (Col)

8. Edward Ellis, Dick Hogan, Robert Stanton, Virginia Vale and Kent Taylor in *Three Sons* (RKO)

9. Bob Hope and Shirley Ross in *Some Like It Hot* (Par)

10. Warren Hull and Movita in *The Girl from Rio* (MoP)

11. Deanna Durbin and Ann Gillis in *First Love* (Univ)

8 △ ▽ 11

9 △ ▽ 10

1   2   3   4   5

6   7   8   9   10

11   12   13   14   15

16   17   18   19   20

21 △ ▽ 26   22 △ ▽ 27   23 △ ▽ 28   24 △ ▽ 29   25 △ ▽ 30

1. Don Barry
2. Robert Bartholomew
3. Gustav von Seyffertitz
4. Norman Willis
5. Enid Stamp Taylor
6. Chico Marx
7. Groucho Marx
8. Harpo Marx
9. Slim Summerville
10. Myrna Loy
11. George Burns
12. Edward Norris
13. Bob Hope
14. Eric Linden
15. Helen Hayes

16. Josephine Hutchinson
17. Joel McCrea
18. Ted Healy
19. Cesar Romero
20. Andrea Leeds
21. Van Heflin
22. Harold Huber
23. Arthur Wontner
24. Helen Broderick
25. Anna Lee
26. Pert Kelton
27. Edward Arnold
28. Bobby Breen
29. Paul Stanton
30. Douglass Dumbrille

31. Randolph Scott in *Jesse James* (Fox)
32. Tyrone Power and Henry Fonda in *Jesse James* (Fox)
33. Bob Livingston and Yakima Canutt in *Cowboys from Texas* (Rep)
34. Gene Autry, Smiley Burnette and Maude Eburne in *Mountain Rhythm* (Rep)
35. Nancy Kelly, Tyrone Power and Henry Fonda in *Jesse James* (Fox)
36. Fay Bainter (s) and Frank Craven in *Our Neighbors, The Carters* (Par)
37. Peter Lorre in *Mr Moto takes a Vacation* (Fox)
38. William Demarest

39. Laraine Day, Tom Brown and Wallace Beery in *Sergeant Madden* (MGM)
40. Adolphe Menjou and Roger Daniel in *King of the Turf* (ES)
41. Gail Patrick and Richard Dix in *Reno* (RKO)
42. Dick Powell
43. Edmund Lowe and Wendy Barrie in *The Witness Vanishes* (Univ)
44. Gladys Swarthout, Broderick Crawford and Lloyd Nolan in *Ambush* (Par)
45. Hal Price and Tex Ritter in *Man from Texas* (MoP)

457

1. George Brent and Bette Davis in *Dark Victory* (WB)
2. Irene Dunne and Fred MacMurray in *Invitation to Happiness* (Par)
3. Ellen Drew and George Raft in *The Lady's from Kentucky* (JL/Par)
4. Mark Lester, Mary McGuire, Edmund Gwenn, Mavis Villiers and Geoffrey Toone in *An Englishman's Home* (AFP)
5. Sidney Toler and Kane Richmond in *Charlie Chan in Reno* (Fox)
6. H B Warner
7. Matty Kemp and Betty Moran in *All Women Have Secrets* (Par)
8. Basil Rathbone in *The Tower of London* (Univ)
9. Edgar Kennedy, Charlie McCarthy and Edgar Bergen in *Charlie McCarthy, Detective* (Univ)
10. Bette Davis and Jerome Cowan in *The Old Maid* (FN)

1. James Ellison, Robert Kent and June Clayworth in *Almost a Gentleman* (GB *Magnificent Outcast*) (RKO)

2. Joel McCrea, Barbara Stanwyck and Robert Preston in *Union Pacific* (Par/CdeM)

3. Jean Arthur and James Stewart in *Mr Smith Goes to Washington* (Col)

4. Cesar Romero, Warner Baxter and Chris-Pin Martin in *The Return of the Cisco Kid* (Fox)

5. Al Jolson, Alice Faye and Tyrone Power in *Rose of Washington Square* (Fox)

6. Akim Tamiroff, John Howard and Dorothy Lamour in *Disputed Passage* (Par)

7. Roy Rogers in *Saga of Death Valley* (Rep)

8. Marie Wilson and Bert Wheeler in *The Cowboy Quarterback* (FN)

9. Nigel Bruce, Ida Lupino and Basil Rathbone in *The Adventures of Sherlock Holmes* (GB *Sherlock Holmes*) (Fox)

10. Nigel Bruce and Basil Rathbone in *The Adventures of Sherlock Holmes* (GB *Sherlock Holmes*) (Fox)

11. Henry Fonda and Don Ameche in *The Story of Alexander Graham Bell* (GB *The Modern Miracle*) (Fox)

12. Don Ameche and Loretta Young in *The Story of Alexander Graham Bell* (GB *The Modern Miracle*) (Fox)

1. William Frawley
2. Fernandel
3. Donald Crisp, Brian Aherne, Bette Davis and Gilbert Roland in *Juarez* (WB)
4. Brian Aherne, Bette Davis and Gilbert Roland in *Juarez* (WB)
5. Michael Redgrave
6. Sigrid Gurie and Basil Rathbone in *Rio* (Univ)
7. Claude Rains, John Garfield and Gloria Dickson in *They Made Me a Criminal* (WB)
8. Sigrid Gurie and Donald Briggs in *Forgotten Woman* (EG/Univ)
9. Brenda Marshall, Joel McCrea and Jeffrey Lynn in *Espionage Agent* (FN)
10. Bob Kortman and George O'Brien in *Timber Stampede* (RKO)

1. Walter Brennan and Spencer Tracy in *Stanley and Livingstone* (Fox)
2. Vera Korene and Victor Francen in *Crime in the Maginot Line* (Tow)
3. Olivia de Havilland and George Brent in *Wings of the Navy* (WB)
4. Nelson Eddy and Ilona Massey in *Balalaika* (MGM)
5. Shirley Temple, Margaret Lockwood and Randolph Scott in *Susannah of the Mounties* (Fox)
6. Warner Baxter and Alice Faye in *Barricade* (Fox)
7. Deanna Durbin in *Three Smart Girls Grow Up* (Univ)
8. Ronald Colman in *The Light that Failed* (Par)
9. Jane Wyatt
10. Rosemary Lane and John Garfield in *Blackwell's Island* (FN)
11. Linda Ware in *The Star Maker* (Par)

1. Binnie Barnes and Isabel Jeans in *Man About Town* (Par)
2. Douglass Montgomery, Paulette Goddard, Bob Hope and John Beal in *The Cat and the Canary* (Par)
3. Edward G Robinson and Ruth Hussey in *Blackmail* (MGM)
4. Ralph Bellamy and Maureen O'Sullivan in *Let Us Live* (Col)
5. Brenda Joyce and Richard Greene in *Here I Am a Stranger* HJB/Fox)
6. Andy Devine, Paul Harvey, Bob Hope, Martha Raye, Gale Sondergaard, Alan Mowbray and Ivan Simpson in *Never Say Die* (Par)
7. Lee Tracy and Peggy Shannon in *Fixer Dugan* (GB *Double Daring*) (RKO)
8. Akim Tamiroff, Patricia Morison and Lloyd Nolan in *The Magnificent Fraud* (Par)

1. Barton MacLane and Eve Arden in *Big Town Czar* (Univ)
2. Bob Burns and Gladys George in *I'm from Missouri* (Par)
3. David Niven, Gary Cooper and Broderick Crawford in *The Real Glory* (SG)
4. Regis Toomey and Kent Taylor in *Pirates of the Skies* (Univ)
5. Cesar Romero, Sally Blane and Sidney Toler in *Charlie Chan at Treasure Island* (Fox)
6. Groucho and Chico Marx in *At The Circus* (MGM)
7. Errol Flynn and Olivia de Havilland in *Dodge City* (WB)
8. Bob Steele
9. Carole Lombard and James Stewart in *Made for Each Other* (DS)

2

4

3

5

6

7

8

9

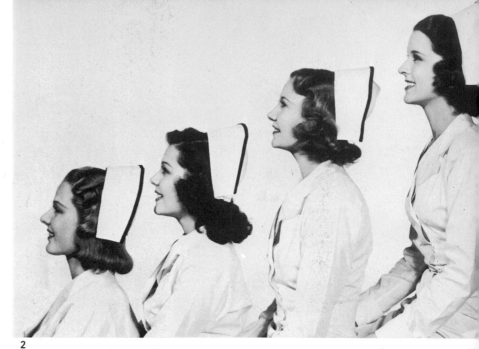

1. Victor McLaglen and Sally Eilers in *Full Confession* (RKO)
2. Florence Rice, Ann Rutherford, Una Merkel and Mary Howard in *Four Girls in White* (MGM)
3. Anna May Wong and J Carrol Naish in *Island of Lost Men* (Par)
4. Butterfly McQueen
5. Leatrice Joy
6. Ralph Bellamy and Fay Wray in *Smashing the Spy Ring* (Col)
7. Walter Pidgeon and Virginia Bruce in *Society Lawyer* (JWC/ MGM)
8. Warren William in *The Gracie Allen Murder Case* (GA/Par)
9. Lewis Stone
10. Randolph Scott and Frances Dee in *Coast Guard* (Col)
11. Marsha Hunt in *Star Reporter* (MoP)
12. Yakima Canutt and John Wayne in *Wyoming Outlaw* (Rep)
13. Louis Hayward and Joan Bennett in *Man in the Iron Mask* (ES)

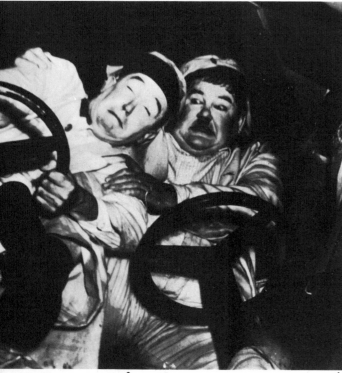

1. Virginia Grey and Chester Morris in *Thunder Afloat* (MGM)
2. Geraldine Fitzgerald
3. June Storey and Gene Autry in *In Old Monterey* (Rep)
4. Laurel and Hardy in *Flying Deuces* (BM)
5. Ralph Bellamy
6. Frances Robinson, Johnny Mack Brown and Bob Baker in *Desperate Trails* (Univ)
7. Betty Field
8. Irene Hervey and Preston Foster in *Society Smugglers* (Univ)
9. Ralph Richardson and June Duprez in *The Four Feathers* (LF)
10. Franciska Gaal, Bing Crosby and Shirley Ross in *Paris Honeymoon* (Par)

1

2 3 4

5 6 7 8

9 10 11 12 13

14 △ ▽ 18　15 △　16 △ ▽ 19　17 △ ▽ 20

23

24

25

26

27△ ▽29

28△ ▽30

1. Boris Karloff and Bela Lugosi in *Son of Frankenstein* (Univ)
2. Basil Rathbone and Boris Karloff in *Son of Frankenstein* (Univ)
3. Robert Young and Ann Sothern in *Maisie* (MGM)
4. Ann Rutherford and Tom Brown in *These Glamour Girls* (MGM)
5. Paul Cavanagh, Virginia Weidler and Margaret Lindsay in *The Under-Pup* (JP/Univ)
6. Bette Davis in *The Private Lives of Elizabeth and Essex* (WB)
7. Ronald Reagan and William B Davidson in *Smashing the Money Ring* (WB)
8. Joe Sawyer and Edward G Robinson in *Confessions of Nazi Spy* (GN)
9. Walter Pidgeon and Rita Johnson in *6000 Enemies* (LH/MGM)
10. Bert Lahr
11. Dick Purcell
12. Michele Morgan
13. Gloria Dickson and Denis Morgan in *Waterfront* (WB)
14. Jessie Matthews
15. Henry O'Neill and Charles Grapewin in *The Man Who Dared* (WB)
16. John Barrymore and Claudette Colbert in *Midnight* (Par)
17. Robert Preston, Gary Cooper, Broderick Crawford, Ray Milland and Brian Donlevy in *Beau Geste* (Par)
18. Cecilia Parker and Dennis O'Keefe in *Burn 'Em Up O'Connor* (MGM)
19. Otto Kruger and Virginia Grey in *Another Thin Man* (MGM)
20. Ronald Reagan, Ann Sheridan and Dead End Kids in *Angels Wash Their Faces* (WB)
21. Humphrey Bogart and James Cagney in *The Roaring Twenties* (WB)
22. Charles Ruggles and Mary Boland in *Night Work* (Par)
23. Allan Lane and Linda Hayes in *Conspiracy* (RKO)
24. Shirley Ross, Sandra Lee Henville, Dennis O'Keefe and Mischa Auer in *Unexpected Father* (GB *Sandy Takes a Bow*) (Univ)
25. Humphrey Bogart and Edward Pawley (c) in *Oklahoma Kid* (WB)
26. Humphrey Bogart and James Cagney in *Oklahoma Kid* (WB)
27. Lucille Ball, Richard Dix and Allan Lane in *Twelve Crowded Hours* (RKO)
28. Melvyn Douglas, Joan Blondell and Joan Perry in *Good Girls Go to Paris* (Col)
29. Pat O'Brien and Wayne Morris in *A Kid from Kokomo* (WB)
30. Byron Foulger and Boris Karloff in *The Man They Could Not Hang* (Col)

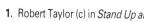

1. Robert Taylor (c) in *Stand Up and Fight* (MGM)
2. Anna Neagle and George Sanders (in helmet) in *Nurse Edith Cavell* (RKO)
3. Peter Lorre, George Sanders and Margaret Irving in *Mr Moto's Last Warning* (Fox)
4. Ian Hunter, Jeanette MacDonald and Lew Ayres in *Bridal Suite* (MGM)
5. Robert Young, Virginia Field, and Annabelle in *Bridal Suite* (MGM)
6. Jane Withers in *Boy Friend* (Fox)
7. Granville Bates, Edith Fellows and Arthur Loft in *Pride of the Blue Grass* (WB)
8. Joan Blondell, Mischa Auer and Bing Crosby in *East Side of Heaven* (Univ)
9. Minor Watson and Preston Foster in *News is Made at Night* (Fox)
10. Gertrude Michael and Jack Holt in *Hidden Power* (Col)
11. Cecilia Parker and Dennis O'Keefe in *Burn 'Em up O'Connor* (MGM)
12. Virginia Field and Douglas Fairbanks Jr in *The Sun Never Sets* (Univ)

1. Smiley Burnette, June Storey and Gene Autry in *Blue Montana Skies* (Rep)
2. Joy Hodges and Thomas Beck in *The Family Next Door* (Univ)
3. Charles Starrett (c) and Iris Meredith in *Outpost of the Mounties* (Col)
4. Robert Preston and Gail Patrick in *Disbarred* (Par)
5. Anna Sten and Alan Marshall in *Exile Express* (GN)
6. Willard Robertson and Anita Louise in *Main Street Lawyer* (Rep)
7. Cary Grant, Carole Lombard and Kay Francis in *In Name Only* (RKO)
8. Kent Taylor, Wendy Barrie and Patric Knowles in *Five Came Back* (RKO)
9. Ann Sothern and Franchot Tone in *Fast and Furious* (MGM)
10. Joan Leslie and James Lydon in *Two Thoroughbreds* (RKO)
11. Virginia Bruce and Walter Pidgeon in *Stronger than Desire* (MGM)
12. John Howard and Gail Patrick in *Grand Jury Secrets* (Par)

1

2

3

4 **5**

6

7

10 ▽

8 △ ▽ **9**

1. Ginger Rogers
2. Marjorie Weaver and Stuart Erwin in *The Honeymoon's Over* (Fox)
3. Evelyn Venable, Donald Woods and C Henry Gordon in *Heritage of the Desert* (Par)
4. Roy Rogers and George 'Gabby' Hayes in *In Old Caliente* (ReP)
5. Melvyn Douglas and Joan Blondell in *The Amazing Mr Williams* (Col)
6. Mary Martin
7. Peggy Moran, Florence Rice, Fritz Feld, Anne Gwynne and Frances Robinson in *Little Accident* (Univ)
8. Don Ameche and Alice Faye in *Hollywood Cavalcade* (Fox)
9. Jed Prouty and Spring Byington in *Everybody's Baby* (Fox)
10. Humphrey Bogart.

470

1

2

3

4

5

6

7

1. Jane Withers and The Ritz Brothers in *Pack Up Your Troubles* (GB *We're in the Army Now*) (Fox)
2. Jane Wyman and Dick Foran in *Private Detective* (FN)
3. Fred Astaire
4. Henry Fonda, Spencer Charters and Alice Brady in *Young Mr Lincoln* (Fox)
5. Loretta Young and Warner Baxter in *Wife, Husband and Friend* (Fox)
6. Ann Dvorak, Chester Morris and Ralph Bellamy in *Blind Alley* (Col)
7. Martin Spellman and Jackie Cooper in *Streets of New York* (MoP)
8. Harry Carey, June Lang and Dick Foran in *Inside Information* (Fox)
9. John Payne, Pat O'Brien and Gale Page in *Indianapolis Speedway* (WB)
10. Fred MacMurray and Madeleine Carroll in *Cafe Society* (Par)
11. Hedy Lamarr and Robert Taylor in *Lady of the Tropics* (MGM)
12. Humphrey Bogart and Rosemary Lane in *The Return of Dr. X* (WB)

8 △ ▽ 10

11

9 △ ▽ 12

1   2

3   4   5

6   7

9   10 △ ▽ 11   8 △ ▽ 12

13   14

15

16

1. Alice Brady, James Ellison, Jean Parker and Billie Burke in *Zenobia (GB Elephants Never Forget)* (HR)
2. Virginia Weidler, Gene Reynolds, Reginald Owen and Guy Kibbee in *Bad Little Angel* (MGM)
3. Jeffrey Lynn, Priscilla Lane and Roland Young in *Yes, My Darling Daughter* (FN)
4. Ronald Reagan.
5. Marie Wilson and Johnnie Davis in *The Sweepstakes Winner* (FN)
6. Michael Redgrave, Margaret Lockwood and Emlyn Williams in *The Stars Look Down* (Gra)
7. Cora Sue Collins, Frieda Inescort and Henry Wilcoxon in *Woman Doctor* (Rep)
8. Jane Baxter and Clive Brook in *The Ware Case* (ASP)
9. Edmund Cobb, Charles Starrett and Iris Meredith in *Riders of Black River* (Col)
10. Tim Holt, George O'Brien, Tom London and Rita Hayworth in *The Renegade Ranger* (RKO)
11. Mary Hart, Roy Rogers, Raymond Hatton and George Meeker in *Rough Riders Round-up* (Rep)
12. Ronald Reagan and Rosella Towne in *Code of the Secret Service* (FN)
13. Ed Brophy, Robert Kent, Edward Gargan, Richard Lane and Horace MacMahon in *For Love or Money* (Univ)
14. Frankie Thomas, Bonita Granville, John Litel and Renie Riano in *Nancy Drew, Reporter* (FN)
15. Griffith Jones, Francis L Sullivan and Anna Lee in *The Four Just Men* (US *The Secret Four*) (CAPAD)
16. Roland Young and Constance Bennett in *Topper Takes a Trip* (HR)
17. Robert Newton, Charles Laughton and Leslie Banks in *Jamaica Inn* (Mfl)
18. The Ritz Brothers in *The Gorilla* (Fox)
19. Roy Rogers and George 'Gabby' Hayes in *Days of Jesse James* (Rep)
20. Ann Shoemaker, Jean Parker, Charles Bickford, Al Bridge and Gordon Oliver in *Romance of the Redwoods* (Col)

17   18 △ ▽ 19   ▽ 20

1

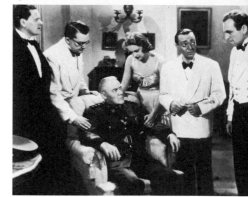

4

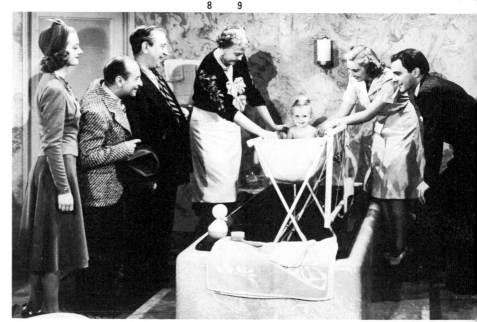

7 8 9

1. Horace MacMahon (s), Clarence Kolb, Leon Ames, Barton MacLane and Willard Robertson in *I Was a Convict* (Rep)

2. Lionel Stander, James Stewart, Lew Ayres and Bess Ehrhardt in *Ice Follies of 1939* (MGM)

3. Cedric Hardwicke and Charles Laughton in *The Hunchback of Notre Dame* (RKO)

4. Betty Grable (c) in *Million Dollar Legs* (Par)

5. Sylvia Sidney and Leif Erickson (l) in *One-Third of a Nation* (FT)

6. Warren Hymer, Jean Hersholt, Charles D Brown, Amanda Duff, Peter Lorre and Richard Lane in *Mr Moto in Danger Island* (Fox)

7. Boris Karloff (s) in *Mr Wong in Chinatown* (MoP)

8. Bruce Cabot (l) and Norman Willis (on stairs) in *Homicide Bureau* (Col)

9. Andy Devine, Anne Nagel, Theodore Von Eltz and Jack Carson (r) in *Legion of Lost Flyers* (Univ)

10. Joy Hodges, Ernest Truex, Hugh Herbert, Kathleen Howard, Sandra Lee Henville (Baby Sandy), Florence Rice and Richard Carlson in *Little Accident* (Univ)

10

DAVID O. SELZNICK'S
production of
MARGARET MITCHELL'S
Story of the Old South

GONE WITH THE WIND

IN TECHNICOLOR, *starring*

CLARK GABLE
as Rhett Butler

LESLIE   OLIVIA
HOWARD · de HAVILLAND
and presenting
VIVIEN LEIGH
as Scarlett O'Hara

A SELZNICK INTERNATIONAL PICTURE

1   **2**   **3**

4△▽6   **5△▽7**

Gone With The Wind (DS) was hailed as a masterpiece when it was first exhibited. On January 26th 1939 filming of Margaret Mitchell's best-selling novel commenced. On June 27th filming was completed. Since its premiere on December 15th 1939 this magnificent four and a half hours movie has acquired more splendour. Across years of stardom, Clark Gable and Vivien Leigh played many parts but in the memories of ardent picturegoers are their interpretations of gun-runner Rhett Butler and wayward, reckless Scarlet O'Hara.

1. Olivia de Havilland
2. Periodical publicity
3. Vivien Leigh
4. Leslie Howard and Olivia de Havilland
5 and 6. Clark Gable and Vivien Leigh
7. Vivien Leigh

Continued on next page

1

2

3

4

5

6 △ ▽ 9

7 △ ▽ 10

8 △

11 12

13 14

Gone with the Wind

1. Clark Gable and Vivien Leigh
2. Vivien Leigh and Leslie Howard
3. Vivien Leigh and Hattie McDaniel
4. Thomas Mitchell, Barbara O'Neil,
Vivien Leigh and Charles Hamilton
5. Clark Gable and Vivien Leigh
6. The Union Army invests Atlanta
7. Leslie Howard and Vivien Leigh
8. Vivien Leigh and Hattie McDaniel
9. Clark Gable
10. Clark Gable and Vivien Leigh
11. Vivien Leigh attends the ball in
widow's weeds
12. Clark Gable and Vivien Leigh
scandalise the officers and their wives.
13. Vivien Leigh and Irving Bacon
(foreground)
14. Vivien Leigh and Thomas Mitchell
15. Vivien Leigh and Olivia de Havilland
16. Thomas Mitchell and Vivien Leigh
17. Clark Gable
18. Vivien Leigh
19. Clark Gable and Vivien Leigh

15 △ ▽ 17

16

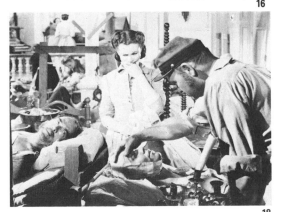

18 19

477

1

5

6

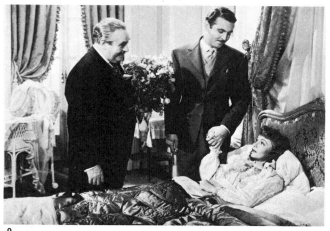

9

7

8

10

11

12

13

1. Neil Hamilton, Wendy Barrie and George Sanders in *The Saint Strikes Back* (RKO)

2. Gracie Allen, William Demarest and Warren William in *The Gracie Allen Murder Case* (GA/Par)

3. Nancy Kelly and Edward Norris in *Tail Spin* (Fox)

4. Clark Gable and Norma Shearer in *Idiot's Delight* (MGM)

5. Anna Lee

6. Anita Louise

7. Claudette Colbert

8. Gilbert Roland

9. Walter Connolly, Allan Jones and Mary Martin in *The Great Victor Herbert* (Par)

10. Robert Young, Eleanor Powell and Robert Young in *Honolulu* (MGM)

11. Rosalind Russell, Joan Fontaine and Norma Shearer in *The Women* (MGM)

12. Lew Ayres, Greer Garson and Robert Taylor in *Remember?* (MGM)

13. Clarence Kolb and Joe E Brown in *Beware Spooks* (RS/Col)

1. Paulette Goddard
2. Larry Fine (of the Three Stooges)
3. Bobs Watson and Lionel Barrymore in *On Borrowed Time* (MGM)
4. Rosalind Russell and Robert Montgomery in *Fast and Loose* (MGM)
5. Jean Parker and Phil Regan in *She Married a Cop* (Rep)
6. Nana Bryant, Harry Carey and Charles Bickford in *Street of Missing Men* (Rep)
7. Emlyn Williams
8. Bob Burns and Susan Hayward in *Our Leading Citizen* (GA/Par)
9. Walter Brennan
10. Greta Garbo, Melvyn Douglas and Ina Claire in *Ninotchka* (MGM)
11. Carole Lombard

1

2

3

4

7

5

6

8

9

10

11

3   4

5   6 △ ▽ 8

1. Irene Hervey
2. Smiley Burnette, Gene Autry and Pat Brady in *Home on the Prairie* (Rep)
3. Barton MacLane and Charles Bickford in *Mutiny in the Big House* (MoP)
4. Gene Autry, Duncan Renaldo, Smiley Burnette and Mary Lee in *South of the Border* (Rep)
5. Mickey Rooney and Lewis Stone in *Andy Hardy Gets Spring Fever* (MGM)
6. Wallis Clark, Linda Winters and Arthur Lake in *Blondie Meets The Boss* (Col)
7. Heather Angel
8. Kenneth Howell, Spring Byington, June Carlson, George Ernest, Jed Prouty and Florence Roberts in *The Jones Family in Hollywood* (Fox)
9. Charles Brinley (I) and Charles Starrett in *Western Caravans* (Col)
10. Sig Rumann, Allyn Joslyn, Jean Arthur, Noah Beery Jr and Cary Grant in *Only Angels Have Wings* (Col)
11. Kitty Carlisle
12. Andy Devine, Beverly Roberts and Richard Arlen in *Tropic Fury* (Univ)
13. Lew Ayres, Lana Turner and Lionel Barrymore in *Calling Dr Kildare* (MGM)
14. Harold Huber, Sidney Toler and Noel Madison in *City of Darkness*
15. Andy Devine, Preston Foster and Ralph Morgan in *Geronimo!* (Par)
16. Preston Foster and Irene Hervey in *Missing Evidence* (Univ)
17. Wally Vernon and Preston Foster in *Chasing Danger* (Fox)
18. Eddie Collins, Jed Prouty and Helen Ericson in *Quick Millions* (Fox)
19. Bob Livingston, Raymond Hatton and Duncan Renaldo in *The Kansas Terrors* (Rep)
20. Iris Adrian
21. Marjorie Weaver, Spring Byington, Jane Withers and Leo Carrillo in *The Chicken Wagon Family* (Fox)
22. Will Hay, Moore Marriott and Graham Moffatt in *Ask a Policeman* (G'boro)

7

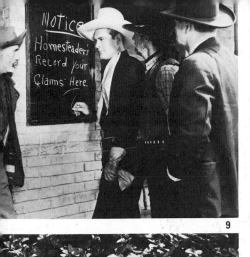

9   10

12   13

14

15   16

17 △ ▽ 20

18 △ ▽ 21   19 △ ▽ 22

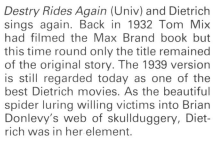

Destry Rides Again (Univ) and Dietrich sings again. Back in 1932 Tom Mix had filmed the Max Brand book but this time round only the title remained of the original story. The 1939 version is still regarded today as one of the best Dietrich movies. As the beautiful spider luring willing victims into Brian Donlevy's web of skullduggery, Dietrich was in her element.

1. Marlene Dietrich
2. Marlene Dietrich
3. Charles Winninger and James Stewart
4. James Stewart and Marlene Dietrich
5. Brian Donlevy, James Stewart and Marlene Dietrich
6. Marlene Dietrich and James Stewart
7. Marlene Dietrich
8. Brian Donlevy and Marlene Dietrich
9. James Stewart and Marlene Dietrich

1
2
3

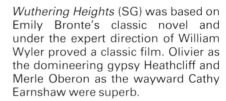

Wuthering Heights (SG) was based on Emily Bronte's classic novel and under the expert direction of William Wyler proved a classic film. Olivier as the domineering gypsy Heathcliff and Merle Oberon as the wayward Cathy Earnshaw were superb.

1. Merle Oberon, Laurence Olivier and David Niven
2. Merle Oberon and Laurence Olivier
3. Laurence Olivier and Merle Oberon
4. Merle Oberon and Laurence Olivier
5. Merle Oberon and Laurence Olivier
6. Laurence Olivier and Geraldine Fitzgerald
7. Flora Robson and Merle Oberon
8. Laurence Olivier and Merle Oberon
9. David Niven, Donald Crisp, Laurence Olivier, Flora Robson and Merle Oberon
10. Laurence Olivier and Merle Oberon

4

5
6

7
8

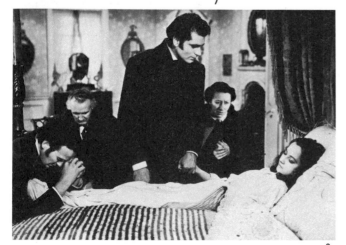

9
10

1

2 3

4

5 6

7

8

9

10

11 12

13 △ ▽ 17

16 △ ▽ 20

14 △ ▽ 18 15 △ ▽ 19

21

22   23

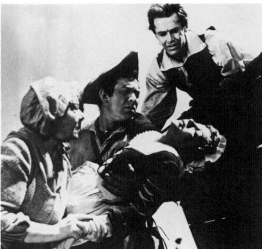

24   25

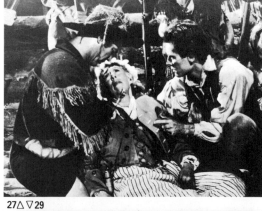

26 △ ▽ 28   27△ ▽ 29

Drums Along the Mohawk (Fox) was based on the best-selling novel by Walter D Edmunds. It relates the adventures of a newly married couple who settle in the Mohawk Valley in the face of merciless attacks by Indians. It was in all respects a worthy addition to Hollywood's various attempts to portray life on the early frontier prior to the Revolution.

1. Henry Fonda and Claudette Colbert
2. Claudette Colbert and Henry Fonda
3. Chief Big Tree, Henry Fonda and Claudette Colbert
4. Henry Fonda and Claudette Colbert
5. Jessie Ralph
6. Claudette Colbert
7. Claudette Colbert and Henry Fonda
8. Arthur Shields
9. Henry Fonda, Dorris Bowdon, Russell Simpson, Elizabeth Jones, Beulah Hall Jones, Claudette Colbert, Jessie Ralph and Kay Linaker
10. Henry Fonda and Arthur Shields
11. Claudette Colbert
12. Roger Imhof
13. Henry Fonda and Claudette Colbert
14. Henry Fonda and Claudette Colbert
15. Henry Fonda and Jessie Ralph
16. Henry Fonda and Claudette Colbert
17. Edna May Oliver, Claudette Colbert and Henry Fonda
18 and 19. Henry Fonda and Claudette Colbert
20. Claudette Colbert
21. Henry Fonda and Ward Bond
22. Chief Big Tree, Henry Fonda and Claudette Colbert
23. Jessie Ralph, Ward Bond, Claudette Colbert and Henry Fonda
24. Edna May Oliver, Henry Fonda, Ward Bond, Jessie Ralph and Dorris Bowdon (r)
25 and 26. Claudette Colbert and Henry Fonda
27. Ward Bond, Edna May Oliver and Henry Fonda
28. Claudette Colbert and Henry Fonda
29. Spencer Charters, Henry Fonda and Claudette Colbert

485

The Wizard of Oz (MGM) was the film for which Judy Garland will always be remembered. Who will ever forget 'Somewhere Over The Rainbow' sung in the dulcet tones of MGM's Sweetheart of the Movies? A splendid supporting cast further enriched this cinematic fairy-tale based on the book written by L Frank Baum.

1. Jack Haley, Ray Bolger, Judy Garland and Bert Lahr
2. Clara Blandick, Judy Garland, Margaret Hamilton and Charles Grapewin
3. Jack Haley, Ray Bolger, Judy Garland and Bert Lahr
4. Margaret Hamilton
5. Judy Garland
6. Judy Garland, Frank Morgan, Charles Grapewin, Ray Bolger, Jack Haley, Bert Lahr and Clara Blandick
7. Bert Lahr, Judy Garland, Jack Haley and Ray Bolger
8. Judy Garland and Frank Morgan
9. Jack Haley, Bert Lahr, Judy Garland, Frank Morgan and Ray Bolger
10. Margaret Hamilton, Judy Garland and Ray Bolger

1

2

3

4

5

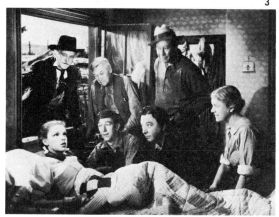

6

7

8

9

10

1

2

3

4

5

6

7

8

9

10

11

12

13

1. Leif Erickson
2. Olivia de Havilland
3. Joan Fontaine
4. Fred MacMurray and Madeleine Carroll in *Honeymoon in Bali* (JL/Par)
5. Lee Bowman and Lana Turner in *Dancing Co-Ed* (GB *Every Other Inch a Lady*)
6. Lynn Bari
7. Mickey Rooney in *The Adventures of Huckleberry Finn* (MGM)
8. Margaret Lockwood, Will Fyffe and Douglas Fairbanks Jr in *Rulers of the Sea* (Par)
9. Priscilla Lane
10. Victor McLaglen and June Lang in *Captain Fury* (HR)
11. Roy Rogers, Chris-Pin Martin and Raymond Hatton in *Frontier Pony Express* (Rep)
12. Moroni Olsen (l), John Wayne and Wilfred Lawson in *Allegheny Uprising* (GB *The First Rebel*) (RKO)
13. John Eldredge and Humphrey Bogart in *King of The Underworld* (WB)

1   2

3   4   5

6 △ ▽9   7   8 △ ▽10

11 12

13 14

15 16

17 △ ▽ 19 18 ▽ 20

1. Edward Ellis, Richard Dix and Joan Fontaine in *Man of Conquest* (Rep)
2. Max Terhune, Richard Dix and George 'Gabby' Hayes in *Man of Conquest* (Rep)
3. Mickey Rooney, Charles Winninger, Judy Garland and Grace Hayes in *Babes in Arms* (MGM)
4. Sally Gray and Lupino Lane in *The Lambeth Walk* (Pin/CAPAD)
5. Grant Withers (l) in *Daughters of the Tong* (TiP)
6. Judith Barrett, Wm Collier Snr and Minor Watson in *Television Spy* (Par)
7. Will Hay, Moore Marriott and Graham Moffatt in *Where's That Fire* (Fox)
8. Karen Verne, Rex Harrison and Joan Marion in *Ten Days in Paris* (IAP)
9. Arthur Lake (l) and Selmer Jackson (c) in *Blondie Brings up Baby* (Col)
10. Herbert Marshall, Claudette Colbert and Bert Lahr in *Zaza* (Par)
11. Frank McHugh, Rosemary Lane, May Robson, Priscilla Lane, Lola Lane, Eddie Albert, Gale Page, Dick Foran and Claude Rains in *Four Wives* (FN)
12. Patricia Ellis, Ernie Adams (s), Jack Holt, Lou Matheaux and Si Schindel in *Fugitive at Large* (Col)
13. Otto Kruger, Mary Maguire and Walter Rilla in *Black Eyes* (ABPC)
14. Laurence Olivier and Valerie Hobson in *Clouds Over Europe* (Col)
15. Louise Platt, Halliwell Hobbes and Melvyn Douglas in *Tell No Tales* (MGM)
16. Elyse Knox and John Hubbard in *Fighting Mad* (MoP)
17. Richard Lane, Joe Penney and Tom Kennedy in *The Day the Bookies Wept* (RKO)
18. John Howard (r) in *Bulldog Drummond's Bride* (Par)
19. Roscoe Karns, Irene Dare and George Meeker in *Everything's on Ice* (RKO)
20. Chill Wills, George O'Brien (c), Harry Cording and Carlyle Moore in *Arizona Legion* (RKO)

The Three Musketeers (GB *The Singing Musketeer*) (Fox) was a musical version of Alexandre Dumas' classic with Don Ameche as a singing D'Artagnan. The Ritz Brothers were in fine fettle as three would-be musketeers.

1. Don Ameche
2. Pauline Moore and Don Ameche
3. Lionel Atwill
4. Miles Mander
5. The Ritz Brothers
6. John King and Gloria Stuart
7. Joseph Schildkraut
8. Pauline Moore, Gloria Stuart, Don Ameche and the Ritz Brothers.

2

1

5

3△ ▽7

4

6△ ▽8

1

3

6

9 △ ▽ 11 10 △ ▽ 12

1. Bruce Cabot, Helen Mack and Thomas Jackson in *Mystery of the White Room* (Univ)
2. Isa Miranda and Ray Milland in *Hotel Imperial* (Par)
3. George E Stone, William Gargan, Joan Bennett and Adolphe Menjou in *The Housekeeper's Daughter* (HR)
4. Warren William and Ida Lupino in *The Lone Wolf Spy Hunt* (Col)
5. Bonita Granville and Frankie Thomas in *Nancy Drew, Trouble Shooter* (WB)
6. Tyrone Power, Linda Darnell and Warren William in *Daytime Wife* (Fox)
7. Leo Carrillo, Rosina Galli and Henry Armetta in *Fisherman's Wharf* (RKO)
8. John Litel, Janet Chapman and Margaret Lindsay in *On Trial* (WB)
9. John Garfield and Priscilla Lane in *Dust Be My Destiny* (FN)
10. Ray Corrigan, Phyllis Isley and John Wayne in *New Frontier* (Rep)
11. Max Terhune, Ray Corrigan and John Wayne in *The Night Riders* (Rep)
12. Lon Chaney, Betty Field and Burgess Meredith in *Of Mice and Men* (HR)

491

1 2

3

4 5

6 △ ▽ 8

7 △ ▽ 9

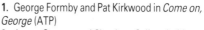

12   13

14

15 △ ▽ 17   16   ▽ 18

10   11

1. George Formby and Pat Kirkwood in *Come on, George* (ATP)
2. James Stewart and Claudette Colbert in *It's a Wonderful World* (MGM)
3. Margaret Lockwood in *A Girl Must Live* (G'boro)
4. Eddie Albert and Zorina in *On Your Toes* (FN)
5. James Gleason and Russell Gleason in *Should Husbands Work?* (Rep)
6. Victor McLaglen, Joan Fontaine and Cary Grant in *Gunga Din* (RKO)
7. Cary Grant, Victor McLaglen and Douglas Fairbanks Jr in *Gunga Din* (RKO)
8. James Ellison in *Hotel for Women* (Fox)
9. Johnny Downs (c) and Constance Moore in *Hawaiian Nights* (Univ)
10. Fay Bainter, Gail Page, Donald Crisp and Priscilla Lane in *Daughters Courageous* (FN)
11. Bobby Breen and Kent Taylor in *Escape to Paradise* (RKO)
12. Harry Woods, Lupita Tovar and George O'Brien in *The Fighting Gringo* (RKO)
13. Wendy Barrie and Tyrone Power in *Daytime Wife* (Fox)
14. Jean Colin and Kenny Baker in *The Mikado* (GSF)
15. Ann Baldwin and Roy Rogers in *Wall Street Cowboy* (Rep)
16. Virginia Dale and Robert Paige in *Death of a Champion* (Par)
17. Maria Ouspenskaya, George Brent and Myrna Loy in *The Rains Came* (Fox)
18. Billy Halop, Billy Benedict, David Gorcey, Huntz Hall and Bobby Jordan (r) in *Call a Messenger* (Univ)

1

2

3

4

5

6

7

8

9

Stagecoach (WaW) Mention the name of John Ford interrogatively to any movie buff and he will instantly answer 'Stagecoach!' for although Ford acted in and directed countless films *Stagecoach* must surely be the epic for which he will always be remembered.

1. The Way Station
2. John Wayne, George Bancroft, Donald Meek, Chris-Pin Martin and Thomas Mitchell
3. Claire Trevor
4. Thomas Mitchell, Claire Trevor and Louise Platt
5. George Bancroft, Andy Devine, Donald Meek, Claire Trevor, John Carradine and John Wayne
6. Berton Churchill, Lon Mason, John Wayne, Andy Devine and John Bancroft
7. Andy Devine
8. Donald Meek
9. John Wayne
10. Louise Platt and John Carradine
11. George Bancroft, Thomas Mitchell and John Wayne
12. The Ambush
13. Claire Trevor and John Wayne

10 △ ▽ 12

11 △ ▽ 13

7 △ ▽ 10

1. Moore Marriott
2. Billy Benedict (c) and Elisha Cook Jr (r) in
Newsboys Home (Univ)
3. Ralph Richardson in *The Lion has Wings* (AK/LF)
4. James Burke
5. Al 'Fuzzy' St John, Nina Guilbert, Art Jarrett and
Dorothy Fay in *Trigger Pals* (Cmt/GN)
6. Robert Kent (c) in *Convicts Code* (MoP)
7. John Hartley, Buck Jones and Helen
Twelvetrees in *Unmarried* (GB *Night Club Hostess*)
(Par)
8. Helen Parrish and Ann Sheridan in *Winter
Carnival* (WaW)
9. Leon Ames (s) and Frankie Thomas (c) in
Code of the Street (Univ)
10. Gay Seabrook, George O'Brien and Marjorie
Reynolds in *Racketeers of the Range* (RKO)

495

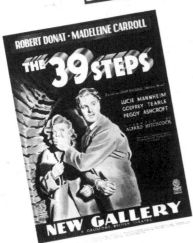

Olivia de Havilland and Errol Flynn in *The Adventures of Robin Hood* (FN) and publicity pages for famous films of the Thirties.

ABBREVIATIONS

ABPC	Associated British Picture Corporation	DS	David O Selznick	KG	Ken Goldsmith	Roc	Rocket
Act	Action Pictures	DZ	Darryl F Zanuck	KM	Ken Maynard	RoS	Robert Sisk
AdP	Admiral Pictures	EaP	Eagle Productions	KV	King Vidor	RP	Robert Presnell
AFP	Aldwich Film Productions	EC	Emmanuel Cohen	Lasky	Lasky	RS	Robert Sparks
AG	Arthur Greenblatt	EG	Edward Grainger	Len	Lenfilm	RW	Roland West
AH	Arthur Hammerstein	EK	Edward Kaufman	LF	London Films	SAWW	Sono Art-World Wide
Aja	Ajax	Emp	Empire	Lib	Liberty	SB	Sandro Berman
AK	Alexander Korda	ES	Edward Small	LL	Louis Lighton	SeP	Select Productions
All	Alliance	FD	First Division	LR	Leni Riefenstahl	SF	Svensk Filmindustri
AIP	Allied Pictures	FFA	Freuler Film Associates	LS	Lone Star	SG	Samuel Goldwyn
Amb	Ambassador	FN	First National	M	Merrick	SGPS	St George's Productions Stirling
AP	Academy Pictures	Fox	Twentieth Century Fox	Maj	Majestic	ShP	Showmen's Pictures
Arg	Argosy	FR	Fanchon Royer	MaP	Mascot Pictures	Spe	Spectrum
Art	Artclass	FrF	French Film	May	Mayfair	Spr	Superior
ASC	American Securities Corporation	FT	Federal Theatre	Mel	Melody Pictures	SL	Sol Lesser
ASP	Associated Star Productions	FZ	Florenz Ziegfeld	Mfl	Mayflower	StL	Stan Laurel
ATP	Associated Talking Pictures	GA	George K Arthur	MCC	Merian C Cooper	Stn	Steiner
Ath	Atherton	Gau	Gaumont	MF	Milton H Feld	Sup	Supreme
Ayw	Aywon	G'boro	Gainsborough	MGM	Metro Goldwyn Mayer	SW	Sol M Wurtzel
B&D	British and Dominion	GF	Garrick Films	MoP	Monogram Productions	SZ	Sam Zimbalist
Bch	Butchers	GK	Garrett Klement	Mosfilm	Mosfilm	T	Toeplitz
Bea	Beacon	Gra	Grafton	MP	Maurice Pivar	TA	Tom Arnold
BeP	Beverly Productions	GN	Grand National	Nero	Nero Films	Tal	Talmadge
Bet	Beaumont	GSF	Gilbert and Sullivan Films	N	Nelson	TFC	Transatlantic Film Corporation
Big	Big	GSBP	Gloria Swanson British Pictures	NF	Northern Films	TFS	Twickenham Film Studios
BIP	British International Pictures	HaL	Harry Langdon	NP	Nazi Party	Tif	Tiffany
BM	Boris Morros	HH	Howard Hughes	NW	New World	TiP	Times Pictures
BN	British National	HJB	Harry Joe Brown	Oberon	Oberon	Tow	Tower
BPS	Budd P Shulberg	HL	Harold Lloyd	OP	Olympic Pictures	Tra	Trafalgar
BZ	Bennie F Zeidman	Hof	M H Hoffman	Par	Paramount	Tre	Treo
Cad	Caddo	HR	Hal Roach	Paris	Paris	Tud	Tudor
Cap	Capitol	HS	Harry Sherman	Pat	Pathe	TK	Tobis Klangfilm
CAPAD	Co-operative Association of Producers and Distributors	HuS	Hunt Stromberg	PB	Pandro S Berman	UA	United Artists
CAT	Cine-Allianz Tonfilm	HW	Herbert Wilcox	Pee	Peerless	Ufa	Ufa Films
CC	Colbert Clark	IA	Inter Allied	Pen	Pendennis	Univ	Universal
CdeM	Cecil B DeMille	IAP	Irving Asher Productions	Pin	Pinebrook	V	Viking
CD	Carl Dreyer	Imp	Imperator	PFP	Pascal Film Productions	Va	Vandor
ChC	Charles Chaplin	Int	International	PLP	Pickford Lasky Productions	Vic	Victory
Che	Chesterfield	Inv	Invincible	PoP	Powers Pictures	Vit	Vitagraph
Cmt	Cinemart	JB	Jack Buchanan	Pre	Premier	Vog	Vogue
Col	Columbia	JC	J V Cremonim	Pri	Principal	VSP	Victor Saville Productions
Con	Concord	JeP	Jefferson Pictures	Pur	Puritan	W	Wester
CoP	Conn Pictures	JP	Joe Pasternak	RaP	Raspin Productions	WaW	Walter Wanger
Com	Commodore	Jew	Jewell	Rbv	Rabinovitch	War	Wardour
Cor	Coronado	JHP	J H Productions	Rce	Reliance	WB	Warner Brothers
Cos	Cosmopolitan	JL	Jeff Lazarus	Reg	Regal	WLB	William Le Baron
Coy	Colony	JN	J L Nounez	Rel	Reliable	Wo	World
Cre	Crescent	JS	Joseph M Schenck	Rem	Remington	WS	William Steiner
Cri	Criterion	JoSt	John Stafford	Rep	Republic	WSm	William Sistrom
DFBP	Dela Films British Productions	JSt	John Stone	Ria	Rialto	WW	World Wide
		JWC	John W Considine Jr	RJ	Ray Johnston	XX	Production Company Unknown
		KBS	KBS	RKO	RKO Radio Pictures	ZM	Zion Myers

(l) Left (r) Right (c) Centre (s) Seated (St) Standing (k) Kneeling (t) Top (b) Bottom

The Private Life of Henry VIII (LF) 1933

The King Steps Out (Col) 1936

Hell Harbor (UA) 1930

The Little Princess (Fox) 1936

Charlie Chan's Secret (Fox) 1936

Stagecoach (UA) 1939

The Private Lives of Elizabeth and Essex (WB) 1939

INDEX TO FILMS

Faithful Heart (G'boro) 1932

A Very Honorable Guy (FN) 1934

The Baroness and the Butler (Fox) 1938

The Chief (GB My Old Man's a Fireman) (MGM) 1933

White Lies (Col) 1934

Hello Trouble (Col) 1932

Stamboul (Par/Brit) 1931

The Three Musketeers (Fox) 1939

Law of the Texan (Col) 1938

Father O'Flynn (Bch) 1935

Sing you Sinners (Par) 1938

Anybody's Blonde (Act) 1931

The Lady in Scarlet (Che) 1935

Dr Jekyll and Mr Hyde (Par) 1932

Blockade (WaW) 1938

Island Captives (Pri) 1937

Having Wonderful Time (RKO) 1938

Crime School (FN) 1938

Wide Open Faces (Col) 1938

The Silk Express (WB) 1933

Swing that Cheer (Univ) 1938

Fighting Thru (Tif) 1930

The Flag Lieutenant (B&D) 1932

The Gentleman From Arizona (MoP) 1939

Damaged Love (SAWW) 1931

Fourth Alarm (RJ) 1930

Union Pacific (Par) 1939

Come Closer Folks (Col) 1936

Mutiny on the Blackhawk (Univ) 1939

Carmen (PoP) 1932

File 113 (Alp) 1932

The Devil is Driving (Par) 1932

The Lottery Bride (AH/UA) 1930

Call Her Savage (Fox) 1932

Police Call (ShP) 1933

Don't Bet on Love (Univ) 1933

The Old Dark House (Univ) 1932

A Doctor's Diary (Par) 1937

Double Alibi (Fox) 1937

The Hunchback of Notre Dame (RKO) 1939

State's Attorney (GB Cardigan's Last Case) (RKO) 1932

Scarface (HH) 1932

The Midnight Special (Che) 1930

One Romantic Night (UA) 1930

Speak Easily (MGM) 1932

Midnight Alibi (FN) 1934

Spies of the Air (BN) 1939

The Devil to Pay (SG) 1930

The False Madonna (Par) 1932

Divorce Among Friends (WB) 1931

The Lady Objects (Col) 1938

Flirtation (FD) 1935

Crashing Thru (MoP) 1939

King of Jazz (Univ) 1930

The Devil and the Deep (Par) 1932

Shop Angel (Tow) 1932

Boys' Reformatory (MoP) 1939

What Would you do, Chums? (BN) 1939

The Spirit of the West (Alp) 1932

If I Had a Million (Par) 1932

The Deadline (Col) 1932

Bill Cracks Down (Rep) 1937

Redheads on Parade (Fox) 1935

Love Under Fire (Fox) 1937

Charlie Chan at the Olympics (Fox) 1937

The Secret Witness (Col) 1931

Happy Landing (MoP) 1934

Charlie Chan's Chance (Fox) 1932

He Learned about Women (Par) 1933

The Fountain (RKO) 1934

Up Pops the Devil (Par) 1931

The Stoker (Alp) 1932

Spring Madness (MGM) 1938

Big Town (Inv) 1932

Men in White (MGM) 1934

Stablemates (MGM) 1938

Girl in 419 (Par) 1933

The White Parade (Fox) 1934

Woman Against the World (Col) 1938

Borrowed Wives (Tif) 1939

Intimate Relations (Tud) 1937

Waterfront Lady (Rep) 1935

Expensive Husbands (WB) 1937

Blaze O'Glory (SAWW) 1930

Juggernaut (JHP/GN) 1937

Brothers (Col) 1930

Advice to the Lovelorn (Fox) 1933

Little Miss Thoroughbred (WB) 1938

Headin' East (Col) 1937

The Last of Mrs Cheyney (MGM) 1937

Romeo and Juliet (MGM) 1936

Bird of Paradise (RKO) 1932

Seventh Heaven (Fox) 1937

Midnight Taxi (Fox) 1937

The Hoosier Schoolboy (KG/MoP) 1937

Slim (WB) 1937

Maid's Night Out (RKO) 1938

The Big Pond (Par) 1930